PLATOON

&

SALVADOR

THE ORIGINAL SCREENPLAYS

OLIVER STONE'S
PLATOON

&

SALVADOR

OLIVER STONE & RICHARD BOYLE

THE ORIGINAL SCREENPLAYS

VINTAGE BOOKS
A DIVISION OF RANDOM HOUSE
NEW YORK

First Vintage Books Edition, November 1987

Copyright © 1985, 1986, 1987 by Oliver Stone

All rights reserved under International and Pan-American Copyright Conventions. Published in the United States by Random
House, Inc., New York, and in Canada by Random House of
Canada Limited, Toronto. Originally published in Great Britain by
Ebury Press, a division of the National Magazine Company, Ltd.,
in 1986. The foreword was originally published
in *American Film*.

Library of Congress Cataloging-in-Publication Data
Stone, Oliver.
Oliver Stone's Platoon; and Salvador
"The original screenplays."
1. Vietnamese Conflict, 1961–1975—Drama.
2. El Salvador—History—1979– —Drama.
I. Boyle, Richard. II. Stone, Oliver. Salvador.
1987. III. Title.
PN1997.P518 1987   791.43′75   87-40153
ISBN 0-394-75629-0 (pbk.)

Grateful acknowledgment is made to Jobete Music Co., Inc., for
permission to reprint excerpts from the lyrics to "Tracks of My
Tears" by Marv Tarplin, Warren Moore and William Robinson.
Copyright © 1965 by Jobete Music Co., Inc. Used by permission.
All rights reserved. International copyright secured.

Manufactured in the United States of America
10 9 8 7 6 5 4 3 2 1

FOREWORD

BY OLIVER STONE

March–May 1986, the Philippines. I was nineteen when I first came out to Asia. It was June 1965, and the Saigon heat and shirts soaked in sweat are what I first remember – and the thread of rickshaw drivers' muscles as their carts beat out squeaky rhythms on the broken streets as I tried to make it home drunk from some whorehouse before the curfew closed me down. It was out here I became a young man – teaching school, working as a wiper in the merchant marine, fighting in the army. The East has been an orphan home to me; life quickens out here, the images sharpen, the neuroticism and slackness of Western living vanish into blood red sunsets, green seas, and a leathery pirate people.

Although I push forty now, not entirely pleased with what I've become, inside me still is that solitary, wide-eyed youth standing under those raggedy Asiatic clouds, looking out at the sea with his fantasies of Lord Jim and Julie Christie, an anonymous infantryman who eagerly believed in Goethe's admonition, to the effect, 'Beware of what you dream to be in your youth for you will become that thing in your mid-age' and I knew then that someday, somehow, I would write my story and join the flow of time.

The basis for *Platoon* was hatched somewhere there in the aftermath of the war, in New York in December 1969, but it wouldn't be written till 1976. Drugs, jail, anxieties would cloud the brain for years until one day, in the summer of the two-hundredth birthday of the United States, broke and going nowhere at thirty, I wrote it as straight as I could remember it.

But nobody wanted to make it because it was 'hard, depressing, grim'. So I buried it again, accepting that the truth of that war would never come out because America was blind, a trasher of history, with no desire to know or to regret, for if we stopped and questioned ourselves, our optimism and self-confidence would be next.

It was reborn, strangely, seven years later, because Michael Cimino had read it and remembered it and he wanted me to write *Year of the Dragon* with him, and somehow we convinced Dino De Laurentiis to make it in a barter arrangement. So I wrote *Dragon*, then cast *Platoon* and went to the Philippines to scout locations. My spirits soared, and then Dino said, 'No'. No American distributor would agree on *any* terms to give the movie a 'commercial' ($3 million) release, so Dino dropped it and, this time, in the summer of '84, my heart broke. Why I wondered, was the film resurrected only to be killed once again? The meaninglessness of it drove me to utter despair.

It was out of this nothingness that another man – Richard Boyle – walked into my life with not a dime to his name, but with a sense of humor and adventure, and we wove the tale that became *Salvador* from pure love and fun, and like two rogue prospectors out of a Huston movie, went off and tried to con the Salvos into making the picture; and somehow life has a way of taking care of you when you relax, when you don't want something so bad it goes away, and *Salvador* became the most joyful picture I ever made. Producer John Daly, who comes from the poor streets of London, was loose and wild enough to defy (with the critical help of Gerald Green) the 'No's' of the American conglomerates who would never in a million years soil themselves on something as radical and ugly as *Salvador*, and it was all done in six months from script to shooting, and it was like a fairy tale. If you persist, I guess, the worm *does* turn, though without rhyme or reason, but that's another story – *Salvador*.

It's the same British unit (Daly, Green, Derek Gibson, and one American, Arnold Kopelson) that's making *Platoon* – with European money – right on the heels of *Salvador*. The ironies continue to amaze and educate me – how could I know that what was solely history in 1976 would wait until now to become a possible antidote to the reborn militarism of Grenada, Libya, Nicaragua? Perhaps, after all, there was a reason all along.

Charlie Sheen is nineteen now and trying to play the part I played. He has the dark-browed, quiet beauty of a young Montgomery Clift in *A Place in the Sun* and *Red River,* part of that throwback-to-the-fifties generation, nothing being too much to ask of him as long as it's 'cool', and if it's not it elicits a cocked, quizzical eyebrow. He moves fluidly with the camera; we're doing a take, and I know I want him to do it again 'cause his body attitude is incorrect, but the moment I think it, he eases into the exact position I want. This happens time and again, an eerie sense of mental bonding between us. I waste few words with Charlie; a thought, an image, he says, 'It's cool', and just does it, wading through water or bellying through mud to hit his mark and a line.

Equally astonishing is his gradual shift in personality. He arrived a bit of a nerd from the teen films he'd done – Malibu in his soul, hot wings at Hamburger Hamlet, tightly cut hair, with a hundred pounds of provisions his mother sent that he would never use. Over the weeks, he's become tougher, sharper, a jungle vet who can hump sixty pounds and walk right up on a deer in the bush without being heard. The changes exactly mirror those in his character in the script, though we leave it unsaid between us. I realize somewhere along the way I'm in the presence of a kid who, unless he screws up, is going to be a movie star; it's in his genes, and when you're six inches from it, you just *know* it, it's like watching Ted Williams hit a ball or knowing the queen's the Queen.

Tom Berenger is Sergeant Barnes, the Captain Ahab of the platoon. He's a quiet actor with the moral stamina and possible longevity of a Frederic March or Spencer Tracy, another Irishman. He buries his natural personality so well in his parts that even in films like *The Big Chill,* people don't see the original stamp and tend to overlook him. Here I want him to play someone with evil in his heart, but play him with an understanding that will shed light on Melville's line, 'O this lovely light that shineth not on me ...', and from watching his coiled performance, I think many people at the end of the film will think he has

7

been wronged by Charlie Sheen, Willem Dafoe, and destiny.

Dafoe, who was so magnificently evil in *Streets of Fire* and *To Live and Die in L.A.*, plays Sergeant Elias, who takes on Barnes and pays for it with his life. It's a sea change for Willem who, because of his exaggerated Scandinavian cheekbones, has been typecast as a villain, though in reality he is closer to Max von Sydow in his gentleness of manner.

The real Elias was about twenty-three in 1968 when I met him during a brief stint in the First Cavalry's Long Range Reconnaissance patrol (I moved around a lot, four units, two wounds). Dashingly handsome, with thick black hair, a flashing white smile, and Apache blood, Elias was everything we were later going to recognize in Jim Morrison and Joplin and Hendrix, he *was* a rock star but played it out as a soldier; real danger turned him on. Everybody seemed to love him except the 'lifers' and the juicers, with their six and seven stripes (Elias had five, and that's as far as he was going), who were making profits out of rear-echelon deals on beer and PX supplies and screwing over the 'grunts' doing the actual fighting. They were the trash of Vietnam and the cancer on the balls with which we tried to fight the war; they were also the guys who ran me out of two units 'cause I wouldn't take their shit. Guys like Elias pissed them off a whole lot more 'cause he smoked dope, which, in '68, was for faggots and hippies and black panthers, and it broke my heart when I heard Elias died on some hill in the Ashau when one of our grenades went off and killed him. It was unlike Elias; he was too smart to get wasted like that, yet how symbolic of this frustrating war – many of our best troops killed by our own side in accidents. There was even the whispered thought that Elias had been done in by one of our lifers.

Sergeant Barnes was equally mythic in retrospect. He really *was* Achilles, a warrior king in his own time. And I – this modern New York City boy who'd never really believed all that Homer stuff in school – was actually hauling his radio, the equivalent, I suppose, of driving his chariot.

He never yelled at me, but his cold, quiet stare withered and terrified me as no man has ever done since. He was the best soldier I ever saw, except, possibly, for Elias. One day he snuck up on two 'gooks' having breakfast and killed them, quick, before the fish heads hit their lips; they died surprised. But, unlike Elias, there was a sickness in him, he wanted to kill too much. The gooks had shot him right above his left eye in '66, and the bullet somehow lodged in there and he spent a year in a hospital in Japan. The resulting scar ran the whole left side of his face in a large, sickle-shaped pattern layered with grafted skin from the indentation above his eye to his lower jaw. It was a *massive* job, indicative of equally massive damage to the nerves and possibly the brain.

Yet when he got out, he came back to the Nam because he *wanted* to. To get even, I guess – either with the gooks or, if they weren't around, with us. When Barnes looked you in the eye, you felt it all the way down to your balls. But there was a tenderness and sensuality in the man's quietude that made him fascinating, equally handsome in a snub-nosed way as Elias, and I found out in time he was married to a Japanese girl he'd met in the hospital. He'd been wounded some six or seven times, though he never talked about it, or the woman, or himself. He'd get drunk at poker and occasionally crack a country smile, but never let you in. The only vulnerability in the man *was* the scar, and such a massive thing it was that it provoked the deepest empathy.

It was from these roots that the essential conflict between Elias and Barnes grew in my mind. *Two* gods. Two different views of the war. The angry Achilles versus the conscience-stricken Hector fighting for a lost cause on the dusty plains of Troy. It mirrored the very civil war that I'd witnessed in all the units I was in – on the one hand, the lifers, the juicers, and the moron white element (part Southern, part rural) against, on the other, the hippie, dope smoking, black, and progressive white element (although there were exceptions in all categories, and some lifers did more dope than I ever dreamed). Right versus Left. And I would act as Ishmael, the observer, caught between those two giant forces. At first a watcher. Then *forced* to act – to take responsibility and a moral stand. And in the process grow to a manhood I'd never dreamed I'd have to grow to. To a place where in order to go on existing I'd have to shed the innocence and accept the evil the Homeric gods had thrown out into the world. To be both good and evil. To move from this East Coast social product to a more visceral manhood, where I finally felt the war not in my head, but in my gut and my soul.

We import twenty-five black, white, and Spanish actors from all over the country, many of them teenagers fascinated by the history of the war; we build a three-mile dirt road into the jungle, dam a stream to create a river, dig a series of tunnels. A Philippine worker dies in a cave-in, his spirit exorcised at a special ritual in the jungle; we construct a ruined French church and a Twenty-fifth Infantry base camp on a plain. The massive crew of 250 is mostly Filipino, with the core unit from *Salvador* coming over (Bob Richardson on camera, production designer Bruno Rubeo, editor Claire Simpson, Gordon Smith for prosthetics, special effects man Yves de Bono), American, Italian, Irish, Canadian, and English respectively, a highly mixed and inflammable group, bringing with it a chaos I enjoy.

The dream is coming true, yet I fear I will screw up the responsibility (dozens of letters pour in from vets begging to work on the film for nothing, admonishing me not to ruin their dreams that the truth will be told). Also, I feel tired (there's not been a single day's break since *Salvador*), and I worry that I am stale and have done the film too many times in my head. Cimino, with his Napoleonic intensity, warns me, 'Don't leave the game in the locker room' – by which he means don't get so excited about casting, rehearsal, storyboards, and executive decisions that, by the time you shoot, you're dead inside, you're not putting it down on film. It's good advice and I try to go with it, finding now that a movie generally comes down to the Day Of – to being the *opposite* of your storyboards, to the insignificant odd moment you never thought would've worked, to just plain luck and the coming together of so many live elements in the proper framework. Renoir, I think, was right: Create an atmosphere, find the right location and light, let your collaborators do their best work, and the rest will flow.

The revolution comes and goes, and though we obviously root for the overthrow of Marcos's putrefying social structure, we are forced, once he goes, to make an entirely new set of under-the-table deals with the new cadre of generals, sergeants, and mechanics for the use of their choppers, jet fighters, tanks, and infantry battalions. The Clark and Subic Facilities and their men are closed to us because the U.S. Defense Department deems our script 'totally unrealistic'. We dig up the extras from bars, floaters, and among school kids. Nigerian tribesmen studying in the Philippines double as black soldiers.

The actors go through an intense two-week training course at a Philippine jungle school under Capt. Dale Dye, Vietnam vet and twenty-year marine, assisted by four ex-marines. Dye, the type of man you find in *The Right Stuff,* brave and laconic and true, imparts the samurai ethic to them, although at times he drives the liberal contingent of the crew nuts with his fervent anti-Communism. But, as someone once said about John Wayne, 'His politics aside, you do *love* the man'.

The actors dig their own foxholes, sleep three hours a night, eat cold rations, hump all day in the jungle, ambush at night. Fights break out, black-white relations get rocky, feet get sore, ligaments twist, evacs occur, field sanitation prevails, yet gradually, inevitably, a spirit of camaraderie – of 'gruntdom' – evolves. The only thing that cannot be taught is the fear of instant, violent death that no one can describe for them except their imaginations.

During the shoot, four or five production people are fired, and there are the usual fights, raging line-producer battles, several broken limbs, one near-fatal viper bite, hordes of insects, early monsoon rains, and too many scary moments in helicopters. Dale Dye and I both know how close we are to buying it, having seen choppers go down in Nam, but we have no choice: Money is tight, chopper time limited, so we go for broke, flying out of the jungle canyons in wild wind currents, shooting film as fast as we can. It's the worst week of fear I've had since Vietnam, yet I feel younger than ever, the years dropping off me now with the terror.

The jungle humidity and the twelve-hour days, six-day weeks take their toll on the crew. An unidentified fever bug hits everyone, and by the forty-second day, half the crew doesn't show up for night shooting. I fear for the script, which, as always, is the first to suffer from cost cutting (this is not a major studio film; we're committed to fifty-four iron days in the jungle and not *one*

11

day more). The script is my flesh and blood, I fight for it like a mad dog, only to end up cutting about fifteen per cent of it months later in a Los Angeles editing room. Editing always seems to me like a calculated rout from my grand plan of attack, but in the end the essence seems to survive in a reduced form, like amoebae in a dish ready to grow again with the audience.

I compromise on some shots, and we finish on the fifty-fourth day, at five o'clock on a May morning. Alex Ho, the Chinese production manager with me since Dino, now beaten to a pulp by cast and crew, comes over and says, not without some irony, 'Congratulations, Ollie, it's been a long two years.' ' . . . No, a long twenty,' I murmur, sad 'cause I know that although I finished the film, a part of it will never be there, any more than the faces of the gawky boys we left behind in the dust. As close as I came to Charlie Sheen, he would never be me and *Platoon* would never be what I saw in my mind when I wrote it and which was just a fragment, really, of what happened years ago. That, too, is gone. And we move on.

I don't want to party with the cast and crew – they're having too good a time and I don't want to bring my director's consciousness to bear on them – so I ride home alone with the driver as the light comes up over the paddies and the water buffalo, and the peasants come out as they always do to work the fields in that first pink light of an Asia dawn. It is just another late spring day in the World (as we called it in Vietnam) and nobody cares that we just finished this little 'thing in the jungle'. Why should they? Yet as I press my face against the window of the silently moving car, in my soul there is a moment there and I know that it will last me forever – because it is the sweetest moment I've had since the day I left Vietnam.

PLATOON

CREDITS

Sergeant Barnes .... TOM BERENGER
Sergeant Elias .... WILLEM DAFOE
Chris .... CHARLIE SHEEN
Big Harold .... FOREST WHITAKER
Rhah .... FRANCESCO QUINN
Sergeant O'Neill .... JOHN C. MCGINLEY
Sal .... RICHARD EDSON
Bunny .... KEVIN DILLON
Junior .... REGGIE JOHNSON
King .... KEITH DAVID
Lerner .... JOHNNY DEPP
Tex .... DAVID NEIDORF
Lieutenant Wolfe .... MARK MOSES
Crawford .... CHRIS PEDERSEN
Manny .... CORKEY FORD
Francis .... COREY GLOVER
Gardner .... BOB ORWIG
Warren .... TONY TODD
Morehouse .... KEVIN ESHELMAN
Ace .... JAMES TERRY MCILVAIN
Sanderson .... J. ADAM GLOVER
Tony .... IVAN KANE
Doc .... PAUL SANCHEZ
Captain Harris .... DALE DYE
Parker .... PETER HICKS
Flash .... BASILE ACHARA
Fu Sheng .... STEVE BARREDO
Rodriguez .... CHRIS CASTILLEJO
Tubbs .... ANDREW B. CLARK
Village Chief .... BERNARDO MANALILI

14

Village Chief's Wife .... THAN ROGERS
Village Chief's Daughter .... LI THI VAN
Old Woman .... CLARISA ORTACIO
One-legged Man .... ROMY SEVILLA
Terrified Soldier .... MATHEW WESTFALL
Mechanized Soldier *1 .... NICK NICKELSON
Mechanized Soldier *2 .... WARREN MCLEAN
Rape Victim .... LI MAI THAO
Medic .... RON BARRACKS

Written and Directed by .... OLIVER STONE
Produced by .... ARNOLD KOPELSON
Executive producers .... JOHN DALY/DEREK GIBSON
Co-producer .... A. KITMAN HO
Production Executive .... PIERRE DAVID
Director of Photography
Production Designer .... BRUNO RUBEO
Film Editor .... CLAIRE SIMPSON
First Assistant Director .... H. GORDON BOOS
Sound Mixer .... SIMON KAYE
Military Technical Adviser .... CAPTAIN DALE DYE (RET.)
                               UNITED STATES MARINE CORPS
Special Effects Supervisor .... YVES DE BONO
Special Make-up effects &
visual continuity .... GORDON J. SMITH
Executive in charge of
production .... GRAHAM HENDERSON
Original Music by .... GEORGE DELERUE
Casting .... PAT GOLDEN/BOB MORONES
                                           WARREN MCLEAN
Production Supervisor .... OOTY MOOREHEAD
Production Manager .... JOE CONSTANTINO
Unit Manager .... CENON GONZALES
Key Second Assistant Director .... GERRY TOOMEY
Second Assistant Director .... PEPITO DIAZ
Script Supervisor .... SUSAN MALERSTEIN
Production Coordinator .... ANGELICA DE LEON
Location Manager .... JERRY O'HARA
Assistant to Oliver Stone .... ELIZABETH STONE
First Assistant Camera .... CHRIS LOMBARDI
Additional
Assistant Camera .... GEORGE ROSALES/CALOY SALCEDO

Supervising Sound Editor .... GORDON DANIEL
Sound Editors .... DAVID CAMPLING/GREG DILLON
JAMES J. KLINGER/TONY PALK
Music Editing .... SEGUE MUSIC
Supervising Music Editor .... RICHARD STONE
Re-Recording Mixers .... JOHN 'DOC' WILKINSON
RICHARD ROGERS
CHARLES 'BUD' GRENZBACK
Voice Casting .... BARBARA HARRIS
Music Coordinator .... JOANNE WEISS
Art Directors .... RODEL CRUZ
DORIS SHERMAN WILLIAMS
Chief Armorer .... CESAR DOMINGUEZ
Assistant Armorer .... ROMAN 'DOC' TIZON/
ELIONG MUNOZ/DIOSDADO FIGUEROA/
DONDI PANGILINAN

Makeup and Prosthetic Special
Effects Assistants .... GIONILDA STOLEE/
DEREK HOWARD/CECILLE BAUN
Special Effects Technician .... ANDREW WILSON
Special Effects Assistants .... ROLANDO SALEM/
JOSE MARQUEZ
JIMMY INTAL/RUDY CANDAZA
FELIZARDO MANALOTO/BOY TERRADO

Assistant Military
Technical Advisers .... STANLEY WHITE U.S.M.C. (RET.)
KATHRYN CLAYTON/MARK K. EBENHOCH/
ROBERT M. GALOTTI, JR.
Vietnamese Technical Adviser .... WYNNE WICKER
Philippine Military Liaison .... EUSEBIO GARCIA
Wardrobe Supervisor .... WYNN ARENAS
Costumer .... KATHRYN MORRISON
Second Unit Director of Photography .... TOM SIGEL
Second Unit Assistant Director .... EVAN KOPELSON
Second Unit Sound Mixer .... TAFFY HAINES
Construction Manager .... FRANCISCO BELANGUE
Stunt Coordinator .... GIL ARCEO
Stunts .... MARK K. EBANHOCH/ROBERT M. GALOTTI, JR.
LEONY VIDAL/ROLLY SILONG/JOSEPH RAMOS
ALEX CABODIL/SONNY TUAZON
Still Photographer .... RICKY FRANCISCO

Publicist .... ANDREA JAFFE, INC.
M/S BILLINGS PUBLICITY, LTD.
Production Secretary .... ANNE G. GARCIA
Assistant to Arnold Kopelson .... MAYES RUBEO
Key Production Assistant .... JOHN KERR

FADE IN:
A QUOTATION AGAINST A BLACK SCREEN:

'REJOICE, O YOUNG MAN, IN THY YOUTH ... '
Ecclesiastes

The sound now of a C-130 air cargo plane roaring over us and we cut sharply to:

EXT: AIRSTRIP – BASE CAMP – VIETNAM – DAY
As the C-130 coasts to a stop, the hatch rotating down on a hot, dusty lifeless airstrip somewhere in Vietnam. Nothing seems to live or move in the midday sun.

TITLES RUN

A DOZEN NEW RECRUITS step off the plane, unloading their duffel bags, looking around like only the new can look around, their hair regulation-clipped, crisp, new green fatigues fitting them like cardboard.

CHRIS TAYLOR is just another one of them – as he turns into a tight closeup, to look at a motorized cart pulling up alongside ... He's about 21. Newmeat. His face, unburned yet by the sun, is tense, bewildered, innocent, eyes searching for the truth.

They fall now on a heap of BODY BAGS in the back of the cart. Two soldiers begin loading them onto the plane. Flies – hundreds of flies – buzz around them, the only cue to their contents.

GARDNER *(next to Chris, Southern accent)* That what I think it is?

SOLDIER 1 *(a look)* I guess so ...

An uncomfortable look between them.

SERGEANT Okay, let's go ...

As they move out, Chris' eyes moving with the body bags being loaded onto the plane. Moving over now to a motley HALF DOZEN VET-ERANS bypassing them on their way to the plane. They look happy. Very happy, chatting it up.

They pass the newboys – and they shake their heads, their eyes full of an almost mocking pity.

VETERANS Well I'll be dipped in shit – new meat! Sorry
bout that boys – 'sin loi' buddy ... you gonna love the
Nam, man, for-fucking-ever.

*Chris looking at them. They pass, except for the last man who walks
slower than the rest, a slight limp. His eyes fall on Chris.*

*They're frightening eyes, starved, hollow, sunken deep in his face,
black and dangerous. The clammy pallor of malaria clings to him as he
looks at Chris through decayed black teeth. Then the sun flares out on
him and he's past. And Chris looks back. Disturbed. It's as if the man
was not real. For a moment there. As if he were a ghost.*

*Chris walking, duffel bag on the shoulder, looks up at the lollipop sun
burning a hole through the sky. A rushing SOUND now. Of frightening
intensity, an effect combining the blast of an airplane with the roar of a
lion as we hardcut to:*

EXT: JUNGLE – SOMEWHERE IN VIETNAM – DAY
*The sun matches the intensity of the previous shot as we move down into
thick green jungle. We hear the sound of MEN coming, a lot of men. The
thwack of a machete. Brush being bulled. We wait. They are getting close.*

The CREDITS continue to run.

*SUBTITLE reads: December 1967 – Bravo Company, 25th Infantry
Division – Somewhere near the Cambodian Border.*

*A sweating white face comes into view. CHRIS – cutting point. Machete
in one hand, whacking out a path for the platoon, M-16 in the other, he
looks like he's on the verge of heat exhaustion. Breathing too hard, pacing
himself all wrong, bumping into things, tripping, not quite falling, he
looks pathetic here in the naturalness of the jungle. An urban transplant,
slightly neurotic and getting more so.*

*His rucksack is coming apart as well, about 70 badly packed pounds
banging noisily.*

*Behind him BARNES now comes, the Platoon Sergeant. Then the RTO,
his radio man, humming lightly. Others are behind, the column snaking
back deep into the brush.*

*We cut around some FACES of the Platoon – all to be seen later. Young
faces, hard and dirty after weeks in the field, exhausted yet alert, fatigues*

filthy, slept-in, torn, personalized, hair way past regulation length, medals, bandanas. A jungle army. Boys.

Chris glancing down at his raw bleeding blisters. Transfers the machete to his other, slightly less blistered, hand. The kid cuts on — struggling but trying, on his last reserves of strength, smashing almost straight forward through brush, not even bothering to look ahead. He smells something, looks around, slows his pace, eyes working . . . around to the base of a tree. He moves past it.

And as he does so, the camera from his POV comes around on a dead decomposing 10-day-old GOOK — eyes starting from its sockets, worms and flies feasting.

Chris draws his breath in, terrified. Barnes suddenly appears alongside, his hard humorless eyes looking annoyed from the gook to Chris.

BARNES What are you waiting for? He ain't gonna bite you. Move out.

Chris looks at him with pent-up hatred and crashes on.

EXT: COMPANY CP – DAY – MOVING
At the COMPANY CP, CAPTAIN HARRIS on the radio.

HARRIS Bravo Two, Six. What's the delay up there, move it out on point. We've got a link up at Phase Line Whiskey at One Eight Zero Zero, over.

EXT: PLATOON CP – DAY – MOVING
At the PLATOON CP, LIEUTENANT WOLFE sweats heavily as he speaks in his radio. He is also new to the field, a dark little feisty guy, about 24, very hairy, especially in the eyebrows, an intense get-ahead look.

LIEUTENANT WOLFE Two Bravo, Two move it out. Six says we're jamming 'em up back there. Over.

Barnes, upfront, turns to SAL, his radio man, under his breath.

BARNES Tell that dipshit to get fucked. Get that other freshmeat up here. Gardner.

As Barnes picks up his pace, irritated now at this reprimand from the

21

CO – coming up on Chris, who is soaked now from head to foot in sweat, dizzy, feeling sick, about to vomit.

BARNES What the hell's the matter with you Taylor! You a sorry ass motherfucker. Fall back.

He grabs Chris' machete out of his hand and bulls his way into the foliage, tearing it apart, setting a new pace.

Chris being bypassed by the column, their eyes on him. He is swatting at the red ants that are all over his neck.

GARDNER, another new recruit, fat, hustling up to replace him.

A big and black medic – DOC – comes over, gentle eyes and manner; with him is Sergeant ELIAS, concerned.

DOC You okay?

CHRIS Ants. I got ants on my neck ... *(shaking them out)*

DOC *(helping him)* Yeah, black ants are killers, you look sick man. You need a little salt. *(reaching into his satchel)*

Sergeant Elias, a handsome, graceful dark-haired Indian kid of 23, the squad sergeant, is taking items out of Chris' pack – air mattress, extra unnecessary clothing, extra canteens, grenades, gas mask, books.

ELIAS *(shaking his head, amused)* You're humping way too much, troop, don't need half this shit. I'll haul it for you but next time you check it out with me okay?

Chris nodding, grateful, panting.

The men passing, watching. Chris sorry about this, trying to keep up face.

BUNNY, a young 18 year-old with an angel's face, is pissing in the dead gook's face.

KING passes, glances at him.

KING You're a sick mother Bunny.

Bunny laughing about it.

22

Chris standing there one moment, fighting for his breath, suddenly passes out, going over with his 70 pound rucksack, hitting the ground with a loud bang.

ELIAS *(concerned)* Hold it up.

On Chris — his eyes opening. He seems all right.

CHRIS *(trying to get up)* I'm okay ... I'm okay.

Chris crumples backwards. Elias helps him.

EXT: COMPANY PERIMETER #1 –DUSK
The COMPANY – about 100 men who seem insignificant amid the size of the surrounding jungle – is digging into a perimeter of some 100-yard radius. A RESUPPLY CHOPPER lifts off in a flurry of blowing leaves. Bare-chested soldiers chop down trees, clear fields of fire, set out claymores, fill sandbags, chow down. Little fires snake up against the greying red horizon.

EXT: COMPANY PERIMETER 31 – DOC'S POSITION – DUSK
We cut close on a pair of grungy feet — the staple of the infantry — moving up to DOC, the Medic, bandaging them for FU SHENG, a Hawaiian kid.

EXT: COMPANY PERIMETER #1 – RHAH'S POSITION – DUSK
Rhah sets his tripflare. Crawford, with him, putting out a claymore.

EXT: COMPANY PERIMETER #1 – RODRIGUEZ – POSITION – DUSK
Back in the perimeter RODRIGUEZ sets his M-60 in the newly dug foxhole. SAL, next to him, is shaving in his helmet.

EXT: COMPANY PERIMETER #1 – KING'S POSITION – DUSK
KING looks like a king. A lion of a black man but with a sleepy, gentle face, not to be roused, is painfully trying to scrawl a letter home with the pencil held awkwardly, mouthing the words. FRANCIS, a young baby-faced black with long lashes and soft eyes, peeks over his shoulder, shaking his head.

FRANCIS Shit, King, it ain't d-e-r-e man, it's d-e-a-r, and

Sara don't have no two r's in it, fool. Shame on you.

King shrugs, a sleepy stoned voice.

KING Don't matter, she knows what it means ... an she
don't read too good nohow ...

EXT: COMPANY PERIMETER #1 – COMPANY CP – DUSK
Sgt. Elias washes himself, attentive to his body, slender and well-muscled, an extremely handsome youth. Of Indian blood, with long black hair, generous smile, wide facial bone structure, gypsy eyes, and the cleanest white teeth, he could be a young Greek god. He is given somewhat to panache, a silver wristband on his arm, a bandana of black parachute silk hanging from his neck, his fatigues tightened down at the ankle, he pulls his pants down, checking for crotch rot, applying talcum powder to the area, his buttocks facing us.

LERNER, a white kid, 19, from Florida, stopping to admire the frontal view.

LERNER Mumm, any time sweetheart.

ELIAS Lerner, you'd choke to death on it.

EXT: COMPANY PERIMETER #1 – COMPANY CP – DUSK
At the COMPANY COMMAND POST a beehive of activity with its four radios, personnel, some Vietnamese scouts milling around. CAPTAIN HARRIS is running down a field map with his THREE LIEUTENANTS. Harris, a broad-shouldered fine-looking military specimen with the requisite Southern accent and football coach mannerism, is directing his remark to 2nd Platoon's LT. WOLFE, who looks a little nervous.

CAPTAIN HARRIS Sky Six reports a fresh company of NVA
moving across from Cambodia to this blue line *(points to position)*. We got a good chance to light 'em up tonight. All platoons will set squad-size ambushes before full dark. Lt. Wolfe *(glances at him)* You 'bush in this area near that ol' Buddhist temple we passed on the hump in. Lt. Hawkins, you take this area in the rubber plantation ...

LT. WOLFE *(eager)* No problem sir ...

EXT: PLATOON PERIMETER #1 – CHRIS' FOXHOLE – DUSK
Elsewhere, Chris scrapes out a foxhole, his shirt off, bandana around
his head, the work hot and heavy.

TEX is out there setting the claymore as BIG HAROLD and JUNIOR start
breaking down their C's.

JUNIOR *(a whining high voice)* Hey Big Harold, gimme your
    peaches for the fruitcake man.

BIG HAROLD *(laughs loudly)* Fuck you bitch.

JUNIOR C'mon man, didn't I do you right that time I give
    you the turkey loaf for the ham and lima beans shit.

BIG HAROLD Tricky bitch, reason you gimme dat turkey
    loaf is nobody else can eat that shit 'cept me so don't
    start your game playing with me Junior.

They're both black, Junior with huge goggle eyes and a face of pimples
and pockmarks, his teeth yellowed and decayed, some of them missing.
Harold is about twice his size, about 250 pounds, a baby huey con-
centrating real hard on preparing his stove to eat with.

JUNIOR Youse a pig man. I hope Manny get dat laundry
    gig for' you do.

BIG HAROLD De fool think he's gonna get it but he ain't
    known for his thinking.

JUNIOR He's a fool alright but you a bigger fool. Hey
    whiteboy, watcha waiting for – dat hole ain't gonna dig
    itself …

Chris looks up, continues working, as Junior chuckles.

JUNIOR Hey Taylor, you don't know it but I saved your ass
    today. I killed a shit-eating dog. *(laughing)*

BIG HAROLD *(getting up)* That reminds me, I gotta take a
    shit.

JUNIOR You gonna wipe your ass dis time?

HAROLD Yeah if you let me have your shirt.

CHRIS (*VOICE OVER, as he digs*) Somebody once wrote Hell
is the impossibility of Reason. That's what this place
feels like. I hate it already and it's only been a week.
Some goddamn week, grandma ... (*checking his raw
blisters*) ... the hardest thing I think I've ever done is go
on point, 3 times this week – I don't even know what I'm
doing. A gook could be standing 3 feet in front of me
and I wouldn't know it, I'm so tired. We get up at 5 a.m.,
hump all day, camp around 4 or 5 p.m., dig foxhole, eat,
then put out an all-night ambush or a 3-man listening
post in the jungle. It's scary cause nobody tells me how to
do anything cause I'm new and nobody cares about the
new guys, they don't even want to know your name. The
unwritten rule is a new guy's life isn't worth as much
cause he hasn't put his time in yet – and they say if you're
gonna get killed in the Nam it's better to get it in the first
few weeks, the logic being: you don't suffer that much.
I can believe that ... If you're lucky you get to stay
in the perimeter at night and then you pull a 3 hour
guard shift, so maybe you sleep 3–4 hours a night, but
you don't really sleep ... I don't think I can keep this
up for a year, grandma – I think I've made a big mistake
coming here ...

*As he speaks, we cut around to various shots of the platoon members on
the perimeter – shaving, eating, cooking, playing, etc ...*

EXT: PLATOON CP – NIGHT
*Towards the end of this voice over, we cut to Sgt. BARNES moving
towards the PLATOON CP. A powerful face, a quiet, angry fixed stare, a
thick trimmed moustache that helps conceal a network of plastic surgery
grafts and scars. The distortion from the jaw up the left side of his face to
his forehead, punctuated by a severe indentation above the left eye where a
bullet once penetrated his skull.*

*Walking with him is Sgt. O'NEILL as they join WOLFE, Sgts. ELIAS and
WARREN at the PLATOON CP where they're huddled over maps. Warren
is a black, thin, tall, paranoid man with untrusting eyes, silent and bitter.*

BARNES *(to all, almost pleased about it)* We got boo-coo movement. 3rd Battalion just got hit 15 kliks north or here.
(the MEN react with wary silence)

O'NEILL *(eager to elaborate)* Yeah, they had claymores strung up in the trees, blew a whole fucking platoon to pieces. BAAD SHIT.

Barnes inflects his next words at Wolfe, who is worried.

BARNES Yeah, they got two Lieutenants and a Captain.

WOLFE Jesus.

Elias quiet. Barnes studying the map.

WOLFE *(to Barnes)* Who do you want on ambush, Sergeant?

Barnes doesn't bother acknowledging the question, barely glancing at the Lieutenant, to him a necessary evil. Everybody knows who's really in charge of the Platoon. Barnes flicks his gaze to Elias.

BARNES Elias – you take your squad and I'll take Tex and Francis from your squad. *(to Warren)* We move out in two-zero mikes. *(concluding)*

ELIAS I thought it was O'Neill's turn tonight.

They all look at each other. O'Neill spits in the dust, a freckled, short red head with a hard worried face, a lifer, 30 going on 60.

O'NEILL Shit! Morehouse and Sal are short. Fu Shen's going on R&R, you don't want to send their asses out on an ambush. You got the fresh meat Elias.

ELIAS *(to Barnes)* They don't know shit Barnes, and chances are we gonna run into something.

O'NEILL So what am I going to do! Get one of my guys zapped so some fuckface fresh from the World can get his beauty fucking sleep!

ELIAS Hey O'Neill why don't you cool it, you don't have to be a prick everyday of your life you know.

O'NEILL Fuck you Elias.

BARNES You get your men ready Elias ...

Concluding the debate, no further argument, Barnes rises. The meeting's closed. Lt. Wolfe hasn't said a word, looking as Elias departs, without a word.

O'NEILL *(watching him)* Fucking guy's got 3 years in and he thinks he's Cochise or something ...

His resentment directed partly at the way in which Elias carries himself, the natural sense of grace — and the dignity it bestows.

CUT TO:
EXT: PLATOON PERIMETER #1 – SQUAD ASSEMBLY POINT – DUSK
Later. On the very edge of the perimeter, darkness coming down fast, the men in the ambush patrol rustle into their packs, all of them bitching.
Tex, carrying the M-60, looks up at the glowering sky.

TEX Shit, looks like rain. All night too. Gonna grow mushrooms in your bad-ass crotch Junior.

JUNIOR *(under his breath)* Goddamn ain't no justice round here, you break your ass for de white man ... gonna get our act together, do some rappin' wid de brothers, change things ...

CRAWFORD What's O'Neill have a nose up the lieutenant's ass already, how come we always get ambush.

FRANCIS Politics, man, politics. We always getting fucked around here.

Chris is scared, nervous with his last-minute equipment adjustments, his pack obviously overweight for a night mission as he hauls it up.

28

Gardner, the other new boy, is jovial in contrast, his wallet extended towards Chris.

GARDNER Hey Chris, I show you a picture of Lucy Jean?

CHRIS *(not to be bothered)* No ...

Gardner shows him his girl. She's real dog u-g-l-y, and what makes it worse is Gardner's put the standard photo of Raquel Welch alongside it, tits and all. But he misses the irony of it.

GARDNER *(admiring)* Yeah she's the one all right ... that's
    Lucy Jean. She's a-waiting for me.

CHRIS *(nodding)* Yeah she's real pretty, you're lucky ...

Gardner puts it away. Elias appears alongside them, checking their packs out, takes out Chris' poncho liner and other items. He carries a modified M-16 with a short barrel and a collapsible stock.

ELIAS *(to both boys)* Don't need this or this ... you're doing
    okay. Just stick close to Tex, do what he does.
    (calling out to Tex) Tex you got Junior and Taylor here on
    your position.

Tex is a sour Texas Ranger type, chews tobacco, spits.

TEX Damn, 'Lias this gun's boss. Put Taylor someplace else.

Chris feels the words like lashes on him.

ELIAS You got Taylor ...
    (to Gardner) ... Gardner you go with me
    (to Chris and Gardner), 'Case somethin' happens to you,
    you get separated or lost don't yell out okay. Sit tight.
    We'll get to you.

His eyes. Chris watching them. A smile in them. Elias moves off, a quality to the man that Chris admires. A natural sense of leadership.

BARNES Okay, let's move it out.

As he follows King, on point, out the perimeter. A single file.

29

EXT: THE AMBUSH NIGHT (RAIN)
Night is coming down. The tone of the jungle sounds has subtly shifted — mellower, more sinuous and certainly scarier.

The file stops. King, an experienced point man, listens.

Chris — carrying Tex's linked ammo — looks around, tense. Behind him is Gardner, trying to smile, starts to whisper something ('Hey Taylor ...') when he's abruptly shushed.

The file moves on. Gardner's pack rattling a little too loud. A weird rush of cold wind now rattles the trees and the MONSOON comes. A hard slanting rain, sudden, tropic.

EXT: RUINS – JUNGLE – NIGHT (RAIN)
A piece of an old Buddhist temple, under a sulky moonlight now in a state of decay, the jungle surging to engulf it.

The Men are setting up quickly and relatively quietly in the ruins — alongside a minuscule trail. The rain is coming down harder than ever.

Chris and Tex setting out their claymore mines, raveling back their detonating cords to their position, drenched. In the far distance, an ILLUMINATION ROUND brightens the sky for a brief moment. Various ad lib curses and directions are lost in the sound of the rain.

EXT: AMBUSH – BARNES' POSITION – NIGHT (RAIN)
At the Ambush CP, Ace whispers into his radio. A soft hissing sound.

EXT: AMBUSH – CHRIS' POSITION – NIGHT (RAIN)
Later. Close on Chris being shaken awake.

TEX Taylor, you're on.

CHRIS *(groggy)* Uh hunh.

The rain continuing to pelt them. Tex hands him an infrared scope.

TEX *(suspicious)* You sure you know how to work the claymore?

CHRIS *(offended)* Sure.

Tex curls up as best he can in his poncho to sleep.

TEX Okay ... don't catch no zzz's on me buddy or I'll sling your motherfucking ass ... You hear me?

CHRIS *(grits his teeth)* Yeah. *(looking at his watch)*
Hey Tex – you're ten minutes fast.

TEX Sin Loi. *('tough luck', closes his teeth)*

Chris lets it go, scans the jungle and trail with the scope. The POV is greasy and blurred. He puts it aside.

Suddenly a series of resonant SNORES crack through the jungle. Chris starts, then sees it's from JUNIOR lying out there, spreadeagled in the rain. Chris prods him.

CHRIS Junior!

JUNIOR Unh? ... Unh.

CHRIS Shaddup! You're snoring ... Shhh.

Bending low into his eardrum. Junior never wakes, rolls over with a growl. Silence.

CUT TO:
EXT: CHRIS' POSITION – NIGHT (RAIN)
Later. A pool of muddy water has formed, in which a pair of buttocks sit. Move up to Chris still on duty, looking at his watch, drawn, drenched, pathetic, rainwater coursing down his face.

CHRIS VOICE OVER *(continuing his letter)* ... 'Course Mom and Dad didn't want me to come, they wanted me to be just like them – respectable, hard-working, making $200 a week, a little house, a family. They drove me crazy with their goddamn world, grandma, you know Mom, I don't want to be a white boy on Wall Street, I don't want my whole life to be predetermined by them.

A large RIPPING SOUND as the wind blows down a big tree branch onto the jungle floor. He starts, peering out. Nothing. He looks at his watch again.

CHRIS VOICE OVER ... I guess I have always been sheltered and special, I just want to be anonymous. Like everybody else. Do my share for my country. Live up to what Grandpa did in the First War and Dad the Second. I know this is going to be *the* war of my generation. Well here I am – anonymous all right, with guys nobody really cares about – they come from the end of the line, most of 'em, small towns you never heard of – Pulaski, Tennessee, Brandon, Mississippi, Pork Bend, Utah, Wampum, Pennsylvania. Two years' high school's about it, maybe if they're lucky a job waiting for 'em back in a factory, but most of 'em got nothing, they're poor, they're the unwanted of our society, yet they're fighting for our society and our freedom and what we call America, they're the bottom of the barrel – and they know it, maybe that's why they call themselves 'grunts' cause a 'grunt' can take it, can take anything. They're the backbone of this country, grandma, the best I've ever seen, the heart and soul – I've found it finally, way down here in the mud – maybe from down here I can start up again and be something I can be proud of, without having to fake it, maybe ... I can see something I don't yet see, learn something I don't yet know ... I miss you, I miss you very much, tell Mom I miss her too – Chris.

He moves towards Junior, shakes him, but Junior seems to be out of this world.

CHRIS Wake up!

Junior opens one dead eye.

CHRIS It's your shift, man ...

Junior scowls, swears, looks around for his rifle in the mud.
Chris crawls back to his position, curling himself up in his soaked poncho, teech chattering from the cold, rain splattering over him. A long beat. He sighs, the sigh kicking off the next image.

EXT: CHRIS' POSITION – NIGHT

Chris jerks awake – very suddenly, very frightened. THE RAIN HAS STOPPED. The jungle sounds are loud. Cicadas, night animals, water dripping hypnotically from leaf to leaf. And the whirr of a million mosquitoes out after the rains, chewing at Chris' face. He looks around, startled.

Tex is asleep. Junior is asleep. What happened? He looks at his watch. The mosquitoes are eating him alive. He buries his head in his green towel which he wears around his neck, but he can't see. A beat. He moves again, miserable from the bites. Another beat. Then suddenly the sounds of the jungle shift – some of the animals dropping out. A different tone. A piece of wood is stepped on, a rustle of bush ...

Chris sees something, lifts an edge of the towel to peek out.

A shadow of a figure is frozen there in front of him about 15 yards. It looks like a man. But it doesn't move. At all. It listens.

Chris, his heart in his mouth, tries to peer through it. It's a bush. It has to be. No human being could stand that still. His heartbeats are up. The moments take forever. But deep down – somewhere in his psyche – he knows who it is.

The figure now shifts, ever so slightly – and moves. It is a human being. Oh my God!

Chris looks around. Tex seems like a mile away. Why doesn't anyone fire! He casts a desperate look at his rifle, at his grenades encrusted with mud, but in spite of all his training, he is frozen with indecision and fear at the sight of his enemy.

The figure seems to whisper something back, then turns and comes down the trail. Now a second and third figure appear behind him – all in helmets and packs. All coming right past Chris' position. Ten yards. Nine.

Chris is rigid with terror. Stark eyes. Pleading with Tex to wake up, but out of reach. He is about to have an anxiety attack, his heartbeats so far up he is sure they will hear him.

The first figure is now directly in front of Chris on the trail, looking left and right. A rattle of his equipment, a creak of leather. A smell. The man's face now catches the moonlight and his eyes come around on Chris.

Oriental eyes. Looking right at him. Startled. Chris staring back, hypno-

33

tized. It all happens very fast. The figure murmurs something in Viet-namese. A warning. He swivels.

A flash of muzzle fire. A raking cough of automatic fire. A grenade explosion.

Chris is hurled to the ground, helmet bouncing off, scattered, confused, jarred. All hell breaks loose around him with NOISE and SHOUTS.

Tex, kissing the ground, is yelling at him.

TEX THE CLAYMORE! GET THOSE FUCKERS!

Chris, not knowing what he's doing, is fumbling with the claymore handles, presses them. INSERT: They won't give. He tries again and again to squeeze the life out of them. Tex is screaming at him.

TEX THE SAFETY! TAKE THE SAFETY OFF YOU ...

Lunges over and grabs the handle from Chris. Clicks the safeties off and blows them.

Three EXPLOSIONS rip out into the night – and one of the ENEMY is caught in a brief instant looking like an X-ray, his body lifted and swirling in the air, then enveloped in swirls of smoke.

Chris, trying to keep up, grabs his M-16, lays out a stream of fire. The sound all around him is deafening.

EXT: GARDNER'S POSITION – NIGHT
Gardner, freaking out, stands crouched, confused, tries to run, collapses.

EXT: O'NEILL'S POSITION – NIGHT
O'Neill throws a grenade, wild.

EXT: CHRIS' POSITION – NIGHT
An explosion. Chris hits the deck.

Tex is now on the M-60 machine gun, yelling at Junior who is cringing on the ground.

TEX Feed me!

He lays out red tracer bullets like laser beams, then suddenly reels back, whiplashed, screaming. A grenade explosion rocks them.

TEX AAAAGHHH! MY ARM! MY ARM!

His hand and wrist are gone, his face in the dirt. Junior is fumbling around, trying to stay down and help him at the same time.

JUNIOR *(grabbing Tex's gun)* DOC! GET UP HERE! TEX IS HIT!

Chris, looking out to his front, has no clue what's going on. Except the fire is slacking. Relayed shouts of 'Medic! Medic!' Other SHOUTS.

SHOUTS HOLD IT UP! HOLD IT UP!

The firing has ceased. A silence, punctuated by occasional shouts and fast moments, has enveloped once more the cemetery. Doc crashes through the bush, kneels over Tex, who continues to howl in deep pain.

TEX *(freaked out)* MY ARM! JESUS FUCKING CHRIST!

DOC Easy Tex easy boy!

Trying to sound calm but his voice on the edge, examining the mutilation with a pen flashlight, he whips out his morphine in a big hypodermic.

VOICE *(next position)* Doc over here! Gardner's hit.

DOC 'right there.

As he slips the morphine into Tex's arm.

TEX *(muttering at Chris)* ... goddamn! goddamn! DUMB FUCKER, DUMB FUCKER!

Chris watching, suddenly feels himself dizzy, instinctively runs his hands over the back of his neck. Feels the warm blood there. A moan comes from his lips. Junior looks at him.

JUNIOR Oh shit, Doc he's hit too.

CHRIS *(weakly)* I'm hit ...

Barnes and Big Harold come hustling up.

Doc finishes tourniqueting Tex, cradles Chris onto the earth, his flashlight probing the wound. Tex in background continues to thrash and moan.

Chris waits, tensely for the verdict, his eyes big with fear on Doc, who takes out his morphine.

JUNIOR *(to Barnes, pointing at Chris)* That dumb fuck didn't blow his claymore!

Chris hearing this. Barnes looks at him.

DOC *(to Chris)* . . . it's a scratch, nothing to worry about.

CHRIS *(suspicious)* Doc . . . tell me the truth, don't lie to me.

The needle goes in. Tex lets out this strange keening moan that sets everyone's teeth on edge.

JUNIOR *(to Barnes)* He let 'em walk right up on us. He was sleeping on his shift.

CHRIS *(muttering weakly)* I was not . . . it was your . . .

DOC *(leaving, to Harold and Junior)* Self-preservation's the first law of nature. Gotta learn how to work your shit Taylor. Watch em, don't let 'em go into shock.

Tex's moans are maddening and scary. Barnes suddenly clamps his hand over Tex's mouth shutting him up and from way down deep in his throat, chokes out the words.

BARNES Shut up! Shut up – and *TAKE IT! TAKE THE PAIN!*

Tex's eyes roll wildly, uncomprehending. Doc and Big Harold looking at Barnes, wondering. Tex is suddenly silent, shocked. Barnes stands, an icy glare, goes. Junior scrambles over to Tex's side. Doc runs off.

Big Harold cradles Chris, his big black hands like a mother, reassuring him.

BIG HAROLD You gonna be okay Taylor, okay, don't you

start worrying now.

Chris looking up at him, eyes blinking slowly, dazed already by the morphine. He's very scared.

CHRIS Do you ... do you know you're gonna die ... Big Harold? ... do you feel like ... like ... everything's gonna be fine and then ...

BIG HAROLD Bullshit man, you gettin outta the field, man. Three hots a day, white sheets, dem pretty white nurses give you blowjobs too you pay em enough, I heard tell bout dem white bitches. Better save yo strength Taylor.

JUNIOR *(muttering darkly)* Don babytalk him man. Cocksucker fell asleep. They walked right up on us, he don do shit.

HAROLD Shaddup bitch.

Chris is getting woozier, feeling he is dying but starting to grin, not caring about it anymore. Yet he is nowhere close to dying.

CHRIS It's not ... so bad ... dying. How long ... it ...

EXT: TRAIL – RUINS – POSITION #1 – NIGHT
Barnes stands over a moaning, ripped up ENEMY SOLDIER. FIRES his M-16 point blank into the head. The Soldier bucks and dies, quivering.

EXT: TRAIL – RUINS – POSITION #2 – NIGHT
ELIAS, checking out a blood trail some distance away, shifts on the shot, looks back.

EXT: TRAIL – RUINS – POSITION #3 – NIGHT
FRANCIS, MANNY, BUNNY and KING are huddled over another mangled enemy corpse.

BUNNY *(stripping the corpse)* That's no NVA man. That's a chink – look at 'em, the cocksucker's six and a half feet tall. Look at his gear – good as ours.

FRANCIS Shit I blew my claymore right in one dude's face
and I seen him walking around afterwards.

MANNY What we fighting here, vampires?

EXT: TRAIL – RUINS – POSITION #1 – NIGHT
*Elias comes up to Barnes swiftly, indicating the blood trail leading off
into the bush.*

ELIAS Blood trail just keeps going and going but no body.

BARNES How the hell did he get away?

ELIAS Fuckers returned fire soon as we lit 'em up. Hard
core fuckin' NVA. They got their shit together.

KING *(coming up, to Barnes)* Sarge – Doc wants you. There's a
problem with the new man.

*Elias and Barnes go with King. Past Chris and Tex who are ambula-
tory and bandaged, being helped along. As Barnes passes, the men
look at him, everybody quickly senses something is wrong.*

EXT: GARDNER'S POSITION – NIGHT
*At one of the positions Doc is working feverishly to knock the life back
into Gardner who lies there, his shirt stripped off on his cottage cheese
belly. A huge sucking chest wound. He's dying. You know it because he
knows it. The eyes do the talking, numb, terrorized yet strangely
detached, accepting, not protesting or concerned any longer.*

*Most of the ambush has assembled and is watching, Chris moving in to
see. Doc is mumbling to him, low key.*

DOC Chopper's on the way Gardner, hang in there, you
gonna be okay ...

*But Gardner seems unconcerned. Things are going on in his head –
who knows what. And in his eyes there are big tears rolling. Then a
morphine smile. A sort of goofy Gardner smile, maybe thinking about
Lucy Jean, who knows. He's dead.*

BARNES *(to all)* Take a good look at this lump o'shit ...

38

(motions to Gardner's body)
Remember what it looks like, all of you. You fuck up in a
firefight and I guaran-goddamn-tee you, a trip out of the
bush – *IN A BODYBAG*. Out here, assholes, you keep your
shit wired tight at *ALL* times ...
(glares directly at Chris)
and that goes for you, shit for brains. You don't *SLEEP
ON NO FUCKIN' AMBUSH*. Next sonofabitch I catch
coppin' z's in the bush I'm personally gonna take an
interest in seeing him suffer – *I SHIT YOU NOT* ...

*He thumps Chris lightly but menacingly in his chestbone and moves
on.*

CHRIS *(drowsy)* I didn't fall asleep, Sergeant, Junior ...

BUNNY *(pissed, cuts in, shoves him hard)* Shut your face chicken
shit! You in big trouble boy!

O'NEILL Excuses are like assholes, Taylor – everybody got
one.

ELIAS Knock it off! We got two men need attention here.
Police up your extra ammo and frags, don't leave
nothing for the dinks. Hoyt, Junior, carry Gardner.

JUNIOR *(muttering)* Let de white boy carry his ass, he this
dude that got him fucked up. Who'd be hauling his ass
if that was a brother laying there?

Elias follows Barnes out of earshot of the others.

ELIAS Man'd be alive if he'd had a few more days to learn
something.

Barnes, registering it, just keeps walking.

EXT: BASE CAMP – DAY (WEEK LATER)
*Chris is driven up in a jeep to his Company CP – marked 'Bravo CP'
on a C-ration box. It's midday on a hot lazy afternoon, few people out
in the 102 degree sun.*

*Chris' Company is on the outskirts of the base camp, their bar-
racks regulation wood, canvas, and fine mesh screening, red
dust everywhere, bunkers down on the perimeter, reams of barbed
wire and concertina, a sand-bagged MESS HALL and CHAPEL,
81 mm mortar pits, observation towers, recoiless rifles, 50-caliber
machine guns.*

*Chris gets out of the jeep, stiff-necked, a bandage around it, still in some
pain. The first man he intersects is KING, carrying crates of beer.*

KING Hey Taylor, what's in the breeze?

In King's mild tone Chris tries to read his standing in the platoon.

CHRIS Okay – got light duty, three days.

KING Shit, too bad we in base camp anyway.

CHRIS What you got there – beers?

KING Yeah, just stole me some from the Top's supply but
he's stealing it from us anyway. *(sees somebody coming)*
Chucks are coming. You better 'didi' man.

*Too late. Sgt. O'NEILL, the redhead lifer accompanied by Spec 4
SANDERSON, a big handsome blond kid, not too bright in the face, both
slightly drunk, come around a corner, beer cans in hand. O'Neill sees
Chris immediately.*

O'NEILL Hey Taylor – you back?

CHRIS *(pause)* Uh, looks like it?

SANDERSON *(spotting King's beer)* Where'd you get that beer
King?

KING *(a funny look)* I found it . . .

SANDERSON You found it? . . . Bullshit! You going on
report. Gimmee that shit.

O'NEILL Awright, come here both of you. You too Taylor
(wags his finger) Got a little special job for you.

They advance toward him reluctantly.

CHRIS I got light duty, Sarge. Doctor said to take it easy couple days.

O'NEILL *(laughs)* ... ain't that tough shit now.

EXT: THE OUTHOUSE – DAY
A wooden cabin with some half-dozen seats built over half barrels cut from empty oil-drums. A guy is in there, pulling up his pants.

Chris, King and Crawford, a California blond with a handsome honeyed look, are sweating heavily as they roll the barrels out from under the outhouse, the smell of human waste strong. A hot midday emptiness, nobody around except the flies.

KING *(pissed)* ... Motherfuckah, motherfuckah, I'm too short to be dealing with *this* shit! They keep *fucking* with us man, no letup ...

CRAWFORD *(equally pissed)* Politics man, fuckin' politics. That O'Neill man got his nose so far up Top's ass he gotta be Pinocchio ...

KING Forty-two days man and a wakeup and I'm a gone motherfucker. Back to de *WORLD.(dreaming in his eyes)*

CRAWFORD Broke a 100. Got 92 to go. April 17. DEROS man. California this summer. Waves are good they tell me, surfin's gonna be good ...

KING March man in Tennessee, sniff the pines ... sniff that crossmounted pussy walkin' down by the river. What you got Taylor? *(a snicker)* Let's see three hundred and *WHAT*?

CHRIS ... 32. 332 days.

CRAWFORD *(groans)* Oh man! Sorry bout that. I can't even remember when I was 332. You gotta count backwards like you got 40 days in – think positive.

KING *(to Chris)* How the fuck you get over here man, you look like you educated ...

CHRIS I volunteered.

KING You *WHAT*? Say 'gain.

CHRIS Yeah, I dropped out of college and told 'em I wanted infantry, combat, and Nam ...

He grins, finding their reactions funny. It's also the first time we've seen Chris crack a smile.

CRAWFORD You volunteered for this shit man?

KING You a crazy fucker, givin' up college man.

King has long sleepy eyelids and cat's eyes, a large pink tongue and big white-edged cotton picker's nails — a lazy, gentle nature, content with the world.

CHRIS Didn't make much sense. Wasn't learning anything ... *(hesitates)* And why should just the poor kids go to the war — and the college kids get away with it.

King and Crawford share a smile.

KING What we got here a crusader?

CRAWFORD Sounds like it.

They pause, wipe the sweat off. King lighting up a half-smoked joint, hitting a few puffs, eyes shooting around, making sure he's not spotted, passing it to Crawford.

KING Sheeit, gotta be rich in the first place to think like dat. Everybody know the poor aways being fucked by the rich. Always have, always will.

Noticing Chris is having trouble with his neck, picking at his bandage.

KING You okay man? Neck botherin' you?

CHRIS Nah ...

KING Here have some of this. Won't feel a thing.

Chris looking at the joint, a little apprehensive. He's never smoked.

CHRIS No, thanks ...

KING Go on, whatcha gotta lose, yo' here now ...

CRAWFORD Kills the smell of shit anyway.

The joint proferred. Chris waits a beat, shrugs, takes it, smokes.

KING Suck it in. Hold it ... That's it. Now let it out.

Chris blows it out.

CHRIS Don't feel it.

King and Crawford chuckle, go on rolling the cans.

KING Dat's what they all say.

CUT TO:
EXT: OUTHOUSE – LATER – DAY
*King, Crawford and Chris pour kerosene over the cans at a secure
distance from the outhouse.*

*King lights it. The cans pop and start crackling. A line of burning
barrels. Rings of dirty black smoke rise against a soft blue sky.*

They watch, stoned. Chris turns to both of them.

CHRIS   ... you know that night we got hit ... I ... *(ashamed)*

KING Fuck it, don't mean nothing, no such thing here as a
coward, done your best man, next time y'do better.

CRAWFORD History, man, history.

*Chris surprised at their attitude. The joint suddenly hits him, a look in
his face, eyes looking around different. Over at King.*

CHRIS *(deadpan)* I think I'm starting to feel that
  stuff ...

Crawford laughs.

KING *(laughs)* Yo getting there Taylor. You be cool now and
  I'll introduce you 'round to some of the 'heads'.

CHRIS What are heads?

KING *(laughs, walks away with Crawford)* Later ...

Chris alone, breathes deep, feeling the full effect.

EXT: BASE CAMP – NIGHT
*A relief against the long harsh, hot day. We see lights on all over the
camp, sounds of music, laughter from the barracks.*

INT: UNDERWORLD HUTCH – NIGHT
*King leads Chris down to a specially constructed cellar-like hutch dug
deep into the ground on an isolated edge of the battalion perimeter.
Ammo casing and canvas are piled over it, and sandbags surround it.
From the outside very little sound can be heard as they go down
through a trap door made of ammo crates. Past a lookout (Adams)
pulling security, hitting a joint but alert. King motions to him, it's cool.*

*Inside is another world. Chris looking around amazed. It's like a
private cabaret for the 'heads' who are there cooling out. Boxes of food
from the States, beers, whiskey bottles, crates functioning as tables,
hammocks hanging from poles, electric fans, tape decks,
paraphernalia.*

*The boys are all dressed up in their Saturday night rags. The clothes
are clean, the headbands, the medallions are out, anything distinctive
and individualistic. On the tapedeck, Jefferson Airplane's 'Go Ask
Alice'.*

*To Chris it is a new world. And RHAH, the resident head, sitting there in
all his finery puffing a huge burning red bowl in a three foot long
Montagnard pipe, seems to be the lord of final judgment in this smoky
underworld.*

Across his naked chest, birds and snakes are tattooed. Around his neck a black skull and white ivory cross side by side. On his knuckles 'Love' and 'Hate' are tattooed. In his eyes, a dancing Satanic fire. A poor rural Southern white, in his grizzled late 20's, he could be a Biker King. Giving Chris the once-over.

RHAH Whatcha doing in the underworld Taylor?

KING *(smiling)* This ain't Taylor. Taylor been shot. This man Chris been resurrected ...

Chris wondering what he's doing here. His eyes roving over LERNER, CRAWFORD, MANNY, FLASH, FRANCIS, HOYT, TUBBS, DOC, others from the Platoon, about 9 or 10 of them.
Rhah eyes him back, hands him the bowl.

RHAH You lame Taylor?

CHRIS What?

RHAH You lame or something?

KING *(smiling)* ... go ahead on, smoke it man.

Chris understands, takes the bowl. Hesitates. Then smokes it. The contact fumes are almost enough to knock him out. He starts coughing. They're all laughing.

RHAH Your shit's in the wind troop. Baaaah!

Lerner replies, his tongue hanging out in parody.

LERNER And Baaaaaaa! back on you.

RHAH *(looking at Lerner with distaste)* If you're gonna do it man, 'least do it right.

Building up to it, his eyes shaking with conviction at the whole insanity of the world, he neighs with all the venom he can muster.

RHAH Baaaaaaaaaaaaaaaaaaaa!

45

They all laugh and applaud. King smoking from the pipe passing it back to Chris who takes another hit, doesn't cough this time, looking around, wondering about these guys.

LERNER   I didn't like it.

RHAH   Bah, you're a child, Lerner. Rhah don't waste time
on you.

They go on ad-libbing with each other, teasing Doc, who's fairly straight, saying he wants to go to med school in the fall. 'Be what?' 'A gynecologist, man.' 'What dat?' Francis suggests, 'Dat's a pussy doctor, man — he's gonna be Doctor Feelgood, man!' They're all cracking up, finding every joke funny. As Chris finishes his hit on the pipe, looks up across the smoke, already dazed, surprised to see ELIAS suddenly there — leaning out of his sling in a far corner of the hooch. A Monkey is draped around his neck with silver bracelets, rings, a necklace — like a sensual little Egyptian whore, Elias playing with it, spaced out in a sleeveless vest, tiger pants. Dancing eyes on Chris, he swings out the hammock, comes over with the monkey.

Meanwhile Manny has broken into a high falsetto snatch of blues directed at Chris, joined by Big Harold and Francis, all of them clicking their hands.

MANNY & FRANCIS & BIG HAROLD & DOC   Oooh Chris, you
look like you is high
Oh yeah, he looks like he is high
Ooooh Chris, you know you gonna be that way all night
Oh yeah I think that you are ... Yeah! up now and up
to par oh yeah

Elias pulls out a Remington 870 shotgun, jacks it to the rear, points it at Chris.

ELIAS   Put your mouth on that.

Chris does so slowly, a little worried. Elias takes a hit and blows it down the bore — 'shotgunning' it into Chris' lungs. Chris staggers back, coughing. Everybody laughs 'hey dude — you done had your ass blown away' etc ...

Elias smiles his big white-tooth smile.

ELIAS First time?

CHRIS Yeah.

ELIAS Then the worm has definitely turned for you man.

Chris puzzled by this expression.

ELIAS *(smiles)* Feel good?

CHRIS *(a sense of euphoria now)* Yeah. No pain in my neck now. Feels good.

ELIAS Feelin' good's good enough.

As he sucks in a huge mass of smoke off the bowl. His eyes performing a funny little hop, skip and jump, as he holds it, his face turning red.

The monkey jabbers and jumps around on his neck, worried. Elias then blows the smoke out in its face, the monkey hating it.

The Group laughs.

ELIAS Hey Crutcher. I hear you got a Dear John from your gal. Told you she wasn't getting 'nuff from you.

Lerner looks up, stoned out of his mind, wearing a ring in his ear.

LERNER Shit. Sold me out for some lame dude with a 4-F.

ELIAS What'd you say her name was again?

LERNER *(recalling her image)* Daisy Mae.

BIG HAROLD Hey look at Charlotte!

The monkey is sitting quietly stoned, its eyes blinking. Laughter off.

ELIAS Daisy Mae! What Daisy Mae look like Crutcher?

MANNY She look huge and got freckles on her ass.

LERNER She look beautiful.

FRANCIS How much she weigh man?

BIG HAROLD She braid her hair under her armpits, Crutcher.

FRANCIS *(sarcastic)* Daisy Mae what?

KING Daisy Mae Highway, that's what. *(laughing)* Well whatcha want, Lerner, your dick been limp for a year, 'cept when you're bopping your buddy Tony up there.

LERNER Fuck that.

ELIAS I fucked this chick in Hawaii man. Couple weeks ago … Ooooh! Wow – outasight. Gracie Slick man, she looked like Gracie man, I shit you not. *(remembering)*

The look on his face ensnares all of them, except perhaps Rhah.

MANNY What happened man. What whorehouse you go to?

ELIAS No whorehouse man. On the beach.

FRANCIS Sure.

ELIAS Yeah, sure. She walked right by me. Long black hair, tits swinging. Ass like French bread. Legs don't end right.

LERNER *(skeptical)* You can plant that shit in Tennessee man, but it won't come up in Texas.

CRAWFORD So what she got, hair on her tits.

ELIAS I just stopped man. My heart's beating like a hardon right I got a hardon sticking through my pants, my bathing suit looks like a hutch …

BIG HAROLD I know dat feeling …

ELIAS So I'm thinking to myself – Elias you walk away from this, you gonna regret this the rest of your natural life.

So I go after her, follow her down the beach. You know find out if she is what she is.

They're all hooked into this now.

KING And?

ELIAS Well she was picking up her kids.

MANNY Dat's dat.

ELIAS No, dat ain't dat.

FRANCIS Get outta here, she married ...

ELIAS Like two hogs in heat. Boy.

Their throats knotting ...

CHRIS *(joining in)* ... But what'd she do?

ELIAS What didn't she do. She fucked the living shit outta me, that's what she did!

CRAWFORD *(sucking in air)* Jesus!

ELIAS Couldn't get enuff ...

CHRIS But what'd she actually do?

ELIAS She was a crossbreed, Chinese and Polish.

BIG HAROLD What dat?

RHAH *(finally hooked in)* And living in Hawaii man?

ELIAS Yeah – and has blonde hair and almond-shaped eyes.

FRANCIS Hey man didn't you say she had black hair?

ELIAS She had blonde hair man. And long tan legs, in those leather sandals you know, with those thongs up to her knees, this musky oil on it ... mmmm smelled good when they were wrapped around my face ...

They groan, dreaming of Hawaii.

DOC Yeah!

CHRIS God!

BIG HAROLD Please, somebody hold my dick!

ELIAS *(in afterthought)* ... and a broken nose.

DOC Broken man?

ELIAS Yeah, otherwise she would've been too perfect,
   y'know what I mean ... some woman. Her name was ...

He forgets it. A grass blackout. Lerner urging him on.

LERNER Susan?

MANNY Tamara?

CHRIS Elizabeth?

Elias shaking his head, trying to remember.

KING Merle?

RHAH Merle? Jesus! ... Patty?

BIG HAROLD Inga?

CHRIS Jennifer?

HOYT Connie?

Elias snapping his fingers.

ELIAS Dawn! That was it!

CHRIS *(repeating it)* Dawn ...

King listening to the sound of it.

KING Dawn?

The others nodding, musing over it.

BIG HAROLD Yeah, Dawn ...

INT: THE BARRACKS – NIGHT
In comparison to the darkness of the hooch, a highly lit atmosphere, attracting bugs ... dusty gear lying around a disordered hooch, loud and finger-snapping COUNTRY WESTERN MUSIC playing from a tape deck, a well-known tune, circa 1967.

BUNNY, the 18 year-old angel face, totters drunk with a Colt-45 beer in hand, over to JUNIOR, the badass black kid with the zits, who just lies there on his cot sweating, doing nothing.

BUNNY *(listening to the music)* Listen to that shit, that's good shit!

JUNIOR *(irritated as always)* Fuck that redneck noise, dude. All dem chicks be rappin' how dey losin' der' ho's and how dey ain't got no bread for beer. Fuck dat honky shit. Got to get me some motown jams, dig it?

BUNNY *(doesn't understand a word of it)* Whaddaya talking shit for man. Hey Junior! Y'ever smoke any shit?

JUNIOR Das right dude. You be tryin' to string de black man out on dat shit and keep him *DOWN*. Time's be coming, my man, when de black man's gonna throw off that yoke.

BUNNY *(lonely in his way for company)* Say I can dig it. Smoke that shit everything kinda gets weird y'know? *(hiccups, sits)* Y'hear that story the gooks is putting chemicals in the grass so's we become 'pacifists' so's we don fight *(to no one in particular)* Where the hell's everybody, theyse gettin high that's what – bunch of hopheads, they think they special ...

JUNIOR *(turns away, bored)* Don you worry Bunny, youse a killer anyway.

51

BUNNY Yeah but I still like a piece of pussy once in a while
– ain't nothing like a piece of pussy cept maybe the
Indie 500.

JUNIOR Youse so fucked up man.

BUNNY Y'ever look at yoself in the mirror Junior, youse
uglier than a dick on a dog man. *(laughing)*

JUNIOR Yeah, you had a piece of pussy on a plate in front
of you, you'd probably kill it.

BUNNY Shit, I bet I been laid more'n you have.

JUNIOR Sure, you probably stick it in tween her knees and
think youse there.

BUNNY Yeah?

JUNIOR Only way you'd get some pussy is your bitch dies
and wills it to you – and then maybe.

*Lt. WOLFE wanders down the aisle, beer in hand, slightly lonely,
bypassing FU SHENG, the Hawaiian and TONY, a mustached hairy-
browed Italian kid from Boston, who are playing some kind of dice game.
They hardly acknowledge the Lieutenant who stops by RODRIGUEZ, the
Mexican-American kid who is on his cot in his neatly arranged area
writing a letter home with a pencil, forming the words with his mouth, as
always minding his own business. Religious objects comprise his few
decorations.*

WOLFE *(amiable)* How you doing Rodriguez?

RODRIGUEZ Good sir.

WOLFE Need anything?

RODRIGUEZ No sir.

*Wolfe winks at him, continues on to the POKER GAME going on in the
center of the barracks, the main action. BARNES, Sgts. O'NEILL and
WARREN, the quiet sullen black, SANDERSON and SAL play as ACE,*

the tiny radio kid, and MOREHOUSE *look on; all of them drinking beer and bourbon chasers from a bottle.*

WOLFE *(to O'Neill)* How's it going Red? *(using his nickname)*

O'NEILL Shit, cocksucker's got all the cards tonight.

WOLFE *(to Barnes)* Looks like you're doing all right Sergeant.

Barnes, raking in the chips, is the big winner, a light bead of sweat on his forehead and a somewhat glassy look to the eye the only indication he is drunk – his shirt peeled off revealing a muscular, scarred body.

BARNES Yeah, and I ain't even cheating yet.

SANDERSON *(the big blond kid)* Have some Kentucky windage Lieutenant. *(passes him the bottle of bourbon)*

Wolfe takes a nip.

BARNES Play Lieutenant?

WOLFE Nah, I wouldn't want to get raped by you guys ...

O'NEILL What are you saving up to be Lieutenant – Jewish?

Laughs. Wolfe forces a smile, glad to move on. There is a continual worried rodent air about him, an anxiety, a desire to fill the vacuum in his leadership with a false masculinity.

WOLFE Catch you men later. Enjoy yourselves.

As he goes, O'Neill shakes his head after him.

O'NEILL Sorry ass motherfucker ain't he. You think he gonna make it Barnes?

Barnes plays a card, glances, a minute movement of his head.

O'NEILL Yeah that's what I figger. Some dudes you jes' look in their faces and you *KNOW* they just ain't gonna make it.

Barnes looks – with some irony – at O'Neill. The Country Western tune has reached a crescendo whine which now mixes into:

INT: UNDERWORLD HUTCH – NIGHT
Francis, the baby-faced black, and Manny, green shades covering his skinny face, lead with a high blues falsetto.

FRANCIS & MANNY *(singing)* 'People say I'm the life of the
    party cause I tell a joke or two
    Although I may be laughing loud and hardy
    Deep inside I'm blue ...'

The Hutch looks now like a Turkish bath with minimum visibility, the smoke fumes dense. They are all up dancing on their feet – King, Tubbs, Big Harold, Hoyt, Lerner, Crawford, Flash, Doc, Elias – a few light gestures with their hands above shoulder level, passing around the grass pipes while they shuffle, fingers clicking. The song – Smokey Robinson's 'Tracks of My Tears' – accompanies them from a vintage tapedeck.

ALL '... Since you've left me, if you've seen me with
    another girl seeming like I'm having fun although she
    may be cute she's just a substitute because you're the
    permanent one ...'

King and Big Harold wave Chris into the Circle and he starts swaying with them, feeling as if he's being accepted into a new family.

Rhah watches it all, puffing away on his magic dragon pipe, the shadows dancing on the walls.

It looks like a Saturday night dance party. A yearning for tenderness, for feminity, for a moment of peace in this nightmare life. Their eyes closed, thinking of dance partners that can't be here tonight. Singing their souls out.

ALL '... So take a *good* look at my face. You'll see the smile
    looks out of place. Look a little bit closer. It's easy to trace.
    The tracks of my tears ...'

EXT: JUNGLE – NVA BUNKER COMPLEX – DAY
*An overwhelming 103 degree heat. Chris is once more on point, a little
better now but obviously struggling with a thick unyielding bamboo
thicket that forces him forward in a caveman crouch. Napalm jelly is
hanging from the trees in great canopies of spider webs, obliterating
the sky.*

CHRIS VOICE OVER New Year's Day. 1968. Just another day.
Staying alive. There's been a lot of movement near the
Cambodian border, regiments of NVA moving across.
A lot of little firefights, ambushes, we drop a lot of
bombs, then we walk through the napalm like ghosts in
a landscape ...

*Chris working his way over twisted, broken stumps, branches. On the
back of his flak jacket he's written, 'If I die bury me upside down so the
whole world can kiss my ass'.*

BARNES Pssst!

The signal for silence. Chris freezes. Barnes edging up to him.

BARNES *(whispers)* Bunker ...

CHRIS Where?

Doesn't see it. Following Barnes' imperceptible movement of his head.

*The bunker, dug into the ground and camouflaged with brush,
is staring right at him, not more than 20 feet away. Chris is a dead
man if ...*

Barnes, checking the terrain, signals radioman Hoyt.

*Barnes edging up to the bunker, eyes everywhere. Chris following. The
tension builds. They come up to the edge of it, peer in. Nothing.*

*Barnes walks around it, slips in from the back. Chris covers him, other
guys coming up now, making a small perimeter.*

*Chris now starts to see things he didn't see. Right in front of his nose –
there is a trench from this bunker to another and another. There is now
in his view a complex of bunkers and thatched hootches and lean-tos all
blending into the forest. A ghost city ...*

55

Elias and others fanning out now, careful . . . whispered conversations in the wind.

Chris moves past a rope with freshly washed laundry stretching between two trees, clothes stirring in the wind. He looks up as King points out a treehouse, then looks down as Lerner whispers something and points — NVA rucksacks are laid out on the ground in an orderly platoon-sized pattern.

CUT TO:
INT: NVA BUNKER – TUNNEL POSITION – DAY
Elias goes down into a dangerous-looking TUNNEL, on a rope with a .45. Barnes watching him. We sense Elias loves the danger, smiling.

EXT: NVA BUNKER – COMPLEX – MAIN POSITION – DAY
Lt. Wolfe signals Manny and Chris out onto the two flanks.

INT: NVA TREEHOUSE – DAY
Rhah and King explore a treehouse. Rice stores. Rhah, an experienced soldier, seems tense, moves cautiously, expecting booby traps.

EXT: NVA BUNKER – WARREN'S POSITION – DAY
Sgt. Warren cautiously explores another bunker, probing a little tunnel in the bottom of it with a stick. Bunny, having a small frame, goes down into it, fearless.

EXT: NVA BUNKER – MANNY'S POSITION – DAY
Manny, the skinny black boy with the coloured beads, is out on flank — alone, smoking a cigarette, humming.

EXT: NVA BUNKER – CHRIS' POSITION – DAY
On the other flank, Chris, also alone, waits, listening to the sounds of the jungle. He too is smoking a cigarette. The eeriness is everywhere. Rays of morning light peeking through the cathedral dome of the jungle. Bird calls.

INT: NVA TUNNEL – DAY
Elias climbs deeper and deeper into the hole, a rope attached to his waist leading out to the surface, his flashlight now coming around on a shaftway demarcating a TUNNEL that seems to stretch for at least 100 yards. The light revealing cobwebs all along it, but tall enough for a small man.

EXT: CHRIS' POSITION – DAY
It's quiet, weird. Chris takes his pants down, squats. He thinks he hears something, tenses.

There is a soft rustling sound now. And as he focuses on it he realizes it is coming from very close to him. Something light and sinuous moving over the leaves. He looks down.

A bright yellow and orange-ringed krait viper is crawling right between his two legs. It stops, senses another life standing over it.

Chris frozen with dread.

The snake crawls on, pulling its long, long 15 foot body behind it.

On Chris, eyes dilated, slowly regaining his breath looking around everywhere now.

INT: NVA TUNNEL – DAY
Elias moving down the tunnel, fearless. We expect something any moment to come out and nail him but nothing does. He stops. His flashlight revealing a kitchen and an NVA hospital set up. A hammock swings as if someone just deserted it. In another hammock is a dead man. Elias advances cautiously.

EXT: NVA BUNKER – COMPLEX – SANDERSON POSITION – DAY
Spec 4 Sanderson, the big handsome blond kid, is moving through an abandoned bunker. With him is Sal, a tough street kid with an intense face, all whiskered. Sanderson noticing now a metal box of 50-caliber ammo, U.S. marking, half-buried in the ground.

SANDERSON Hey look at that.

He opens the case. Official-looking documents are inside, they glance through them, lighting cigarettes, the search over, successful, they relax.

SAL *(a worried type)* Leave it willya – it's gook shit.

SANDERSON Nah this stuff's important.

He puts the documents back in the ammo case, lifts it. It's the last thing he ever does.

EXT: NVA BUNKER – SANDERSON POSITION – DAY
The ensuing explosion shakes the ground, obliterating both boys,
branches, smoke and dust flying out.

EXT: NVA BUNKER – CHRIS' POSITION – DAY
Out on flank, Chris hits the ground, hugs it.

EXT: NVA BUNKER – COMPLEX – SANDERSON POSITION – DAY
Barnes runs up. Black smoke sweeping through the trees. Sal suddenly
appears, stepping out of the smoke, stunned. The front of his body is
soaked in blood from a thousand shrapnel holes, his clothes shredded,
he stares at Barnes, dazed. Both his arms are gone and blood is
geysering out like a water fountain. He crumbles – dead or dying.

BARNES Corpsman!

He runs over to Sal, gets a hold of his face in a vicelike grip, enraged,
tries to yell some sense into him.

BARNES *(directly to Sal)* Goddamit! Are you fucking kids ever
    gonna learn! Don't you understand how easy it is to die!

The Doc running up – one look tells us all we need to know.

DOC Holy Jesus!

EXT: NVA BUNKER COMPLEX – MAIN POSITION – DAY
Lt. Wolfe, shaken, is on the radio with Cpt. Harris, words garbled
through the air, trying to describe a primal horror.

EXT: NVA BUNKER COMPLEX – SANDERSON POSITION – DAY
Barnes moving through the wreckage – sees severed limbs sticking in a
sandbag.

EXT: NVA BUNKER COMPLEX – MAIN POSITION – DAY
Rhah crouches over a piece of leg tied into a hipbone and a rib.

EXT: NVA BUNKER COMPLEX – DAY
Elias coming out of the tunnel, filthied.

EXT: NVA BUNKER – MAIN POSITION – DAY
Elias coming abreast of Wolfe.

ELIAS Tell Six we need engineers here, this pos. is crawling with traps.

WOLFE They're on their way ... *(consulting his map)* There's a gook village half a klik downriver, Battalion wants us to move in and search it ASAP, something's going on ... where's Barnes?

INT: NVA BUNKER – SANDERSON POSITION – DAY
Barnes is still there in the wrecked bunker, squatting there staring as if his mind has disconnected for a moment. He reaches up, touches his scars. The look on his face suggests he is deeply wronged by this tragedy, that he is taking it very personally.

EXT: NVA BUNKER – MAIN POSITION – DAY
Chris watches him from outside the bunker, awed.

Barnes notices Chris watching him, takes a breath, stands.

BARNES You gonna sit there and play with yourself Taylor or you gonna be part of my war ... Awright, saddle up, let's go – Tubbs you got point.

The men moving into jungle formation, silently.

Chris walking over into line, stops for a moment – noticing a freshly-severed eyeball partially buried in dirt, staring up at him. He turns away, sickened.

EXT: NVA BUNKER COMPLEX – MAIN POSITION – DAY

O'NEILL Where's Manny?

WARREN Manny! ... Hey Buchanan.

There is no answer. The men in the platoon start to look at each other, sensing more trouble.

Elias heads into the bush after him. Barnes watches him go.

Francis, his friend, and Tubbs and King follow.

FRANCIS Hey man whatcha doing ... where you at? Get
your black ass back in here!

EXT: NVA BUCKER COMPLEX – MANNY'S POSITION – DAY
Out on the flank position, where he once stood, Elias walks out, looks.
The jungle is silent once again. Francis, Tubbs, King follow. The
others – Barnes, Lt. Wolfe, Warren, Chris, Rhah ...

FRANCIS & OTHERS *(whispering loudly)* Manny? ... Manny?

Their voices trailing off. Bird cries come back.

Elias combing the ground for clues ... nothing.

Chris looking on, can't believe it, none of them can, a collective chill
running through the platoon.

EXT: JUNGLE – DAY
The Platoon moving downslope in the Jungle, their faces grim, quiet,
deadly. King is on point.

CHRIS VOICE OVER We had to get to the village before dark
so we left Elias with some men to keep looking and to
wait for the engineers ... But it was King found him ...
about 1000 yards downriver, not far from the village –
It was the end of the mystery ...

A moving shot approaching Manny. He's trussed with rope, arms
behind his back. Throat cut, eyes startled open, mouth shaped in a
scream of terror.

Barnes, the other men looking ... Chris. Barnes says it for everyone,
'The motherfuckers...'

EXT: VILLAGE – TRAIL – DAY
They come up out of the jungle onto the side of a CART TRAIL,
where a tiny village overlooks the river. The VILLAGE is poor, a series
of thatched hutches made of C-ration cardboard and aluminum beer
can sidings, faint whiffs of smoke coming from cook fires. Pigs and
dogs wander about.

An OLD VILLAGER watches them pass from his tillable plot, smoking a cigarette, one leg wrapped around his hoe, resting, no expression.

CHRIS VOICE OVER ... the village, which had stood for maybe a thousand years, didn't know we were coming that day. If they had they would have run ... Barnes was at the eye of our rage – and through him, our Captain Ahab – we would set things right again. That day we loved him ...

A pig loiters along the trail, rooting.

Bunny coming up on it with a smile.

BUNNY Hey pig, pig – come here, pig, pig.

The pig grunts. Bunny leveling his shotgun, fires point blank. A horrible squeal.

Chris, directly behind him, looks disgusted.

EXT: VILLAGE – DAY
Tony suddenly points, excited, calls to Barnes.

TONY There goes one!

Their POV – a young VILLAGER fleeing down the slope.

Barnes doesn't hesitate, nails him with a short volley of well-placed shots.

BARNES *(to Tony)* Check him out

He turns back into the village.

EXT: VILLAGE – DAY
Troops fanning out over the village, some TWO DOZEN VILLAGERS scattering to collect their children, dogs barking.

SGTS. O'NEILL & WARREN Get em out! Get em out!

EXT: VILLAGE TUNNEL – DAY
In another part of the village, Barnes hovers over a hole leading into some kind of tunnel.

BARNES Get out of there you fuckheads move! Move!

Fires a warning shot. Three VILLAGERS climbing out of the spider hole, arms raised, but not showing any emotion. Barnes turning to his radioman Hoyt and Big Harold accompanying.

BARNES *(to Harold)* Put 'em in the pig pen. *(to Hoyt)* There's more down there. Gimme your Willy Pete.

Hoyt, with reluctance in his eyes, hands over a specially shaped grenade.

Barnes stands over the hole, the grenade in hand.

The three VILLAGERS who just came out of the hole, yell from the distance, to others still in the tunnel, pleading with them to come out.

BARNES FIRE IN THE HOLE!

Barnes throws the phosphorus in. A muted EXPLOSION. Then sizzling acidic fumes. Frying sounds. A hideous scream from somewhere deep in the hole.

Hoyt, watching, is sickened. Barnes businesslike.

The Villagers, in grief, howl and tear at their faces.

FU SHENG *(hustling up to Barnes)* Sarge, we found some shit!

Barnes going with him.

EXT: VILLAGE – OUTSIDE HUTCH – DAY
The sun is sitting there hot and high in the sky.

Chris, strangling in heat, a demented look on his face, staggers into a hutch with Francis.

INT: HUTCH – VILLAGE – DAY
Threadbare, poor, a typical Buddhist shrine in the corner, motes of light crisscross through the poor matting and c-ration sides.

Chris edges over, pries up a floorboard, flips it over, scared.

There's a tunnel inside. A long dark dangerous hole.

CHRIS La Dai! La Dai! GET THE FUCK OUTTA THERE!

FRANCIS Hey take it easy man. They're scared.

CHRIS They're scared? What about me! I'm sick of this shit
man, I'm sick of this shit! They don't want us here!
Who do you think they're fighting for! GET OUTTA
THERE!

*Francis doesn't recognize him in his rage. Bunny now coming in,
followed by O'Neill, drawn by the shouting.*

EXT: VILLAGE – WEAPONS CACHE – DAY
*Barnes stares down at a WEAPONS CACHE buried cleverly underneath
the rice urns. Ace, Fu Sheng, Sgt. Warren, Lt. Wolfe, others, are digging
it out. It's in white plastic wrappings – a load of AK-47s, rockets,
grenades, claymores, carbines, flares, NVA uniforms. A real find.*

SGT. WARREN *(to Barnes)* ... and over here there's enough
rice to feed a whole fuckin' regiment ...

*Barnes walking with him over to an undercover rice silo being dug out
by Tubbs and Junior. Barnes looks it over.*

BARNES *(to Warren)* ... bring the honcho over here. *(to Tubbs
and Junior)* Burn it.

INT: HUTCH – VILLAGE – DAY
*An Old Woman and her Son, a young man with one leg, throw up their
hands, climbing out of the hole with stupid confused looks as Chris,
shaking with his own sort of confusion and rage, cuffs them, hustling
them out. The Young Man uses a pair of crutches for his blown-off
limb, hobbling like a mangy three-legged dog.*

BUNNY Hey look at this! Ma and Pa Kettle here. Look at
them – greasy gook motherfuckers!

CHRIS Get up out of there! ... You see I didn't wanna hurt
you. Why didn't you come out, when I said so hunh!
Why? WHY! WHY? DON'T YOU LISTEN ... WHAT
ARE YOU SMILING AT HUNH! FUCKING
ASSHOLES!

The couple, hands raised, muttering things in Vietnamese, don't understand a word, shaking their heads stupidly and smiling that impassive Oriental smile which sends Chris into a rage only he can understand.

His finger closes on the trigger of his 16.

Francis, the baby-faced black, looks nervously, sensing the danger . . . Bunny amused, drawn in by Chris. O'Neill watches passively from the lip of the hutch.

The Young Man continues to grin, not seeming to realize the degree of danger he's in, which is what Chris wants — a token sign of acquiescence. There is also the added element of showing off his manhood in front of an audience now.

BUNNY *DO,* 'em man, do 'em!

Chris. The trigger. He pulls. But he can't quite bring himself to kill. The bullets exploding in the dirt at the edges of the young man's feet.

CHRIS *(demonic)* DANCE YOU ONE-LEGGED
     MOTHERFUCKER, DANCE!!!

The Young Man hops up and down in a reflex fear of the sounds of the bullets as they thud into the dirt. Yet his eyes remain fixed on Chris in wonderment.

Chris, firing out the magazine, seems to expend his bloodlust. He ceases, noticing — for the first time — the eyes of the Young Man. They aren't stupid — nor fearful — but filled with resignation and despair — a despair that Chris, in disgust of himself, recognizes.

Chris lowers the rifle, silent.

The Young Man's impassive face shines now with tears. That sad young look — as if death itself would've been a release. Chris turns his eyes away, an awkward sense of shame.

FRANCIS *(leaves)* Let's get out of here man.

But Bunny takes up the slack, moves forward on the young man.

BUNNY *(to Chris)* You chickenshit man, they're laughing at

you, look at them faces. That's the way a gook laughs.

The Young Man nodding affably to Bunny and mumbling ingratiating words in Vietnamese.

BUNNY Yeah sure you are, you're real sorry ain't you. You're just crying out your hearts about Sandy and Sal and Manny – they're laughing at us! Their family is out there in the fucking bush blowing us away and they're laughing at us!

O'NEILL *(checking out the hutch)* Forget it will ya, let's go. . .

Chris standing there, watching, sensing something awful is going to come and unable to do anything about it. It comes – suddenly and without any warning. Bunny is looking at O'Neill, the Vietnamese couple are muttering something. In one fluid move, Bunny swivels and with unbelievable savagery clubs the young one-legged man in the side of the head with the butt of his 16.

O'NEILL *(stunned)* Hey what are you doing!

BUNNY Fucker!

The young man is groaning on the floor of the hutch. Bunny smashes him – again and again.

BUNNY That's for Sandy! And this is for Sal! And this is for fucking Manny! This is for me!

Chris watches, horrified. Never in his life has he seen something so horrifying as this. And yet he does nothing. Can do nothing. He is part of it.

BUNNY *(stepping back, examines what's left of the head, amazed)* Wow! You see his fucking head come apart? Look at that ... I never seen brains like dat before. Jesus fucking Christ ...

The Old Lady is shrieking, hovering over the body of her son. Bunny studying her.

BUNNY Betcha the old bitch runs the whole show. Probably helped cut Manny's throat. Probably cut my balls off if she could. *(to Chris)* Come on, man, let's do her.

She cowers from him. Chris staring, transfixed, out of his mind.

BUNNY ... Don't even look like a fucking woman. Look at them ugly tits. Broken fucking eggs.

He clubs her. Chris steps back, horrified. As is O'Neill, more puzzled than horrified.

BUNNY *(hitting her again)* Let's zap all these motherfuckers! Let's do the whole village!

He backs out of the hutch, scared. Evidently Bunny is temporarily insane. But he spots O'Neill, yells at him.

BUNNY GET BACK HERE YOU FUCKING COWARD O'NEILL. THIS IS FOR SANDY ... THIS IS FOR SANDY MAN! AND SAL! AND MANNY!

As he clubs her to death.
On Chris' face, blood and brain tissue flying up into it.

EXT: CENTRAL AREA – VILLAGE – DAY
A tiny knot of men are ringed around Barnes who is questioning a sturdy-looking man who is the VILLAGE CHIEF. He has been stripped of his shirt, scars all over his body, scared. He has his ID papers out, trembling, showing them to Lerner who speaks some pidgen Vietnamese.

BARNES Where'd he get these wounds?

Lerner translates, the man talking back.

LERNER He says he was hit in a bombing raid.

TONY He's a dink fosure.

BARNES Ask him what the weapons are doing here?

LERNER He says they had no choice. The NVA killed the old honcho when he said no. He says the rice is theirs.

BARNES Bullshit ... who the hell was the dink we just nailed on the riverbank?

Chris and O'Neill come up, watch. Others coming from different places — sensing the narrowing drama. But half the platoon is still at work in the village. We hear shouts, grenade explosions, occasionally gunfire.

LERNER ... He says he doesn't know, NVA haven't been around in a couple of months. Maybe it was a scout or ...

The men around Barnes grumble.

BARNES Yeah sure it was. What about all that fucking rice and the weapons ... who they for? *(looking at the Village Chief)* Cocksucker knows what I'm saying ... don't you Pop? *(a blank look)*

ACE You're goddamn right he does!

Lerner translating. The Village Chief's WIFE is now on the scene, a middle-aged woman with angry features, yelling at Lerner trying to answer for her husband, a high-pitched barrage of indignant words directed mostly at Barnes, and interspersed with the spitting of her betel nuts on the ground.

The Village Chief trying to talk her down. But things are definitely getting out of control. And the heat from the sun is only aggravating the situation, pounding down on the actors in the drama, their fatigues soaked in sweat and anger.

LERNER *(finally)* He swears he doesn't know anything! He hates the NVA but they come when they want and ...

JUNIOR He's lying through his teeth!

TONY Waste the fucker, then see who talks.

BARNES What's the bitch saying?

LERNER *(overwhelmed)* She's going on, I don't know – why
    are we shooting the pigs, they're farmers . . . they got to
    make a living, all that crap . . .

*The Woman is still ranting when Barnes turns to her, quite casually
levels his M-16, and puts a bullet in her head. She goes down as if
pole-axed.*

*A stunned pause. The Chief looking at his wife. The Villagers in
background reacting.*

*Wolfe looking . . . Chris looking, shocked. Doc, possibly the straightest
of them all, very uncomfortable. They are all shocked in some way, but
do nothing against the power of Barnes. Barnes walks over to the pig
pen with the other Villagers, very casually, confronts them.*

BARNES *(to Lerner)* Tell him he talks or I'm gonna waste
    more of 'em.

*Lerner shaken up, muttering to the Village Chief who is in shock,
kneeling next to the body of his wife, muttering in a high whine of pain.*

BARNES Go ahead, Lerner, ask him.

A group of Villagers huddle to one side.

Lerner, shaken, is yelling at all of them, demanding an answer.

LERNER They don't know Sarge, they don't know! *(half
    believes it)*

*Barnes turns his attention on the other villagers, his intentions appar-
ent. Everybody feels them. They're next. Barnes is unperturbed, very
much in command of the situation, no rage, no emotions expressed.*

*Chris has never seen such a thing in his life – but can't react. Can't stop it,
just watches it like he's not quite there.*

*The same goes for Lieutenant Wolfe, for all of them. The very outrageous-
ness of Barnes' killing seems to quell all protest.*

ACE *(sensing the impending massacre)* Hey Sarge can we get in on this.

Tony advances, the hairy Italian kid from Boston.

TONY Let's go all the way, let's go for it! Let's do the whole fucking village. Come on, Sarge!

Chris' eyes . . . Rodriguez next to him, is neutral but willing.
Francis is hesitant.
Fu Sheng and Junior are ready to go for it. Lt. Wolfe is powerless, frozen.
Sgt. Warren stepping up. The massacre is just about to break.
The Villagers know it, kneel in prayer, mutter.
Barnes suddenly grabs and drags a young 19 year-old Woman, the Village Chief's daughter, across the pen, throws her down on her knees, in front of the stunned Village Chief. She's screaming.

BARNES This his daughter, right?

Lerner nods. Barnes pulls his .45, puts it alongside her head.

BARNES *(to Village Chief)* You lie . . . You Vee Cee . . . I caca dao Vee Cee!

He chambers the .45, the Woman begging Barnes for her life, cradling his knees. He sticks the gun down above her skull.
Chris wanting to cry out, to do something — but can't!
A FIGURE suddenly flares out in the sun, advancing on them. It is Elias.

ELIAS BARNES!!!

Barnes looks around. They all look around.
Elias walks right up to him, followed by his men — King, Rhah, Crawford, others from the rear party. He looks around. The corpse of the Wife . . . the Young Daughter sobbing.

ELIAS WHAT THE FUCK YOU DOING!

BARNES *(pissed)* Stay out of this Elias. This ain't your show.

ELIAS YOU AIN'T A FIRING SQUAD, YOU PIECE OF
SHIT!!

*The stock of his rifle swings up fast and hard smacking Barnes full in
the face, breaking two teeth.*

*Barnes staggers back, hurt, bleeding. Elias is on him like a leopard.
Battering him with his fists.*

*They struggle in the dust, two titans, their faces equally consumed with
rage, clawing, spitting, punching, kicking, pounding each other's
skulls in the dirt. A dust storm swirls around them, the men closing
around like excited apes at a bloodfeast.*

*Most of the men seem to be pulling for Barnes — Chris just watching,
neutral.*

LT. WOLFE BREAK IT UP! ELIAS! BARNES!

*But they roll on, smashing each other's faces in. Both quick, fast, agile,
mean fighters. Sgts. O'Neill and Warren drag them apart.*

Wolfe and Big Harold jump in, hold them apart.

BARNES You're dead, you're fucking dead Elias!

ELIAS *YOU* – you're going to fuckin' jail, buddy, you ain't
getting away with this one!!!!!

WOLFE All right! All right! All right!!! NOW BREAK IT
UP. LET'S GO ...

*They compose themselves, the Villagers looking on, grieving over their
loss.*

WOLFE Alright, Six says torch this place! Blow the weapons
in place. Round up all suspected Vee Cees and shake it
up! We ain't got much light left.

ELIAS *(to Wolfe)* Why the fuck didn't you do something
Lieutenant!

70

WOLFE What are you talking about! *(turns away, goes about his business)*

ELIAS *(spins him around)* You know what I'm talking about!

WOLFE No I don't. I don't know what the fuck you're talking about, Elias! *(goes)*

Who wants to be reminded? A silence of shame. The Men moving away, Warren, Ace, Tony, Rodriguez, Barnes looking back once, a cold glare.

The Village Chief is a broken-looking man, huddled over his wife's body.

Elias stands there, frustrated.

Chris glances at him, moves out.

EXT: SMALL VILLAGE – DAY
A zippo cigarette lighter with the engraved initials: 'From Mai lin to my Bunny Boy'. It sparks a thick flare as Bunny lights the dry straw on the roof of the Hutch where he killed the Old Woman and Young Boy.

Their legs sticking out at the threshold. The hooch burning fast, aided by the strong sun.

Bunny watches with awe.

EXT: SMALL VILLAGE – DAY
Sgt. Warren and Rodriguez lighting another hooch on fire.

EXT: VILLAGE RICE STORE – DAY
Fu Sheng yelling 'FIRE IN THE HOLE!' throws white phosphorus into the rice stores.

EXT: VILLAGE – WEAPONS CACHE – DAY
Barnes and Huffmeister, a big German kid from Texas, are laying the cord to blow the weapons cache.

EXT: SMALL VILLAGE – WELL – DAY
Adams and Parker are poisoning the well with a white phosphorus grenade: 'FIRE IN THE HOLE!'

EXT: SMALL VILLAGE – DAY
Wolfe, Ace, Tubbs, Warren, Rodriguez rope the DOZEN SUSPECTED
VILLAGERS together to take them back for questioning.

Elias watches the Villagers mourn their losses. In the background, explosions, hooches popping with flames, the yells of the violations of the Village winding down.

EXT: SMALL VILLAGE – DAY
Chris wanders through this wreckage in the sun, like a dazed visitor from another planet, not believing it. He sees something, goes towards it – knows what it is.

EXT: VILLAGE – EDGE OF WOODLINE – DAY
Hidden at the edge of the woodline, King hands back a bowl of grass to Rhah, the chief head. They're puffing away.

KING Whew! – where that come from?

RHAH Found it. Growing in a garden.

KING *(smokes)* Sheeit, beats burning hutches anyway ...

They meditatively look out at the Village – burning hutches sending up spirals of smoke. Shouts. Shots. Chaos.

RHAH Yeah – stoned's the way to be ...

EXT: VILLAGE – DITCH – DAY
In a ditch running alongside the Village, partially concealed by foliage and anthills, Tony, Morehouse, and the ubiquitous Bunny have a 12-YEAR-OLD VIETNAMESE GIRL pinned to the ground, gagged and squirming, naked. They are fucking her to death. Junior looks on, both curious and disgusted, but doesn't take part.

TONY Take her up the ass ...

As they roll her over, like excited dogs in heat.

Chris, coming up, sees their heads dipping up and down on the other side of the anthill, knows what they're doing. He makes a conscious decision to do something. He runs over.

CHRIS LET HER GO! YOU HEAR ME! YOU
ASSHOLE! LET HER GO!

He strides right into them, shoves them off hard. The girl is in tears.

TONY What the fuck you want – she's a dink.

CHRIS NO – YOU STUPID FUCK ... DON'T ...
DON'T ... YOU TOO BUNNY. MOREHOUSE.
OFF! NO! ... NO! DON'T ... DON'T!

*He seems disconnected, dazed by the sun, like he's talking to dogs –
loud, repetitive words coming out of an anger he can barely control,
trying to restore some sanity to a world gone totally nuts today. Don't
they understand? Don't they have any sense of a mind? Any kind of
decency?*

*The Men looking at him as if he's the one who's gone nuts, not them.
Bunny looking at Morehouse looking at Tony looking at Junior. The irony
is lost on them, as Chris pushes through to help the poor girl put her scanty
clothes back on.*

CHRIS *(to the girl)* It's okay ... it's okay ...

*Elias appears behind Bunny and the others, sees what's happened. He
signals them to move out.*

ELIAS Get outta here.

The men grumble and slink off quietly. Elias watching as ...

*Chris helps her to her feet, wounded in the intestines, she can barely
stand, blood soaking in her nether regions. Chris slings her up as
gently as he can and carries her.*

CHRIS *(as if to himself)* It's okay, it's okay ...

EXT: VILLAGE – PIG PEN – DAY
*Near the pig pen, a DOZEN SUSPECTS are being led away on ropes by
Tubbs, Warren, Rodriguez. The others left behind look back at their
village in ruins, homes burning, livestock dead or scattered, belongings*

thrown and broken in the dirt. BABIES wail, the adults squat there on their heels watching with absolutely no trace of outward emotion.

Past this Bosch-like canvas, Chris — carrying the girl — walks dazed by the horrors of this long afternoon.

EXT: VILLAGE TRAIL – DAY
The soldiers depart the village. A huge EXPLOSION now rocks the earth and sends a spray of smoke into the blue sky as the weapons cache explodes in stages that sound like the end of the world.

EXT: PERIMETER #2 – JUNGLE – LATE AFTERNOON DUSK
The Company is digging into another overnight perimeter on a ridge with a view of the Valley where the Village was. C-Ration fires all around the perimeter.

EXT: COMPANY CP – DUSK
At the Company, Elias, Captain Harris, Barnes, Lt. Wolfe are huddled. Close on Harris, looking from face to face, assuming a judicial attitude.

CAPTAIN HARRIS   ... and you Lieutenant?

LT. WOLFE   I didn't see anything sir.

ELIAS   I did.

LT. WOLFE   That dink was reported to me as NVA sir by Sergeant Barnes. Sergeant Barnes.

Squirreling out of any responsibility.

ELIAS   My report sir, will include Lt. Wolfe as being witness to the shooting ...

HARRIS   All right, Elias. Sergeant Barnes, I want a report from you ...

BARNES   You got it sir – and I can throw in plenty of eye-witnesses if you want sir ...

HARRIS   Not now. We'll get into this when we get back to

base camp. Right now I need every man in the field, I want your guys to stick together ... Elias? Barnes? ... You hear me? This is no time for fighting with each other. *(pause, they nod)* Tomorrow we're going back into that bunker complex – from the East. *(continuing)* First Platoon will lead ... Brigade thinks they might be back there tomorrow. That's all ... Get some rest. *(turns away)*

Barnes, Elias eye each other and move off.

EXT: PERIMETER #2 – DUSK
Wolfe walks alongside Barnes.

WOLFE Don't worry about it Sergeant, he won't be able to prove a thing, he's a troublemaker but ...

Barnes is obviously worried, although he doesn't let on.

BARNES Elias' a waterwalker ... like them politicians in Washington. Want to fight their war with one hand tied round their balls. Ain't no time or need for a courtroom out here ...

Wolfe leaves him as Barnes turns into his foxhole where Bunny and O'Neill await him anxiously.

O'NEILL How'd it go.

Barnes shrugs.

BUNNY Thataway Sarge, fuckin' Elias man, fuckin' squeal that's what he is, gonna get everybody in the platoon in shit. Somebody oughta fix his ass ...

Barnes fixing his coffee.

O'NEILL *(worried)* Gonna be an investigation or something Bob?

Barnes says nothing, a cryptic look.

O'Neill worried, Bunny, taking his cue from Barnes, slaps him on the back.

BUNNY Ya worry too much O'Neill ...

EXT: PERIMETER #2 – CHRIS' POSITION – DUSK
Elsewhere on the perimeter, Chris is digging out a foxhole with Rhah,
as King and Lerner prepare the C's for dinner.

RHAH I know Barnes six months and I'll tell ya something
    – that man is *MEAN*, red in his soul like a dick on a dog.

KING Barnes gets killed, his jaws'd go on clacking ...

CHRIS Where's he from?

RHAH Barnes comes from Hell.

LERNER Tennessee someplace. Hill country.

RHAH Barnes took a bullet right there. At Ia Drang Valley
    ... *(points to his forehead)*
    And the cocksucker *SURVIVED* – that's *BAAAD* man.
    That's his high, baby. High on *WAR*!

His eyes flare out dramatically. Chris, enthralled in spite of himself.

KING He done a year in Japan in the hospital, then when
    he gets out, the first thing he done is re-up. Four years
    he been in the field ...

RHAH ... and you know how many times he done been
    shot? *(Chris shakes his head)* Seven times! *(with his fingers)*
    Seven.

CHRIS And he still wanted to come back?

LERNER Does a pee wee wanna take a wee wee?

RHAH The Good Lord works his revenge in strange ways.

KING Yeah, you done said it. Revenge on *US*.

CHRIS Does he have a metal plate in his head?

RHAH *(smiles)* You mean he's crazy? No more crazy'n the rest of us been out in the bush too long.

LERNER Well he ain't normal that's fosure.

RHAH That's what he is ... Baaaa!

His hand flashes forward in front of Chris. 'HATE' is written across the left hand knuckles in a sloppy, purplish-black tattoo. Chris looking at it.

RHAH ... and he's *FILLED* with it. He's roaming these jungles looking for little yellow devils to kill. Remember the Devil does God's work too. *(pause)* ... and this here's Elias ... Baaaa!

The other knuckle is out – 'LOVE' tattooed across it. Rhah smiles his crazy smile. Chris stares fascinated at the two knuckles side by side. A moment on his face.

KING Love, yeah!

LERNER *(makes a cuckoo sign)* Here we go again with the crazy preacher stuff. Rhah seen too many movies.

RHAH Baaa, got no time to go to the movies. Love and Hate too busy fighting for possession of my soul.

CHRIS Where's Elias come from?

RHAH *(interjecting)* 'Lias come naturally.

LERNER ... don't know. Done some time. Heard he worked the oil wells in Oklahoma, made some bread and washed up in El Lay.

KING Yeah, get married to some crazy El Lay bitch, an actress or somethin', she blew all his bread – LSD, gurus, all that California shit, and then she turns him into the cops on a drug rap.

RHAH Not the only man to meet his Jezebel either.

KING So he got a reduced and come over here. Nam's his freedom man, Nam's his pussy. Three years he been here.

CHRIS Three years, Jesus, he's crazy as Barnes ...

KING Well sometimes a man jes don' wanna go back. How you gonna talk to civilians man? People back in the world just don't give a shit, y'know what I mean, to them you're a fuckin' animal is all –

LERNER *(to Chris)* I was home on leave y'know and everybody's just worried 'bout making money, everybody's out for themselves, they don't even want to talk about it man, it's like the fucking Twilight Zone back there – you wouldn't even *KNOW* there's a war on here. My sister says to me why you have to go there like I started this ...

RHAH Baaaa! Fuck it, they sold us out – so what! What'd you'all expect? Civilian life is phoney *BULLSHIT* man. They're *ROBOTS* man – watchin' dopey television and drivin' dopey cars, and they fuck up, nobody dies. That's all right, you keep fuckin' up, politicians keep lyin'. Cause it don't really matter. Don't mean shit. So what! Whatcha want – a parade! Fuck that too! No war time no grunt never got no respect. Till he was dead – and even *THEN*! You're fighting for *YOURSELF* man! You're fighting for your *SOUL*, dat's all. Remember dat. And it's some goddamn battle too – if you'se a man, wrestle with that angel ...
(swings his entrenching tool in a rhythmic chain-gang style)
... Love and Hate – the whole shitbang show, that's the story then and now and it ain't hardly gonna change ...

EXT: PERIMETER #2 – JUNGLE – NIGHT
The stars are out in magnificent splendor. A breeze rustling through the trees.

EXT: PERIMETER #2 – CHRIS' POSITION – NIGHT
Chris is turning in his sleep, perturbed, writhing. The whispering is
more and more urgent. Death is all around. He shoots up out of his
poncho liner as if shot, stunned. Scared. Looks around. All is quiet.
Men sleeping.

Elias is huddled in his poncho on guard next to his foxhole. Chris joins
him, sitting, wiping the sleep from his eyes.

CHRIS   ... I can't sleep, why don't you get some sack time.

ELIAS   ... don't feel like it either.

CHRIS   ... beautiful night.

ELIAS   Yeah. I love this place at night. The stars ... there's
no right or wrong in them, they're just there.

CHRIS   That's a nice way of putting it.

Elias cuffs a joint, keeping its glow hidden in the dark. A pause, both
of them meditative.

CHRIS   Barnes got it in for you, don't he?

ELIAS *(philosophically)*   Barnes believes in what he's doing.

CHRIS   And you, do you believe?

ELIAS   In '65 – yeah. Now ... *(pause)* No. What happened
today's just the beginning. We're gonna lose this war ...

CHRIS *(surprised)*   You really think so ... us?

Elias' eyes seem to go to some inner place, his passion surging.

ELIAS   ... we been kicking other people's asses so long I
guess it's time we got our own kicked. The only decent
thing I can see coming out of here are the survivors –
hundreds of thousands of guys like you Taylor going
back to every little town in the country knowing
something about what it's like to take a life and what

that can do to a person's soul – twist it like Barnes and
Bunny and make 'em sick inside and if you got any
brains you gonna fight it the rest of your life cause it's
cheap, killing is cheap, the cheapest thing I know and
when some drunk like O'Neill starts glorifying it, you're
gonna puke all over him and when the politicians
start selling you a used war all over again, you and
your generation gonna say go fuck yourself 'cause
you know, you've seen it, and when you know it, deep
down there ...

*He plants his fist in Chris' gut, expelling his breath such is the force of
the blow – like a power passed between them.*

ELIAS   ... you know it *till you die* ... that's why the survivors
remember. 'Cause the dead don't let em forget.

*His eyes blazing, reliving the deaths in the village, licking the wounds
for the platoon, mourning the failure of its heroism. Chris looking at
him, a little awed by his intensity. Elias looks away, embarrassed that he
has sermonized, looks back at the stars.*

ELIAS   Oh shit! Sometimes there's things in my head ...
man. Grass does that to me, fucks me all up like a crazy
Indian ...

CHRIS   Do you believe that stuff about ... knowing you're
gonna die?

ELIAS   Yeah, those are the guys that live. I really don't think
Death gives a shit, it's like a giant garbage can, I think it
takes whatever it can get ... you never know where it's
gonna come from anyway ... so why spin your wheels?

He shrugs, a certain bravado masking his own uncertainty.

CHRIS   ... You ever think about reincarnation, all that
stuff?

*A lightning quick movement follows. Elias' hand passing over his face
like a mime, a click of the fingers and he leans closer to Chris. A new*

expression on his face. Devil's eyes, mocking child, danger in his soul, excitement, sex — the Elias that Chris saw in the smoking session in base camp. Chris smiles, sucked in, almost laughs and then the face is gone again.

ELIAS Sure, goes on all the time. Maybe a piece of me's in you now, who knows. But when you die – really die – that's a big return ticket. *(soft)* I like to think I'm gonna come back as ... as wind or fire – or a deer *(likes the image)* ... yeah, a deer ...

He smiles at the thought. Chris looks at him, looks away. A shooting star falls suddenly and dryly through the cosmos. Their eyes.

EXT: JUNGLE – STREAM – DAY (RAIN)
The Platoon moves along a shallow STREAM bordering the jungle. A thick RAIN falls amid cracks of distant thunder. Chris, Rhah, Francis, Big Harold, others are at the rear of the platoon, their ponchos pulled over them like big sad grey tents. There's a holdup ahead and the Men rest on rocks or stand. The rain makes a pointilistic pattern, the men collages of grey, their rifles slung upside down to keep dry.
Barnes is up ahead, out of the stream bank, on the radio.

EXT: JUNGLE CHURCH – DAY (RAIN)
Lerner's on point, resting in the shadow of a decaying old French Catholic Church from the 19th Century. The jungle has long ago won the battle, vines creeping into the cracks, remnants of arches layered around the church at the epicenter. Behind Lerner is Sgt. Warren and his radioman.

EXT: JUNGLE CLEARING – DAY (RAIN)
Elias, further back, is checking out the jungle alongside the clearing, noticing a number of old spider holes long since abandoned. He goes over and checks them.

EXT: JUNGLE – STREAM – DAY (RAIN)
Back at the stream, Rhah, looking old and whiskered under his poncho hood, lights up a roach, puffs it. Another crack of thunder. Chris comes over, sits with him on his rock. Rhah passes him the joint. He smokes.

Charlie Sheen as Chris: arriving.

Charlie Sheen as Chris,
Chris Pedersen as
Crawford, and
Francesco Quinn
as Rhah.

Charlie Sheen
as Chris.

Left to right: Charlie Sheen as Chris, Corey Glover as Francis, Chris Pedersen as Crawford, Willem Dafoe as Sergeant Elias, Forrest Whittaker as Big Harold, and Keith David as King.

Tom Berenger as Sergeant Barnes.

The platoon leaving the burning village.

Tom Berenger as Sergeant Barnes and Willem Dafoe as Sergeant Elias.

Running to safety.

Charlie Sheen as Chris.

Charlie Sheen as Chris and Keith David as King.

The platoon.

Big Harold pulls a leech out of his open crotch area.

HAROLD Shit, lookit this little fucker trying to get up ma glory hole.

FRANCIS Hey Big Harold, put dat in your turkey loaf it won't come out your back end.

KING *(ribbing)* Yeah, big boy, thought you had that laundry gig all laid out?

BIG HAROLD *(pissed)* Shit, got to paint myself white get one of dem jobs. Get ma request in for a circumcision.

KING Gonna be a rabbi man?

FRANCIS Gonna cut your pecker down to size hunh Big Harold?

HAROLD Dat's okay wid me, better to have a small one den no one at all.

KING Your girlfriends gonna look for new lovers, man. Best thing a bro's got's his flap.

HAROLD I'll drink to your flap in Chicago, King. All I gotta do is stretch it out to 15 days and I'll be short 15 and the Beast just wouldn't dare send me back to the bush.

FRANCIS You gonna get some for me back in the World, Harold? Whatcha gonna do? *(dreaming of it)*

HAROLD The world's gonna be ma oyster man. First's I gonna EAT – all the hamburger and french fries and steaks soaked in onions and ketchup I can get.
Then I'se gonna FUCK and SUCK Sandy Bell till I sore all over and can't fuck no more, and den I'se gonna SLEEP for DAYS, for WEEKS! Den I'se gonna think bout what comes next ...

The words carry over Chris staring out at the rain, feeling a leaden, fatigued high. Passes the roach, down to a millimeter, back to Rhah who points to his face.

RHAH ... you got one right there.

Chris feels for, finds the leech on the edge of his lip, cursing under his breath.

LT. WOLFE *(in the stream, on radio)* All right move out.

The men start slogging on against the rain.

Junior is drinking from the stream, as Fu Sheng passes.

FU SHENG Don't drink that asshole. You gonna get malaria.

JUNIOR Shit I hope so!

EXT: JUNGLE – CHURCH – DAY (RAIN)
On point, Lerner moves out through a remnant of an old arch, somewhat casual in his approach to point.

LERNER Hey Sarge, you wanna tell me which way or do I get to figger it out?

Sgt. Warren, picking up a quick azimuth on his lensatic compass, points. Lerner moves in the new direction.

EXT: JUNGLE – DAY (RAIN)
Elias looking around, frowning, falls into the line of march.

EXT: JUNGLE – FORWARD POINT – DAY (RAIN)
Lerner moves away from the clearing, working up a slight incline when the MACHINE GUN FIRE erupts out of the jungle, spinning him – throwing him into the dirt like discarded garbage.

The man are down, yelling.

SGT. WARREN Ambush! Incoming! Fucking incoming!

Suddenly an RPG rocket breaks out of the bush, sounding like an atom bomb as it devastates the front of the Platoon. Radio Talk is continuous now, back and forth between the three platoon radios, through the ambush.

O'NEILL DOC, UP HERE! Lerner's hit! . . .

More machine gun fire.

FRANCIS DOC! Over here – we got . . . one . . . two down.
    Warren's hit.

EXT: JUNGLE – CHURCH – DAY (RAIN)
Chris moving up with Rhah and the others out of the stream, they hit
the ground next to Sgt. O'Neill, who looks pretty scared, obviously not
about to move.

CHRIS What's going on?

O'NEILL Shit they got RPGs on our ass. Fucking ambush –
    they was waiting for us to break trail!

KING WATCH OUT! ROCKET!!

Another rocket whistling in. A huge roar. Trees shredded, dirt, dust
rising.

CHRIS Who's on point?

O'NEILL Lerner and Warren

Chris uses his M-16 to lever himself up into a crouch and suddenly
dashes forward, passing Rhah.

RHAH Where you goin' man!

Chris tearing up. Past Flash – the hip black head with the colored
beads. He's dead, torn and shredded, his face and eyes stuffed with
dirt. Next to him Doc is frantically tourniqueting Tubbs, shot in the
legs. He's screaming.

Chris keeps moving to the front as if compelled.

EXT: JUNGLE – BARNES' POSITION – DAY (RAIN)
Barnes is laying out fire.

BARNES Goddamit, you assholes get fucking' firepower out
    there! *(to Hoyt on radio)* Get Two Bravo up here. Get me

a gun. *(to others)* Spread it out! More to the flanks! Look for a fuckin' target!

Another explosion.

EXT: JUNGLE – FORWARD POINT – DAY (RAIN)
Chris comes alongside Francis near the point, throws himself down. Banging his head against his helmet as he falls. The incoming rounds are tearing up the front of the platoon.

CHRIS *(to Francis)* Where's Lerner?

FRANCIS *(terrified)* Out there man – behind the log.

Looking. A body – moaning, sort of moving, wriggling, as if trying to escape the pain.

CHRIS Oh Jesus!

His eyes moving to Sgt. Warren lying alongside a tree – calmly trying to stack his intestines back into his ruptured stomach. Another RPG comes in.

Chris makes a conscious decision, moves up – bit by bit, shielding himself with tree stumps, ant hills, laying out fire, trying to get closer to Lerner.

Francis following his progress, bug-eyed.

Fu Sheng now comes up with his M-60 – Harold his loader, belts of ammo flapping against their bodies. He fires from the hip, providing cover fire for Chris, then pops down.

EXT: FORWARD POINT – JUNGLE – DAY (DRIZZLING RAIN)
Chris, firing out another magazine, crawls closer to Lerner, trying to ascertain if he's still alive.

CHRIS Lerner! Lerner, can you hear me man?

Lerner groans. A fresh burst of AK fire rakes the area. Lerner jerks spasmodically with the impact of the rounds.

Chris spots the sniper. In a hole in the ground. Twenty-five metres off. Snapping the magazine out of his AK to reload. A live gook.

85

Chris tears off a volley at him but the gook disappears in the hole. This is the moment, Chris realizes it, it's now or never if Chris intends to get the gook. He's got to make a move before the man has reloaded his weapon.

He pulls his grenade, pops the pin. He lets the spoon fly off, activating the grenade-timer, as he jumps to his feet and runs for the gook hole, concentrating, concentrating. That head is going to pop up any second with a freshly-loaded weapon and tear his head off.

Chris won't make it to the hole. The throw has to be perfect. He won't get another chance. He heaves the frag, drops and rolls away. The throw is perfect, the golden arc of flight from the outfield nailing the baserunner. It twists cleanly in the hole. The explosion muffled but deadly.

Chris scrambles to his feet, a look of almost total surprise on his face. He can't seem to believe he did it. Pointing his M-16 before him, he advances on the hole, looking over the muzzle to see the badly-mangled NVA man twisted at the bottom.

Chris hurries over to Lerner. He's in bad shape, hit in several places, vaguely conscious.

CHRIS Gator! Gator! *(Lerner groans)* I'm gonna get you out man. You're gonna be okay Gator ... okay?

Fu Sheng laying out fire to protect them, Harold splitting off to get more ammo.

Chris getting Lerner to his feet, hauling him back with all his strength, past Francis ...

EXT: JUNGLE – WOLFE'S POSITION – DAY (RAIN)
Lt. Wolfe seems disoriented, struggling with the rain water washing off his map, trying to read the coordinates for an arty fire mission.

WOLFE *(into the radio)* Redleg, Redleg ... Ripper Bravo Two Actual. Fire mission. Grid six-four-niner ... four zero-two. Direction six-one-zero-zero. Dinks dug in bunkers. Danger close. Adjust fire, over ...

RADIO VOICE Rog, Two Bravo. Solid copy, stand by for shot, out.

ACE Sir, Bravo Three is inbound from the Sierra Whiskey.

Should be here in two zero mikes if'n they don' hit any shit.

WOLFE Fuckin' A!

Elias runs up to him. Fire all around, incoming and outgoing, makes them yell to each other.

ELIAS Lootenant, they're kickin our ass, they know we're gonna bring heavy shit on 'em pretty soon so they're gonna get in tight under the arty. I spotted a cut running around to the left. Lemme take some men and roll up that flank ... *(pointing)* I can work right up on 'em ...

Wolfe unsure, looks up for the artillery.

WOLFE *(to Ace)* Get me Barnes ... I don't know 'Lias, we got four down up there, if I split you off, we ...

Elias grabs a stick, urgent, starts drawing their position in the dirt for Wolfe.

ELIAS Look, Lootenant ...

Wolfe looks up, relieved as Barnes splashes into the CP group. Thunder peals.

BARNES *(yelling at Wolfe and Ace)* Where the fuck is red platoon! Tell 'em to get their asses up here! What the fuck you doin' back here Elias? Round up your assholes and move 'em up front, we're getting chopped to shit.

ELIAS *(yelling back)* Barnes, listen to me ... there's 5–6 spiderholes back there *(points)* next to the church. *(draws it in the ground as he talks)* Third Platoon's coming up the stream to reinforce us. Flank's wide open, dinks get 3–4 snipers in these holes, when Third Platoon comes up, they'll get us in a crossfire with 'em. We'll shoot each other to shit, then they'll hit us with everything they got. It'll be a massacre!

Barnes looking at the drawing.

WOLFE Sounds pretty far out to me 'Lias.

ELIAS Maybe but I seen it happen at Ia Drang in '66, First
Cavalry and they cut us to fuckin' pieces! *(back to Barnes)*
Give me three men, if I'm wrong, I can still roll up that
flank.

BARNES *(a look)* Take off, but keep your radio here.

Elias goes, stops, looks at Barnes ...

ELIAS ... You keep pouring out that suppressing fire,
Barnes. I don't wanna be caught out there with my ass
hanging out you hear me?

BARNES Don't tell me how to fight this fucking war, 'Lias,
you go crying to fucking brigade on your time. Out
here you belong to me. Now move.

*A look. Elias goes fast. More thunder peals. As the 155 mm howitzers
— sounding like deep tom-toms some three miles distant — beat out their
shells. An ominous sound. Closer.*

ACE Sir! Shot out. Arty's on the way!

BARNES *(hurrying back to the front)* Get that asshole O'Neill up
here willya!

EXT: JUNGLE – FU SHENG'S POSITION – DAY
*Fu Sheng is laying out fire when he senses something, looks up. The
artillery shell sounds too close. Getting bigger and bigger on the
horizon. Too big, too loud. A groan of fear on his face, then knowledge.
Then ... a huge EXPLOSION engulfs him.*

EXT: JUNGLE – HAROLD'S POSITION – DAY (RAIN)

BIG HAROLD Short round! It's short, man! They fuckin' got
Fu Sheng! BARNES! OVER HERE!

EXT: JUNGLE – DAY (RAIN)
*Barnes hearing it, starts forward. Another huge shell starting to
whistle in on them.*

BARNES That fuckin' idiot!

It explodes. This is about three times the intensity of the RPG. The jungle floor shakes, trees splinter. Barnes is knocked to his knees, grimaces in pain. Hoyt, Barnes' radio operator, screams out as a fist-sized chunk of hot shrapnel sticks in his back. He's screeching, frantically trying to shuck the radio from his back, his fatigue shirt smoking.

Barnes jerks the radio off Hoyt's back, knocks the man to his knees and unsheathes his bayonet. Ripping off the back of his shirt, Barnes sets to digging out the shrapnel.

EXT: MOREHOUSE'S POSITION – DAY (RAIN)
Morehouse is decimated by a third explosion, chunks of shrapnel whirring like battleaxes into the tree trunks.

EXT: JUNGLE – HAROLD'S POSITION – DAY (RAIN)
Big Harold is tearing blindly away from the front, helmet gone, rifle dragging in the mud when he stumbles, sprawling face down. He jumps up, looks back, sees now the wire over which he tripped. It takes a second to register. He shares a look with Bunny who's already on the ground.

BUNNY Satchel charge! GET DOWN!

Harold goes for the ground the same instant the satchel explodes.

EXT: JUNGLE – CHURCH – DAY (RAIN)
Chris, further back, dumps Lerner with Doc who's got more than he can handle.

CHRIS Take care of him Doc! Please!

Doc looking at him, a dark look of hopelessness. Lerner is a mess, groaning, reaching for Chris' hand.

LERNER   ... don't ... don't leave me man ...

A look between them. Rhah intersecting.

RHAH Taylor – get your ass over here. Move!

CHRIS Hang tough, Gator. Hang in there, man, you're

gonna be OK ... just hang on.

Feeling like a liar, peeling the man's hands off him, leaving him there looking numb. Chris is shaken, Lerner's blood all over him.

He tears out after Rhah, linking up with Elias and Crawford. Elias motioning them to hurry. Another huge artillery round exploding out to the front.

EXT: JUNGLE – O'NEILL'S POSITION – DAY (RAIN)
Sgt. O'Neill, scared out of his mind, hugging the earth, tries to crawl into a small cut in the ground but finds it occupied by a cringing Junior.

EXT: JUNGLE – WOLFE'S POSITION – DAY (RAIN)
Barnes rushes up out of the forest like Achilles, towering in his rage, at Lieutenant Wolfe, ripping his handset from him as the Lieutenant reads off the coordinates off his map.

BARNES YOU IGNORANT ASSHOLE! – What the fuck coordinates you giving! You killed a bunch of people with that fucked up fire mission! You know that? ... ah shit!

Wolfe stares at him, open-mouthed. Disgusted, Barnes hunkers down to read the coordinates from his own map into the handset.

BARNES Redleg Romeo ... Ripper Bravo Two. Check fire, check fire, you're short on our pos! I say again, check your fuckin' fire! ... From Registration point, add one five zero, left five zero, fire for effect!

New incoming fire drowns out Barnes.

EXT: JUNGLE – ELIAS' POSITION – DAY
Elias – a defiant look on his face – moves fast but cautiously back across the Church landmarks. Chris following then Rhah and Crawford. The RAIN has now settled into a mist hugging the ground.

ELIAS Move it! Move it!

Elias comes to a stop, looks. Behind them we hear the sounds of battle, gauging their distance from the main body.

The spider holes are still empty. But he listens, senses something out there getting closer.

ELIAS They're coming ...

Chris looking at Rhah. How does he know?
Elias points out an imaginary line across the breaking mist.

ELIAS Stagger yourselves across this line, shoot anything that moves. They'll be coming from here.

RHAH *(team leader)* Gotcha.

ELIAS One of them gets through it's curtains.

RHAH Where you going?

ELIAS Down along the river 'bout 100 metres, 'case they try to flank us there. Third Platoon's coming up on our rear so watch for 'em.

CHRIS I'll go with you.

ELIAS No ... I move faster alone. *(a grin)*

Elias, his pack stripped, is gone, like a fleet leaf, vanishing into the Jungle.

RHAH *(stringing them out)* Okay Crawford – over here. Taylor – down twenty yards behind that tree.

EXT: JUNGLE – WOLFE'S POSITION – DAY (MIST)
Barnes has finished correcting the fire mission, hurls the handset back at Wolfe, a wild look in his eyes, studying the incoming fire. Makes a decision.

BARNES Let's move back, link up with Three. Let the arty do a little work. *(to Ace on radio, ignoring Wolfe)* Push Two Alpha and Two Charlie. Tell 'em to haul ass and re-group at the church. Tell 'em *NOT* to fire. *(Ace transmits)*

WOLFE What about Elias? We pull back they'll be cut off. He needs cover fire.

BARNES *(looks at him like he's stupid)* I'll get him. *(with a threatening undertone)* You just haul ass too lootenant. *(going, to Ace)* ... don't send Bravo Three up till I get back to the CP. Now move out, all of you.

As he snaps his weapon onto full auto and runs off after Elias in a crouch ... a man with a mission.

EXT: JUNGLE – RHAH & CHRIS' POSITION – DAY
Next to the Church deployed in the jungle, Rhah looks on, silent.

Chris in his position, waits. It is so silent in comparison to the racket from the battle across the forest. The Mist clings to the trees, moist and lovely. Then, a flicker of movement, sound.

Chris hears it, tightens. His POV – at fifty yards. An evanescence of beige and green uniforms moving towards him very fast, scurrying. They look like headless ghosts.

Chris opens fire.

CHRIS GET EM!!!!!!!!

Rhah and Crawford open up. A racket of sound, one of the figures seems to go down, then another but at this distance through jungle it is difficult to say. The firing just as suddenly breaks off and the silence returns.

CHRIS *(ecstatic)* Yeah! I got two of them fuckers ...

RHAH I got one ...

CHRIS ... See them go down? Like fuckin' target practice man, fuck you Charlie!! Ho Chi Minh sucks dead dick! ... Crawford! *(sees him, stunned)*

Crawford, the blond-locked California beach boy, lies on the earth, hit in a lung, having difficulty breathing, moaning in a soft undercurrent. Chris runs up on him.

CHRIS Oh man! ... man!

Attending him. Rhah runs up.

RHAH   Looks like a lung babe. But you're gonna be all right, you only need one of them fuckers.

CRAWFORD   Oh shit man I never thought I'd get hit, I was ... *(gagging)*

RHAH   Stay cool. We gonna carry you out.

Barnes appears, running towards them, looking down at Crawford, at Rhah.

RHAH   Sarge, 'bout five gooks tried to ...

BARNES   Where's Elias?

RHAH   ... came through right over there. We got three of them, we ...

BARNES   Didn't you hear the arty shift? We're pulling back. Get your wounded man and get the fuck back to the church. Get going.

CHRIS   *(indicating jungle)*   ... but 'Lias is still out there.

BARNES   I'll get him. You get the man in, Taylor *(indicating Crawford) NOW.* Or I'll Article 15 both your asses. Move!

Chris and Rhah look at Barnes sullenly, then reluctantly start moving Crawford onto a poncho liner they use as a litter.

BARNES   Move it, MOVE IT!

He's in his blackest rage, the force of his words almost physically pushing the men to move out with Crawford. Barnes turns now to deal with Elias.

EXT: ELIAS' JUNGLE – DAY
Elsewhere, Elias stands silently, listens to the forest. In the distance the firefight can hardly be heard. His helmet gone, his hair hanging free, he is at his best now – alone. He hears it. Somebody running through the jungle, about 100 yards, boots on leaves, coming towards him.

He begins to move lateral to the sound. His steps unheard, better at this than the enemy.

THREE ENEMY FIGURES now appear, crouched and moving very fast with light equipment through the mist.

Elias swerves up in immediate foreground, his back to us, FIRING. All three Figures fall.

A quick glimpse of Elias, not bothering to stop, moving to his next position.

EXT: BARNES' JUNGLE – DAY
Barnes, moving through the jungle, reacts to the fire, resetting his course. Like a hunter stalking a deer. Suddenly there's more firing. Then silence –

EXT: ELIAS' JUNGLE – DAY
TWO MORE ENEMY lie dead in the jungle. A rustle of movement, then a CRY – chilling, jubilant, a war cry.

A pair of feet moving lightly over the jungle. A glimpse of Elias. In his full glory. Roaming the jungle, born to it.

EXT: BARNES' JUNGLE – DAY
Barnes fixing on him, moving.

EXT: ELIAS' JUNGLE – DAY
An NVA SOLDIER, jungle-whiskered, dirty, smart, crouches, listens, looks to his PARTNER. What are they fighting here? The First One mutters something sharp and they split fast in the direction they've come.

They get about six steps when Elias suddenly rises up from the bush, not ten yards in front of them, his shots ripping into them, driving the surprised life from them. Elias is gone.

EXT: NVA JUNGLE – DAY
Elsewhere, another three NVA stop, turn and flee back from where they came.

EXT: JUNGLE CHURCH – DAY
Chris and Rhah get Crawford back to the church grounds, lay him down. No activity around them. Chris plunges back into the jungle where they left Barnes.

RHAH Taylor!

EXT: ELIAS & BARNES' JUNGLE – DAY
Barnes moving, stops, listens. Something is running towards him. But

it's hidden by the bush. He brings his rifle up smooth and quick, waits, then as the bush parts, Elias is standing there. Looking at Barnes.

Barnes sees him, starts to lower his rifle, but then stops. He raises it back an inch, sights it. Pause. A cold sealing look of hatred coming over his face.

In that moment, Elias understands. Quick as a deer, he makes his move, trying to plunge back into the bush.

Barnes fires. Once, twice, three times – the blast rocking the jungle.

Elias jerking backwards into the bush, mortally wounded. Bird cries. A crime against nature.

Barnes calmly lowers his rifle, and walks away from it.

EXT: CHRIS' JUNGLE – DAY
Chris, cutting through the jungle, hears the shots. He stops, listens. Someone is moving through bush towards him, leaves and foliage shaking.

Chris tightens, raises his rifle.

Barnes steps through into his sight – sees him.

Chris lowers his rifle. Barnes walking past him as if he weren't even there.

BARNES Elias is dead. Join up with the platoon. Move it.

CHRIS *(shocked)* He's dead! Where? ... You saw him?

BARNES Yeah. Back about 100 metres. He's dead, now get going, the gooks are all over the fuckin' place.

Moving on quickly. Chris has no choice but to follow, looking back one more time.

EXT: CHURCH GROUNDS – JUNGLE – DAY
TWO CHOPPERS are coming into a LZ in front of the Church. The two platoons, Second and Third, reinforcing, are being evacuated as quickly as possible, one load (6–8 men, depending on wounded) after the other. The choppers are spraying dust all over the place. A scene of chaos, radio talk layering it. Doc is out of supplies, making do with improvised bandages, etc.

WOLFE MOVE IT MOVE IT MOVE IT.

Lerner goes by, horribly wounded on a makeshift litter, into the chopper, Doc attending, holding the IV.

Chris catching a glimpse of him, waiting to get on the chopper, turning to look as:

Hoyt and Sergeant Warren, both wounded, are hurried aboard on litters. The chopper lifting off.

Chris and others now running to the corpses of Flash, Morehouse, and Fu Sheng lying under dirty ponchos, their boots sticking out. The ponchos are blown away in a burst of wind off the chopper blades, revealing their faces — dirt stuffing their eyes and mouths, waxen figures.

Chris and the others lifting them and carrying them towards the next chopper now coming in.

They throw the bodies on. Tubbs and Crawford, both wounded, now move past Chris, into the chopper. Chris running back, with King carrying a litter — their eyes falling on:

Barnes talking with Wolfe and Ace, making signals under the roaring sounds of the chopper. Shaking his head. No. No Elias.

Chris and King looking at each other, mute. They numbly start loading Big Harold, minus his leg, onto the stretcher.

The Third Chopper is down now, waiting, roaring blades silhouetting off the face of the cathedral. A ROCKET BLAST suddenly goes off not too far from the chopper, incoming fire. The DOOR GUNNER signaling for them to hurry, laying out fire.

INT/EXT: CHOPPER – JUNGLE – DAY

Chris and King hustling Big Harold's 250 pounds into the chopper. Climbing in with him. Wolfe, Barnes, Ace running in with them. The perimeter is bare.

Chris' eyes flitting over Barnes as he jumps in. The chopper lifting off as another explosion rocks the area. The Door Gunner sees something, opens up.

Big Harold, cursing, looks chalky but hog happy as he manages a glance down at the jungle. His right leg is gone. Tears are rolling out of his eyes.

KING Man, you gonna be in Japan this time tomorrow, Big Harold.

BIG HAROLD Yeah, I'se lucky dis time, what's a leg to get the fuck outta here ... *(at the NVA)* Eat ma shit, you motherfuckers!

He sinks back, sick. Chris' eyes suddenly fix on something. He can't believe it. He shoves King, points. King sees it. Both stunned.

Barnes is looking. So's Lt. Wolfe, so's Ace. So's the Door Gunner.

Elias is coming out of the jungle. Staggering, blood disfiguring his face and chest, hanging on with all his dimming strength, looking up at them – trying to reach them.

Chris shakes Wolfe, his words drowned out by the roar.

The Chopper Captain looking down, dips. His co-pilot pointing.

The NVA are coming out of the jungle, closing on the spot where Elias is.

Incoming rounds are hitting the chopper. The Door Gunner maniacally firing.

Barnes looking down at the man, can't believe it.

Elias is on his last legs now, obviously being hit by the incoming fire of the NVA. He falls to his knees, still stretching upwards for life.

The Chopper Captain shakes his head at Wolfe.

The Chopper dips one more time firing at the NVA, low and fierce over the jungle.

Chris looking back in horror.

Elias crucified. The NVA coming out now by the dozens from the treeline.

Elias crumbling to the ground. Obviously dead or dying.

HELICAPTAIN ON RADIO ... we still got one on the deck. Bring the gunships in.

Barnes drawing in.

Chris looking at him in revulsion. He knows. Barnes sees his look, ignores it, all of them sitting there silent, living with that final horrifying image of Elias.

EXT: UNDERGROUND HUTCH – BASE CAMP – NIGHT
The 'heads' are assembled – what's left of them. Rhah, King, Francis,

Doc, Adam, a quiet black kid, and Chris, who is impassioned tonight.

CHRIS He killed him. I know he did. I saw his eyes when he came back in ...

RHAH *(puffing on his bowl)* How do you know the dinks didn't get him. You got no proof man.

CHRIS Proof's in his eyes. When you know you know. You were there Rhah – I know what you were thinking. I say we frag the fucker. Tonight.

He looks to King who puffs on a joint, his eyes red.

KING I go with dat, an eye for an eye man.

DOC Right on, nothing wrong with Barnes another shot in the head wouldn't cure.

RHAH *(to Chris)* Shit boy you been out in the sun too long. You try that, he'll stick it right back up your ass with a candle on it.

CHRIS Then what do you suggest big shot?

RHAH *(to Chris)* I suggest you watch your own asses cause Barnes gonna be down on *ALL OF 'EM*.

FRANCIS How you figger that?

RHAH Shit man – Human nature.

Flashes the old knuckle – 'HATE'.

KING Then you jes gonna forget 'bout Elias and all the good times we done had? Right in here.

RHAH He dugged his own grave.

DOC *(correcting)* He dug it.

RHAH He *DUGGED* it too.

CHRIS Fuck this shit!

RHAH You guys trying to cure the headache by cutting off the head. 'Lias didn't ask you to fight his battles and if there's a Heaven – and god, I hope so – I know he's sitting up there drunk as a fuckin' monkey and smokin' shit cause *HIS PAINS HE DONE LEFT DOWN HERE.* Baaaaaaaaaa! (*a vehement movement of his head*)

CHRIS You're wrong man! Any way you cut it Rhah, Barnes is a murderer.

KING Right on.

RHAH I remember first time you came in here Taylor you telling me how much you admired that bastard.

CHRIS I was wrong.

RHAH (*snorts*) Wrong? You ain't *EVER* been right – 'bout nothing. And dig this you assholes and dig it good! Barnes been shot 7 times and he ain't dead, that tell you something? Barnes ain't meant to die. Only thing can get Barnes . . . is Barnes!

Barnes stands there, silhouetted in the trap door, looking down at the men who are stunned to see him here.

He steps down into the hutch, his face now lit by candle light. A bottle of whiskey in his hand, drunk, ugly, sweating, but as always, with dignity, possessive of his silence. He feels their fear in the silence, enjoys it.

BARNES (*soft*) Talking 'bout killing?

He totters slightly as he circles the outer edge of the hutch. No one talks.

BARNES Y'all experts? Y'all know about killing?

He takes the bowl from Adams, smokes it.

BARNES You pussies gotta smoke this shit so's you can hide from reality? . . . (*smokes again*) Me I don't need that shit. I *AM* reality.

Confronting Chris, he moves on, taunting them all.

BARNES There's the way it oughta be and there's the way it is. 'Lias he was full of shit, 'Lias was a crusader – I got no fight with a man does what he's told but when he don't, the machine breaks down, and when the machine breaks down, *WE* break down ... and I ain't gonna allow that. From none of you. Not one ...

Walks past Rhah, past King, throws the pot bowl into the dirt of the floor.

BARNES Y'all love Elias, want to kick ass, I'se here – all by my lonesome, nobody gonna know. Five you boys 'gainst me? *(pause, very soft)* Kill me.

Almost an appeal – naked, intense. Rhah, Francis, Doc look away.

King, the biggest one there, is about to say something, but the moment passes.

Chris waits, his anger on the rise.

Barnes takes a swigger from the whiskey, then turns away contemptuously.

BARNES I *SHIT* on all o' you.

CHRIS KILL YOU MOTHERFUCKER!!!!!

Chris slams into Barnes, rushing him off his feet. Pounding his face, solid blows.

KING & OTHERS Get that mother, babe, go ... Kick his ass, kill that cocksucker!!!

But Barnes is too quick and very strong and takes the blows, getting inside Chris' arm, twisting and flipping him in a wrestler's grip – throwing him hard onto his back on the dirt floor.

The expression of the Men watching slumps, their hopes dashed.

Barnes springs around on Chris, straddles him, one hand pushing his face back, hits him hard. *Once. Twice.*

Chris grimaces, groans, helpless now. A flick of sound.

A knife whipped out of Barnes' boot and pressing against Chris' throat. Chris bleeding from the nose and mouth.

Rhah suddenly spinning into action, fast now, realizing what Barnes intends to do.

RHAH EASY BARNES, EASY MAN!!!

Barnes is on the verge – about to kill again.

Chris waiting.

Rhah coaxing him, moving closer.

RHAH You'll do dinky dau in Long Binh Barnes. Ten years – kill an enlisted. Ten years, Barnes, just climb the walls. *DON'T DO IT . . .*

Barnes' eyes tremble in the candle light, his scars ugly, a spasm clenching and locking his facial muscles. Then suddenly he is calm again, very calm. We sense a man of enormous self-control.

Suddenly he flicks his knife across Chris, leaving a mark below his left eye.

Chris gasps. Looking up at Barnes rising off him. The boots alongside his face.

The Men looking on, the tension lowering.

BARNES *(contemptuous)* Death? What do you guys know about it?

He walks out. Quietly.

EXT: AIR SHOTS – JUNGLE, CHURCH – DAY
Chris sits at the very edge of a Huey Chopper, bandana around his forehead, long hair blowing in the wind, Barnes' mark below his eyes, slicked out now like a jungle veteran, looking down at the VILLAGE where the massacre occurred.

The Village is still a smoking ruin, a few peasants and water buffalo straggling like ants to reconstruct.

101

Bunny, next to Chris, pops his gum, indifferent. Barnes, next to him, shifts, reads a map.

Rodriguez is praying, his mouth moving without audible words, getting ready for the drop.

King is making last minute adjustments in his pack.

Bunny now nudges Chris, points. The Church in the Jungle where Elias was killed is visible. An outline of the Cemetery. Uncomfortable memories play over Chris' face.

CHRIS VOICE OVER They sent us back into the valley the next day – about 2,000 metres from Cambodia – into a battalion perimeter. Alpha Company had been hit hard the day before by a sizeable force and Charlie Company had been probed that night. There were other battalions in the valley, we weren't the only ones but we knew we were going to be the bait to lure them out. And somewhere out there was the entire 141st NVA Regiment.

The BATTALION PERIMETER now breaks in the clear ahead. Smoke grenades of various colors are being popped on the cleared LZ. It's not big, its radius 200 yards, heavily sandbagged, deeply dug, rolls of barbed wire protecting it, radio antennas sprouting from the CP – and surrounded on all four sides by jungle.

The First Chopper rocking down, whipping up dust clouds. Chris jumps out, moving out fast as the Second Chopper starts in.

EXT: BATTALION PERIMETER #3 – DUSK
The crack between the two worlds. The sun is down and the night hesitates before coming on. The men are digging in, last adjustments all along the perimeter, trip flares laid out, food eaten. Filth and garbage is everywhere. The Battalion – albeit one at half strength – seems insignificant in this jungle.

EXT: BATTALION CP – PERIMETER #3 – DUSK
At the Battalion CP, the Major confers with Captain Harris and two other Captains. Two NVA PRISONERS are sitting on their knees, interrogated by Vietnamese Kit Carson scouts and a U.S. Sergeant, their

hands tied.

The Scout slaps the shit out of the NVA.

EXT: PLATOON CP – PERIMETER #3 – DUSK
All this is watched from a distance by Ace and Doc and Lt. Wolfe at the
Platoon CP. Ace and Doc are digging the foxhole, the ace of spades in
Ace's helmet band, sharing the information with Tony and Francis.

ACE ... they caught 'em last night pulling some shit on
    Charlie Company. They found maps on 'em, man – got
    a friend at Battalion says they had every fuckin' foxhole
    here fixed on it. Distances, treelines, our claymores, trip
    wires, everything? I shit you not.

DOC Shit, so what the fuck are we doing here? Why don't
    we move ... *(no answer)* Bad vibes, man, I got bad vibes
    here. Where are the new guys they provided us anyway.

TONY I heard we's in Cambodia right fuckin' *NOW.*

TONY I heard we's in Cambodia right fuckin' *now.*

FRANCIS You kidding man ...

Rhah comes up, a walking stick in hand, huge pirate kerchief on his
head, semi-naked.

RHAH You wanted to see me sir?

WOLFE Jackson, looks like you got Elias' squad now.

RHAH Squad? I didn't know we was still referrng to this
    platoon in terms of squads sir. *(with a snicker for Ace and*
    Doc)

WOLFE *(indicating a rough drawing in the dirt)* These two holes
    are yours ...

RHAH Begging your pardon Lieutenant but my holes are
    far enuff apart you could run a regiment through there
    and nobody'd see them – I got five live bodies left ...

WOLFE I don't want to hear your problems, Jackson. You'll get new men any day. Time being you make do like everybody else.

RHAH Hey Lieutenant I didn't ask for this job, I . . .

WOLFE *(leaves)* I don't want to hear about it Jackson.

RHAH *(amazed, looking off at him)* You don't want to hear about it?

WOLFE *(turns)* That's right. I don't want to hear about it 'cause to tell you the truth, I don't give a shit okay . . . I just don't give a shit anymore.

RHAH *(shrugs, to himself)* Right . . .

WOLFE *(passing Ace digging the CP hole)* This is one time we could sure use Elias.

ACE *(to Doc)* 'Some people say I'm wishy washy. Maybe I am. Maybe I aint.'

EXT: PERIMETER # 3 – CHRIS' FOXHOLE – DUSK
On the edge of the perimeter, King puts out his claymore, unraveling it back towards his FOXHOLE, intersecting MEN from the Third Platoon, who file out on a night ambush, skirting the trip wires, demoralized, silent. Eye exchanges, but no words.

Chris sits on the foxhole watching the ambush go out, smoking a joint by himself, depressed. King comes in with the claymore wires, attaching them to their detonators. Their foxhole – as are all of the Platoon's – is positioned just inside the treeline bordering the LZ, so that they are quite isolated from the center of the perimeter where they first landed.

KING Glad I ain't going with 'em. Somewhere out dere man is de Beast and he hungry tonight . . . Man, what a bummer. Ten days and a wakeup and I'm still dealing wid this shit – fuckin' etcetera and ad infinitum man . . .

The LAST SOLDIER in the file recedes into the foliage.

KING *(noticing Chris' silence)* What's the matter wid you? ...
How come you ain't writing no more? You was always
writing something home. Looks like youse half a bubble
off, Taylor.

He doesn't answer, makes a futile gesture.

KING What about your folks? That grandma you was
telling me about? ...

Chris shakes his head.

KING Girl?

Chris' eyes answer negatively.

KING Must be somebody?

CHRIS ... there's nobody.

KING *(shifts, uncomfortable)* You been smoking too much shit
babe. Gotta control that. Takes a man down ... I
remember when you first come out to the bush, you was
straight as a ...

CHRIS Who gives a shit!

*He shifts, annoyed, prepares his grenades along the sand bags. King
shrugs, preparing his meal, sings himself a snatch of song, a good-
natured man.*

KING *(soft)* 'People say I'm the life of the party
cause I tell a joke or two
although I may be laughing loud and hardy
deep inside I'm blue ... '

CHRIS Y'ever get caught in a mistake King and you just
can't get out of it?

KING Way out of anything, man. Just keep your pecker up,

your powder dry, the worm *WILL* turn. How many days you short?

CHRIS Not just me ... it's the way the whole thing works. People like Elias get wasted and people like Barnes just go on making up rules any way they want and what do we do, we just sit around in the middle and suck on it! We just don't add up to dry shit.

KING Does a chicken have lips? Whoever said we did, babe. Make it outta here, it's all gravy, every day of the rest of your life man – gravy. Oh shit, superlifer!

O'Neill comes up, jerks his thumb at King.

O'NEILL Get your gear together, King, your orders just come through.

KING *(speechless)* You jokin' me man? ... shit, you ain't kidding! Cocksucker. Oh wowww ... the lifers made a mistake, they cuttin' me some slack, they cutting me some slack Taylor! *(dances)*

O'NEILL Collect your shit and move out King. You got 10 minutes make the last chopper. Cee ess em oh or your ass is mine. *(to Taylor)* Francis coming over. *(hurries off)*

King packing up, double time. Chris comes over, helps him, trying to share his happiness but not succeeding.

CHRIS Hey that's great King, that's great ... you take it on home for me, you tell 'em King ... got your address right? You know where you can reach me, man. Anytime!

KING I gotta didi man. Don't wanna miss that chopper. I'll send you a postcard. After I get me some. I'll send you some tapes too man. This new guy Jimi Hendrix man, whew ... you okay Taylor? Just 'member take it easy

now, don't think too much, don't be a fool, no such
thing as a coward cause it don't mean nuthin. Jes keep
on keepin' on. Okay my man ...

*Chris, fighting his depression, slaps hands with King. A brief moment,
they look at each other. A friendship that was forever and is now over.
They both sort of know they'll never see each other again.*

CHRIS I'll walk you out ...

Francis coming up, hauling his pack.

EXT: PERIMETER #3 – RODRIGUEZ FOXHOLE – DUSK
*On another foxhole, Rodriguez positions his M-60, brings up his
ammo belts (no loaders left). Tony eating, nervous, watches him, shakes
his head.*

TONY Rumor goin' round is they got tanks. Soviet shit,
T-34s ... *(pause)* Hey Rodriguez, don't you ever say
nothing?

RODRIGUEZ *(a thick Mexican accent)* What do you want me to
say, it's all the same ol' shit.

Tony shrugs, back to his food.

EXT: PERIMETER #3 – JUNIOR'S FOXHOLE – DUSK
*On another foxhole, Barnes in full pack checks the soles of Junior's
bare feet. Bunny and O'Neill looking on. Junior is moaning as if he's
dying, overdoing it by a mile.*

BARNES So what's the problem?

O'NEILL Says he can't walk.

BARNES Shit. Get your boots on Martin, next time I catch
you putting mosquito repellant on your fuckin' feet I'm
gonna courtmartial your nigger ass.

JUNIOR *(cracks)* DEN COURTMARTIAL ME
MOTHERFUCKAH, bust my ass, send me to fucking

Long Binh, do your worst but I ain't walking no more.
De white man done got his last klik outta me. Get some
chuck dude to hump this shit.

BARNES *(suddenly soft)* Get me that centipede, O'Neill.

O'Neill is puzzled. What centipede?

O'NEILL Sarge?

BARNES Yeah that long hairy orange and black bastard I
found in the ammo crate. I'm gonna put it in this
asshole's crotch, see if he can walk.

*Junior's eyes bulge with suspicion and sudden terror, his demeanor
totally alert now.*

O'NEILL *(understanding)* Oh yeah, right away Sarge.

JUNIOR No! Wait! I'll walk, fuck you I'll walk, I don't need
this shit! I don't need this shit!

BUNNY Fucking pussy, fuck it Sarge, I gotta have him on
my hole?

Barnes going. O'Neill catching up with him.

O'NEILL Uh ... Bob. Like to speak to you. Take a minute.

BARNES *(stops)* Yeah, what is it?

O'NEILL *(shuffles, reluctant)* Bob, I got Elias' R&R ... It's
coming up in 3 days. Going to Hawaii. See Patsy.
(pause, no reaction from Barnes) I never asked you for a
break, I was hoping you ... you'd send me in on the
chopper with King ... what do you say Chief? *(a friendly
punch)*

BARNES I can't do that for you, Red ... We need every
swinging dick in the field. Sorry bout that ...
(starts to go)

O'NEILL (*pleads*) Hey Bob, come on! Talk to me hunh, it's your friend Red, I'm only asking you for three days chief ...

BARNES I'm talking to you Red and I'm telling you no. Get back to your position.

O'NEILL (*grabs him, desperate*) Bob, I gotta bad feeling about this, I ... I'm telling you I got a bad feeling, man, I don't think I'm gonna make it ... y'know what I mean?

BARNES (*quietly*) ... everybody gotta die sometime Red ... Get back to your foxhole.

A look in his eyes. Very remote, very cold, silencing O'Neill. Barnes walks off.

EXT: PERIMETER #3 – BATTALION LZ – DUSK
At the LZ, King runs out, gets on the last SUPPLY CHOPPER with some other men. It lifts off, swirling dust, the last rays of daylight.

Chris watches from a Battalion CP area, waves back – the chopper sound receding in the horizon, the comparative silence of the jungle now creeping up on the perimeter. He turns and starts back to his foxhole.

A man is watching him. He's sitting on a sandbag, face in shadow. It startles Chris, something about him. Something different. A deep West Virginia drawl.

SMOKING MAN Got a light?

CHRIS Uh sure ...

Goes over reluctantly, flicks his lighter, cupping it from the wind. The flame catches a sudden, uneasy expression in Chris' face as he sees the Smoking Man.

We come around and see what Chris sees in the light of the flame. A face that smiles at him like a death's head, a large, ugly blister on his mouth, whiskered, pale – but smiling. A sick man wouldn't smile like this, but he is smiling too intimately, as if he knows Chris from way back. But he doesn't. Or does he? Perhaps it was the man Chris first saw at the airstrip when he came in-country. The same expression of evil, of a man who has seen too much and died, but still lives.

Chris feels an unnatural fear passing through him.

The Man stands, sucking on his cigarette, stretches. He is thin and very tall, towering over Chris.

SMOKING MAN   ... later.

He goes. Chris watches him, wondering. The man never looks back, a leisurely, confident stroll. In that moment, there is an EXPLOSION from way out in the jungle, about a quarter of a mile. Then another, then small arms fire. Chris looks, knows.

EXT: PERIMETER #3 – RHAH'S FOXHOLE – DUSK
On their foxhole, so do Rhah and Adams.

RHAH   Wo – watch out, there goes the fuckin' ambush. Somebody sure stepped on their dick in this op. They ain't even waiting for later, theyse hungry *NOW*.

Adams scrambling his gear together.

EXT: PERIMETER #3 – JUNIOR'S FOXHOLE – DUSK
On his foxhole, Junior listening to the distant firing. Bunny is intro-spective – talking to Junior as if he were his best friend, although they have nothing in common.

BUNNY   ... y'know some of the things we done, I don't feel like we done something wrong but sometimes y'know I get this bad feeling. Not all that shit the Chaplain's jamming up our ass 'bout the Good Lord ... just a fucking bad feeling, y'know what I mean? Don't know why. I told the Chaplain the truth is I really like it here. You do what you want, nobody fucks with you. Only worry you got's dying and if dat happens you won't know about it anyway. So what the fuck ... (*chuckles*)

Junior looks at him likes he's really crazy. Back to the distant firing.

JUNIOR *(pissed now)* Fuck! I gotta be on this hole with *YOU* man. I just know I shouldna come!

Bunny finds it funny, laughs.

BUNNY Don't you worry bout a thing Junior, you with Audie Murphy here, my man ...

EXT: PERIMETER#3 – COMPANY CP – DUSK
At the Company CP, Captain Harris is talking urgently into the radio.

HARRIS Bravo Three Alpha! Send me a grid. Send me a grid, over!

A young inexperienced VOICE screams back into the radio amid intense background FIRING filtered by radio and sounding disembodied.

RADIO VOICE We're pinned down sir, they're in the fucking trees! The trees –

HARRIS OK, Three Alpha, calm down now, son. I'm gonna get you a fire mission ASAP. Smoke'll be first ...

RADIO VOICE *(panic)* Lieutenant's dead sir, radioman looks dead sir, I don't know where the map is Captain! They're all around us sir. They're moving! Hundreds of em! I can hear em talking gook!!! Jesus Christ!

HARRIS *(calming him)* ... Just spot the smoke son and tell me where to shift. We'll get you out of there. Just hang tough and tell me where the rounds hit, over.

EXT: PERIMETER #3 – PLATOON CP – DUSK
At the Platoon CP, Barnes stands, legs akimbo, watching the jungle, anticipating the coming fight as overhead we now hear the 155 SHELLS whistle from a 10-mile distance – passing above them – then pounding down into the jungle in the near distance. Barnes turns, glances at Wolfe, smiles.

EXT: PERIMETER #3 – COMPANY CP – DUSK
At the Company CP, Captain Harris is back on the radio.

HARRIS Bravo Three Alpha six. How bout those rounds
    son? Can you adjust fire? *(waits)* Three Alpha, if you
    can't talk, just key the handset twice over. *(waits)*

*Silence, then a vague MURMURING — becoming clearer and clearer.
It's in Vietnamese. The radio is then bashed in, the sound like thunder in
the Captain's ear. He looks at his RTO, both of them shocked.*

EXT: NVA JUNGLE – NIGHT/DUSK
*In the Jungle itself, the ENEMY is moving. Flurries of movement and
sound, blurred visuals. Hands taping a piece of cloth to a tree, moving on
— revealing a luminous arrow pointing left ... Figures moving past it.*

Hands unraveling a thin wire waist-high, backwards.

*Hands sliding along another wire. We now see a moving helmet with a
luminous plaque on the back of it, leading a file up the wire. To a Jump-
off point about 50 yards outside the U.S. perimeter. Figures crouch.
Whispers. Movement. A pen flashlight on a drawing of the foxhole
positions. The NVA moving out in several directions at once.*

EXT: PERIMETER #3 – CHRIS' FOXHOLE – NIGHT
*On their foxhole, Chris and Francis wait anxiously. Overhead the
ARTILLERY keeps pounding into the ambush area. Now SMALL ARMS
FIRE can be heard picking up at random spots along the perimeter. The
battle, like a tide, is obviously moving closer to them.*

FRANCIS Oh shit me I wish I was back in Memphis now,
    oooh baby this is gonna be a motherfucker!

*Chris says nothing. Suddenly off to their right, about 80 yards, a
BLUE FIZZLE of light erupts.*

CHRIS Trip flares! ... Rodriguez's hole.

*Rat-tat-tat-tat, rat-tat-tat. Machine gun, outgoing, followed by a
sharp explosion. A ROCKET!*

CHRIS RPGs! Shit!

VOICE *(crying)* MEDIC!! DOC! DOC!

A FIGURE thrashes up through the foliage behind them.

RHAH *(a fierce whisper)* Taylor! Francis!

CHRIS Over here!

Rhah jumps into their hole with them, out of breath.

CHRIS Rhah! What's going on. Rodriguez's hole just got ...

RHAH *(gets his breath)* Okay, here it is – one, we got gooks in the fuckin' perimeter.

FRANCIS Oh shit! Dat's it, dat's it ...

RHAH They got through Alpha Company! Anything behind you don't identify itself, blow it away. Two – air strike's coming in. They gonna lay snake and nape right on the perimeter so stay tight in your holes and don't leave 'em.

FLARES now shoot up over the perimeter. Reds, greens, yellows, squeaking as they float down on their parachute hinges throughout the ensuing battle. The perimeter is illuminated at spotty intervals – sometimes arctic bright, sometimes unexplainably dark til new flares shoot up.

Chris, Francis, Rhah all look up at the light, and hug their holes even tighter, feeling naked in the light. Flares cut both ways.

RHAH ... they're probing us, they gonna go up and down this line all night trying to get through. Stay cool ... I'll be back ...

Runs out of the foxhole. Chris suddenly reacting to a noise out front, gripping Francis and pointing to the sound.

A BODY is thrashing towards them, about twenty-five yards, not yet visible but a little awkward and lungy in its movement, as if desperate.

Francis, tense, is about to pop his grenade when Chris grabs him.

CHRIS Hold it!
  (loud whisper)
  WHO IS IT!

But the body keeps coming, lurching now, falling.

FRANCIS Come on man!

CHRIS No!

A POP! — then a fizzle of BLUE LIGHT as the Figure hits their trip flare — revealing itself to be large, with no helmet, and gasping, terrified of the trip flare.

TERRIFIED SOLDIER DON'T SHOOT! DON'T SHOOT!

CHRIS It's the ambush! *(calling out)* In here, man! Hurry.

The SOLDIER now runs in like a fullback going down for the tackle, sprawling into the hole, knocking Chris and Francis down beneath him.
He is sweating, terrified, a white boy with an unrecognizable, filthy face, no rifle, no helmet, his fatigues torn all over.

TERRIFIED SOLDIER Water! Water!

Chris gives him his canteen, his shoulder and neck hurting from the collision. The Soldier sucks down the canteen.

TERRIFIED SOLDIER *(between gulps)* They'se all over the
    place, hundreds of em moving this way! They wiped us
    out man, we didn't have a chance! Where's the CP?

FRANCIS *(points)* Back there.

The Soldier struggling out of the foxhole.

TERRIFIED SOLDIER You guys get outta here! They're right
    on my ass and they ain't stoppin' for shit!

He tears off, leaving Francis in a state of incipient panic. He looks at Chris.

FRANCIS Taylor, let's di-di man!

Chris adjusting position, facing the front, anger in his voice.

CHRIS You go.

Francis hesitates, stays.

INT: PERIMETER #3 – BATTALION CP – NIGHT
At the Battalion CP, the Major is inside his BUNKER, busy between his radio nets.

MAJOR *(to RTO 1)* Get me Bravo!

RTO 2 Charlie Company reports hand to hand on the
    perimeter sir. Three holes are down. They need help!

MAJOR *(looks at his watch, to his XO)* Okay move two squads
    from Alpha down there. Where's that goddamn air
    strike, you bet your ass if we were the First Cav they'd
    be here now.

RTO 1 *(handing him the transmitter)* Bravo Six sir.

EXT: PERIMETER #3 – BATTALION CP – NIGHT
Just outside the Bunker, a MASTER SERGEANT spots something in the flarelight. TWO FIGURES with helmets running towards him at an angle.

MASTER SERGEANT Hey you boys! Which Company you ...

A sudden burst of FIRE cuts the Sergeant down in his tracks and the Figures fly by.
Soldiers in the immediate area spot them.

SOLDIER #3 SAPPERS!

SOLDIER #4 THE BUNKER!

A burst of fire. One of the RUNNING FIGURES goes down. An Explosion engulfs him.

INT: PERIMETER #3 – BATTALION CP – NIGHT
But the SECOND SAPPER runs right into the bunker in a kamikaze

charge, the light from inside momentarily revealing a bulky satchel strapped on his person and the face of the astounded Major.

RTO #3 SIR!!!

*EXT: PERIMETER #3 BATTALION CP – NIGHT
The Bunker EXPLODES with a deafening roar.*

*EXT: PERIMETER #3 – CHRIS' FOXHOLE – NIGHT
In their foxhole, Chris and Francis look at the curling ball of flame, stunned.*

CHRIS Oh no!

*EXT: PERIMETER #3 COMPANY CP – NIGHT
At the Company CP, Captain Harris has a similar reaction.*

HARRIS Jesus fucking Christ!

RTO *(to Harris)* Sir, Brigade is down, you got the Air Net now!

Harris grabbing the handset.

*EXT: PERIMETER #3 – CHRIS' FOXHOLE – NIGHT
In their foxhole, Chris points.*

CHRIS There!

SHAPES moving in the trees. Chris blows his claymore handles. One explosion on top of the other out front. Then return fire. Flashes from a muzzle, rak-a-tak, rak-a-tak, rak-a-tak, the heavier sound of an AK-47.

Chris opening up with his 16. Then being blown down by a grenade explosion at the edge of the foxhole. Then nothing. A pause. Chris' ears ringing, slightly concussed.

Suddenly from down the perimeter there is the sound of a faulty LOUDSPEAKER crackling out from the jungle. A pidgen English, the words mauled, then a snatch of patriotic North Vietnamese music, played from a scratchy old record.

Chris uneasy, looking at Francis who looks terrified. The SOUND now of a whistle. Two hoots, then a sharp third. Then yelling.

Chris grabbing Francis' arm, pointing. There is a VOICE directly out to the front of them – muttering something in Vietnamese, no more than 20 yards away but unseen. It's like hearing a casual conversation from another room, then the sounds of several bodies moving in separate directions – encompassing the foxhole.

CHRIS *(to Francis, a whisper)* Out of the hole! Fast!

Chris crawls out, stops, looks back. Francis won't leave, hugs the shelter.

CHRIS *(a fierce whisper)* Goddamit Francis! Move your
　　fucking ass. Now ... THEY GONNA BLOW IT!

Reaches in and yanks him with all his strength half out of the hole. Francis, finally sparked, now moves out. Both of them bellying it into the brush behind the hole.

Not a moment too soon. An RPG ROCKET whistling in.

The FOXHOLE takes a direct hit, caving in, whirls of smoke spinning off it.

Chris and Francis look back covered with debris. They hear movement.

SHADOWS are swarming towards the foxhole, firing into it to finish them off.

Francis grabs Chris' leg, indicating they get out of there. Chris hesitates – a moment, a decision made now in angry passion – rises up and charges the NVA.

SHADOWS scatter and tumble, caught by his surprise close-range fire.

Chris moving forward into them, blasting, agile, his instincts finely tuned, and totally insane in this moment of time, indifferent to his life. He YELLS insanities, pumping himself up with the adrenaline of courage.

CHRIS DIE YOU MOTHERFUCKERS!!!
　　YAAAAAAAA!!!

Screams from the dark shadows, they fall.

Chris smashing a wounded SHADOW with the butt of his gun down into the foxhole. He jumps back into it, reoccupying it. Blasting the dead gook.

Opening fire out to the front, driving the Shadows back.

Francis watching this, amazed. After a moment of doubt, he too tears back out to join Chris in the foxhole, unbelieving, as he jumps in with him.

FRANCIS *(joining in the frenzy)* YAAAAHHHH!!!
KILLLLL!!!

Then stunned again to see Chris suddenly rise up out of the foxhole and charging forward into the jungle. He is now over the edge.

CHRIS *(charging off into the jungle)* DIE YOU
MOTHERFUCKERS!!!

EXT: PERIMETER #3 – BUNNY'S FOXHOLE – NIGHT
In his position, Bunny is experiencing the same 'high' as Chris, yells out at them.

BUNNY Come on MOTHERFUCKERS, COME ON!!!

Junior, huddled in the hole with him, speechless and terrified, looks at him with huge eyes. The guy is nuts. An incoming grenade explosion shakes the hole.

BUNNY *(laying out more fire)* Come on you can do better than
that!

JUNIOR Fuck this shit! I ain't dyin' in no white man's war!
Ise didi-ing this motherfuckah!

Junior freaks out, throws his rifle down and hobbles out of the hole on his damaged feet at an incredible speed.

BUNNY *(yelling after him)* Get back here you gutless shit ...

A SHAPE suddenly out of nowhere, looms up fast behind Bunny, running at him.

Junior, insane now with fear, runs smack into a tree, knocked senseless and reeling to the ground.

Bunny turning back too late. The crazy drug-high Shape is yelling something like:

NVA SOLDIER Diiiiikaaeeeeeee!

And jumps right into the hole blasting Bunny point-blank in the chest.

*Bunny struggling to consciousness at the bottom of the hole. THUCK!
A boot in the gaping hole where his chest was. Bunny, his eyes uncomprehending. A muzzle is jammed into his mouth, breaking his teeth with
an ugly sound. Another yell from the NVA trooper. A flash of orange red
light. Bunny's face blown to bits.*

Junior, dizzy from the blow to his head, looks up.

*A yellow flare somewhere out there and a SHADOW above him digging a
bayonet into his belly with a grunt. A long oozing sigh of belly gas.*

*An explosion. The Shadow with the bayonet staggering blind without eyes,
holding his brains with his hands.*

*Barnes throws open the empty LAAW rocket casing he has just fired off
and charges forward with a yell, cutting down another NVA in Bunny's
old foxhole. Jumping into the hole, the bottom of which is a liquid pit of
guts, blood, ooze. Another Enemy running in on him. A short burst of fire.
Barnes hit. Firing into each other. Barnes dragging him down into the pit
with him, grappling alongside the corpse of Bunny. Barnes uses an
entrenching tool to finish him off.*

*EXT: PERIMETER #3 – PLATOON CP – NIGHT
At the Platoon CP, small arms fire is all over the place, the NVA closing
the ring. Ace, in the foxhole, yells to Wolfe.*

ACE Negative contact. Can't raise Barnes, Two Bravo, Two
     Charlie, nothin'!

WOLFE Get me Six!

*Nervously aiming his rifle as a man comes running towards them,
staggering.*

ACE It's Doc!

Doc plops down, out of breath, drained, bleeding all over his chest.

DOC They're coming through all over! I can't... I can't do...

WOLFE   Where's Barnes!

DOC   I think he's dead ... it's awful, they're all dying.

Wolfe is stunned, Barnes his last crutch against the chaos. Ace handing him the handset.

ACE   Six!

CAPTAIN HARRIS' VOICE   Yeah! Send traffic or clear this goddamn net!

WOLFE   We've been overrun Captain, we're pulling back. Over!

EXT: PERIMETER #3 – COMPANY CP – NIGHT
At the Company CP, things are just as bad. A Radioman is sprawled over a smashed radio. Captain Harris is in a bunker working the radios himself, as his Radiomen fire at yelling, running FIGURES scurrying all over the inner perimeter.

HARRIS *(furious voice)*   Bravo Two, Six! Goddamit where the hell you plannin' to pull back to! They're all over the perimeter. Be advised Lieutenant, you *WILL* hold in place and you will *FIGHT* and that means *YOU,* Lieutenant. Out!

EXT: PERIMETER #3 – PLATOON CP – NIGHT
At the Platoon CP, Wolfe is astounded by the message. Ace looking at him straight in the eye.

ACE   You're an asshole Lieutenant, you know that.

As he abandons his radio, grabs up his 16 and moves to an adjacent position. Doc, a quiet man up to now, is treating a wounded Parker who is now hit by bullets and thrashes wildly and jerks to a stop. He is obviously dead but Doc goes on trying to finish the bandage. Suddenly he goes beserk, grabs a 16, starts firing and yelling.

EXT: PERIMETER #3 – COMPANY CP – NIGHT
At the Company CP, Harris gets on the radio with the air strike. One of the RTOs on a separate radio calls over.

RTO #5 Captain, Third Battalion Armored's on its way with tracks 'bout 2 kliks west!

HARRIS *(ignores it, into radio)* Snakebite leader, Ripper Bravo Six, we're gonna need you soonest be advised I've got zips in the wire down here, over!

PILOT'S VOICE 1 *(distorted high frequency)* Roger your last Bravo Six, Snakebite lead we can't run it any closer. We're hot to trot and packing snape and nape but we're bingo fuel. It's your call, Six actual, Over.

Harris looks around. The decision made.

HARRIS Snakebite leader, Bravo Six, for the record, it's my call. Dump everything you got left *ON MY POS*. I say again, I want all you're holding *INSIDE* the perimeter. It's a lovely war. Bravo Six Actual and Out.

Pilot's reaction. Very calm. A Farmboy twang.

PILOT'S VOICE Roger your last Bravo Six. We copy it's your call. Get em in their holes down there. Hang tough, Bravo Six we are coming cocked for treetops. Whiskey to Echo ... Snakebite Two, this is lead. Last pass on zero niner. Watch my smoke to target, expend all remaining. Follow my trace ...

The transmission drops out. Harris now looking up into the darkened skies. The planes in no way evident – but they're there. And they're coming.

EXT: PERIMETER #3 – PLATOON CP – NIGHT
At the Platoon CP, the NVA are sweeping fast, crouched, using cover, yelling. Small fires are raging all over the perimeter.

Ace putting out fire, is hit. The NVA are coming over his sandbags. A burst of fire. Ace goes down.

Doc has cracked up, firing at anything, indifferent to his safety. One of the NVA goes down. The Doc is hit in the side, wounded, struggles, is hit again, but keeps trying to fire. He's hit a third time — in the jugular vein. Nearby, Wolfe is firing madly at the oncoming NVA. One goes down. A second is wounded, yelling in pain. Wolfe reloading his 16, popping up, too late. One of them is coming over the sandbags. He sees Wolfe. Wolfe sees him. In the same moment.

Wolfe hesitates, frozen up. The gook unloads his AK-47, a magazine worth, into Lieutenant Wolfe, who crashes down, sprawled unnaturally on the jungle floor. A spasm shakes his body. Then stops. Dead.

Boots run by.

EXT: PERIMETER #3 – O'NEILL'S FOXHOLE - NIGHT
At his foxhole, O'Neill peeks up out of the hole. Several NVA are darting through the jungle 20 yards away, coming towards him, talking loudly to each other. He quickly slips back down in the hole, entwining himself with the approaching NVA, clinking metal.

The NVA stop, glance in the hole. Something is muttered. They run out.

O'Neill opens his eyes, breathes.

EXT: PERIMETER #3 – BARNES' FOXHOLE – NIGHT
BARNES swings his mashed M-16 full into the FACE of an enemy SOLDIER who screams and goes down, Barnes chopping at him with his club. His helmet is gone, his shirt ripped to shreds, his shoulder bleeding, making his last stand against the hated Gooks.

Nearby HUFFMEISTER is hit in the shoulder by a running FIGURE and collapses into the bottom of the foxhole, crying out in pain.

The running FIGURE runs past right into the full force of BARNES' swinging rifle. SMACK! He crumples.

INTERCUT

CHRIS bellies into the area, see Barnes, recognizes him, amazed.

An ENEMY fires, taking Barnes high in the left thigh. A patch of skin blowing off. Barnes rigidly goes down on his left knee like a wounded horse. Holds there, staring into the Enemy, waiting for the coup de grace.

A series of SHOUTS and the Enemy staggers dead as:

Chris lays out a curtain of fire. A GRENADE goes off near him, blowing off his helmet. Dazed, Chris rushes forward firing from the hip – sucked into Barnes' suicidal vacuum. He cuts down an Enemy as:

Barnes, given a new lease, limps angrily forward and tackles a wounded Enemy trying to crawl away, terrified at the sight of Barnes coming after him. Barnes lets out a vivid scream.

And beats the soldier mercilessly, half the stock of his M-16 flying apart broken.

Chris swivels alert on his knees. A pause. No more enemy. Turns to Barnes, his back to Chris still beating at the dead corpse.

CHRIS Barnes!

Barnes swivels instinctively off the corpse and for a petrifying moment Chris sees:

A maddened scar of a face, lips specked with foam. The EYES – refracted in a red-green flare overhead – the pupils distorted into angry red points.

For Chris it is no doubt the most frightening single image he has seen in his life. It will be in his nightmares forever. The essence of evil: wrath, obsession, anger, fear, hatred, permanence – he is paralyzed.

Barnes smashes him full across the face with the broken stock of his M-16. Not even consciously, for at this point, his mind has gone over the edge and the entire world is his enemy. American or Vietnamese, it makes no difference as he strikes Chris harder and harder.

Chris struggles, moans, his teeth and nose cracked. Barnes emits another chilling yell and springs like a humpback up on his good right leg, the left bent – set to deliver the killing blow, the mangled rifle pulled to its highest arc.

CHRIS Nooooooooooooo!

The PHANTOM FIGHTER JET comes now like a great white whale. One big beautiful monstrous beat of deafening sound. Its silver and white belly hurtling low over the treeline in one giant leap of sound momentarily illuminated by a flare. Then a monstrous ROAR of anger.

The bomb ripping Barnes off the body of Chris and spitting Chris across the jungle floor — crashing into a tree some 30 yards away.

FADE OUT

EXT: PERIMETER #3 – CHRIS' JUNGLE – DAWN
FADE BACK IN. Vague sunlight. Blurry. Chris fluttering his eyes. A sharp MOVEMENT in the bush. His eyes fight their way open.

SOFT EYES are watching him from behind foliage. A soft, furry head, alert, rigidly still.

Chris fights his way up to his elbow, in pain, looking at the eyes. The head turns and in one fluid move, bolts. Gone. Like the wind. A deer. A big brown deer. Or was it? Chris will never be quite sure. But whatever it was, it was surely a sign of grace — the grace of Elias. This he knows as he feels himself for the first time alive.

And in pain. His left hand torn and bleeding, shrapnel in his side, cuts on his face, dried blood caking him. Looking around his garden of eden. A messy jungle floor. Cordite fumes. Burned bush and trees. Torn sandbags. Dead NVA. Bird songs somewhere in the distance. It is the very crack of dawn, a pink-red sun casting long oblique light patterns through the trees. A holy light.

Chris pushes himself to his feet, feels his weight and the pain. He walks. In the near distance, towards the LZ area, there's the sound of Armored Personnel carriers grinding, men moving, calling out in Americanese. But Chris is alone here.

He fishes up an AK-47 from a dead NVA. Checks it, a weapon. Walks on.

EXT: PERIMETER #3 – BARNES' FOXHOLE – DAY
Past scores of NVA bodies. Past the Foxhole where Bunny lays dead in the bottom, faceless. Looking over at Junior bayoneted to the ground, dead. NVA everywhere around the hole, some of them still moving, badly wounded.

Chris looking around, then noticing a movement a little further out in the Jungle. Then he sees who.

The uniform is shredded, the figure obviously hurt in several places (thigh, back, neck, hand) but not mortally so, now struggling to right itself, dragging its face up from a belly-down position. Streaked with dirt and blood, we see Barnes once again re-emerging from the dead.

Chris steps over to him, a solemn look on his face. Barnes looks up, begs.

BARNES Get me a Medic will ya. Go on ...

Chris doesn't move. Barnes looks at him again, reading the intention that has crossed Chris' mind. An expression of surprise crosses his face, then amazement, almost shock.

BARNES Fuck you in hell ...

Chris shoots him. Once. Twice. Three times. Silence ...
Barnes is finally dead.

Chris looking at the corpse, numbed, no exultation in his expression. Just cold satisfaction and little feeling left.

Behind him, the SOUND *of a big machine moving. He turns.*

A huge Nazi flag on an antenna looms up in the bush, followed by the great belly of a turreted dragon crunching down a tree for its breakfast.

A big tough GERMAN SHEPHERD *comes bounding at him sniffs, followed by a flak-jacketed* MONSTER MAN — *filthy, and greasy, unshaven face, earring in his left ear, 'DEATH CORPS' scrawled on his shirtless flak jacket and a drawing of a death's head, he looks like a cross between a pirate and a hell's angel. Behind him, a* SECOND MONSTER MAN *and the* ARMORED PERSONNEL CARRIER *grinding its engine, a human skull hanging from its turret.*

MONSTER MAN *(to Dog)* Bozo! Get back here!

His eyes passing on Chris like so much meat.

MONSTER MAN *(to Chris)* Can you walk outta here?

Chris nods. The Soldier pointing to the LZ behind him as a sign he should go that way. The other Soldier already stripping the NVA dead, as the APC grinds on into the jungle, reconnoitering.

Chris walks out of the jungle, head bowed, nauseated, mixed feelings roiling him.

EXT: PERIMETER #3 – FRANCIS' FOXHOLE – DAY
In another foxhole, Francis waits, the sounds of the approaching APC cutting through. He thinks about it a moment. It must be fast. It must be a hard cold decision. Now!

He pulls out his K-bar blade and with one last anguished hesitation, drives it into his thigh muscle.

Francis yells out and collapses in his hole.

EXT: PERIMETER # 3 – O'NEILL'S FOXHOLE – DAY
In another foxhole, O'Neill, unscratched but covered with dirt, waits tentatively as SOLDIERS arrive at his hole. They're a little awed by the sight of the tough-looking O'Neill emerging from his foxhole like Sgt. Rock, dozens of dead NVA littered around him.

APC SOLDIER #1 You alone Sarge?

O'NEILL Fuck yeah. They all left me, bunch of fuckin' faggots.

APC SOLDIER #2 Man, you gonna get yoself a silver star.

O'NEILL Fuck the silver star. You got any booze?

EXT: PERIMETER #3 – RHAH'S FOXHOLE – DAY
Rhah, alive and well, is poking around the NVA corpses with a long gnarled walking stick, looking like a crazy Johnny Appleseed with his pants rolled up on his thin hairy ankles and wearing a red bandana tied in a four-knot around his head.

As one of the APC SOLDIERS carves an ear off a dead NVA, Rhah works his way through the torn bloody pocket of an NVA Troop in full rigor mortis, extracting what he thought was there – a wrapped cellophane of heroin.

Rhah's face glows with satisfaction as he tastes it, then snorts it. With a certain satisfaction of triumph over the grim circumstances.

RHAH *(to the powder)* Yeah, that's good shit ...

EXT: PERIMETER #3 – LZ – DAY
CHRIS is hauled out on a litter. Morphined, his eyes watching it all from somewhere deep in his brain. Passing:

Groups of SOLDIERS looking like bowery bums and moving like rats through the smoke and garbage snooping for souvenirs with wheezy tired eyes and grunts of greed.

Passing a bulldozed PIT with heaps of NVA BODIES in them. A BULL-DOZER pushing another set of bodies in, like photos of a Nazi death camp.

Nearby, two burly SOLDIERS lift a WOMAN NURSE and with a once-through build for momentum, toss the fresh body into the pit.

Chris, numb, goes by.

RADIO OPERATOR *(into radio, exhausted)* – 37 U. S. KIA, 122 wounded and still counting. Estimate 500 Victor Charlie KIA, 22 wounded and still counting. Over.

2ND RADIO OPERATOR Sir, a television crew's coming in with the General –

CAPTAIN HARRIS doesn't respond; at this point he doesn't give a shit, standing apart from the radios looking numbly at the remnants of his boys filtering by on litters.

Chris intersects him now, Harris' eyes looking blankly, then nodding sickly trying to give him encouragement. Just coming to the edge of tears, choking it back, and turning back. These are his sons who are lost. A good officer.

Rodriguez, wounded, is lifted up in his litter and moved out to the waiting MEDIVAC CHOPPER, a huge red cross painted on a white square.

Doc goes by on another litter, then Ace, Adams, Huffmeister, etc.

Then Francis is littered by, bandages around his leg, a big smile on his face.

FRANCIS Hey Taylor, you okay man?

CHRIS Yeah. How 'bout you?

FRANCIS Jes' fine man, jes fine! Ain't never felt better! Both of us two timers man, we're out. *(gives him a slap as he goes by)* See you at the hospital man, we gonna get high-high yessir ... *(goes off)*

The Medic points to the chopper.

MEDIC *(to Chris)* That's your ride man, you ready?

CHRIS *(tries a smile)* You bet.

Chris starts towards it, the Medic assisting him.

EXT: PERIMETER #3 – LZ – DAY
Sgt. O'Neill watches the loading process forlornly from the distance.
Captain Harris intersects him.

HARRIS You got Second Platoon Sergeant.

O'NEILL *(reflexively)* Yes sir –

And as Harris moves away, O'Neill is left thinking. Finally there is a
certain frustration to his actions; he has taken such great pains to stay
alive that the tuition he pays is precisely to stay in this Jungle.
Inevitably his time will come – one way or the other.

His eyes now follow the MEDIVAC CHOPPER upwards, whatever is left
of his shrunken soul yearning to go with it.

EXT/INT: PERIMETER #3 – LZ CHOPPER – DAY
As the Chopper rises off the battlefield, Chris, who is sitting at the edge
so that he has a full view out the open door, waves back at Rhah.

EXT: PERIMETER # 3 – DAY
Rhah, at the edge of the treeline, vigorously shakes his walking stick at
him, his other hand a fist, waving them, emitting his cry.

RHAH Baaaaaaaaaaaa!!!!!!!!!!!!!!

Defiance. Pride. Dig me, I'm Rhah – and there isn't nobody like me in
the world.

EXT/INT: PERIMETER #3 – LZ CHOPPER – DAY
The chopper – with its huge red cross painted on – now rising to meet
God. Smashed on morphine, Chris looking out at the waving ants
below.

Now the trees, the skyline and the chopper is moving fast over the devastation. The jungle forever locked in his memory, Chris looks back, copious, quiet tears flowing from his eyes.

CHRIS VOICE OVER   I think now, looking back, we did not fight the enemy, we fought ourselves – and the enemy was in us ... The war is over for me now, but it will always be there – the rest of my days. As I am sure Elias will be – fighting with Barnes for what Rhah called possession of my soul ... There are times since I have felt like the child born of those two fathers ... but be that as it may, those of us who did make it have an obligation to build again, to teach to others what we know and to try with what's left of our lives to find a goodness and meaning to this life ...

The music surges now to its full strength as we replay bits of film with each actor's name listed – some with silly, clowning looks, others sober, haunted. Gardner, Tex, King, Rhah, Lerner, Sanderson, Manny, Big Harold – all the boys ... and then Barnes staring quietly into the camera, and lastly Elias – shirt off, bowl of grass in hand, his big, beautiful smile.

THE END

SALVADOR

CREDITS

Richard Boyle .... JAMES WOODS
Dr. Rock .... JAMES BELUSHI
Ambassador Thomas Kelly .... MICHAEL MURPHY
John Cassady .... JOHN SAVAGE
Maria .... ELPEDIA CARRILLO
Major Max .... TONY PLANA
Jack Morgan .... COLBY CHESTER
Cathy Moore .... CYNTHIA GIBB
Col. Hyde .... WILL MacMILLIAN
Pauline Axelrod .... VALERIE WILDMAN
Archbishop Romero .... JOSE CARLOS RUIZ
Col. Julio Figueroa .... JORGE LUKE
Army Lieutenant .... JUAN GERNANDEZ
Human Rights Leader .... SALVADOR SANCHEZ
Assistant Human Rights Leader .... ROSARIO ZUNIGA
Maria's Brother .... MARTIN FUENTES
Australian Reporter .... GARY FARR
French Reporter .... GILES MILINAIRE
Major Max Assistant .... RAMON MENENDEZ
Roberto, Restaurant Owner .... JOHN DOE
Woman Rebel .... LETICIA VALENZUELA
Rebel Youth .... ROBERTO SOSA JR.
Dog Attendant .... DARIA OKUGAWA
Cop In San Francisco .... SUE ANN McKEAN
Immigration Officer On Bus .... JOSHUA GALLEGOS
Boyle's Wife .... MARIA RUBELL
Sister Stan .... DANNA HANSEN
Sister Burkit .... SIGRIDUR GUDMUNDS
Sister Wagner .... ERICA CARLSON
Kelly Assistant .... KARA GLOVER
Maria's Grandmother .... MA. DEL
Romero Assassin .... ARTURO BONILLA

Captain Marti ...... Special Appearance by MIGUEL EHRENBERG
Boyle's Baby .... SEAN STONE
Landlord San Francisco .... TYRONE JONES

Directed By .... OLIVER STONE
Executive Producers .... JOHN DALY/DEREK GIBSON
Screenplay By .... OLIVER STONE/RICHARD BOYLE
Produced By .... GERALD GREEN/OLIVER STONE
Associate Producers .... BOB MORONES/BRAD H. ARONSON
Editor .... CLAIRE SIMPSON
Director of Photography .... ROBERT RICHARDSON
Music By .... GEORGES DELERUE
Production Designer .... BRUNO RUBEO
Executive in Charge of Production .... BRAD H. ARONSON
Post Production Supervisor .... MICHAEL BENNETT
First Assistant Director .... RAMON MENDEZ
Costume Designer .... KATHRYN GREKO MORRISON
Music Supervisor .... BUD CARR
Music Editor .... JOAN BIEL
Special Effects Supervision .... YVES DE BONO
Property Master .... RON JEREMY DOWNING
Casting .... BOB 'BLACKIE' MORONES
Still Photographer .... GARY ANTHONY FARR

AMERICAN CREW

Camera Operator .... THOMAS JULIAN RICHMOND
Assistant Cameraman .... CHRISTOPHER LOMBARDI
Still Photographer .... GARY ANTHONY FARR
Stunt Co-ordinator .... BILL CATCHING
Executive Secretary .... PATRICIA GREEN
Production Secretary .... EILEEN ZANNINO
Main Title Sequence Designed By .... ROBERT DAWSON
Associate Editors .... CARLOS PUENTE/TOM FINNAN
Sound Designer/
Supervising Sound Editor ..... DAVID LEWIS YEWDALL, M.P.S.E.
Dialogue Editors .... STEVE RICE/FRANK T. SMATHERS
Sound Effects Editors .... R.J. PALMER/F. HUDSON MILLER
Foley Artist .... JOHN POST/TED GOODSPEED
Sound Assistant .... MICHAEL FISHMAN
Sound Engineer .... JOHNATHAN D. EVANS
1st Assistant Editor .... LISA LEEMAN
Assistant Editors .... JULIE MONROE/DAVIE BRENNER

Apprentice Editor .... JULIE ROGERS
Re-Recording Mixers .... BOB MINKLER/NEIL BRODY/
BILL MUMFORD
Set Dressing, US Locations .... MILO NEEDLES
Sound Recording/San Francisco .... PHIL PERKINS
Production Supervisor/San Francisco .... MARY M. ENSIGN
Location Manager/San Francisco .... LAURIE NOLL

MEXICAN CREW

Supervising Production Manager .... ANUAR BADIN
Production Unit Manager .... FEDERICO SERRANO
Production Manager .... ALEJANDRA HERNANDEZ
Production Co-ordinator .... CONCEPCION TOBOADA
Public Relations .... CHRISTINA ESPINOZA
Assistant Production Manager .... CARLOS GUTIERREZ
Production Assistant .... SERGIO PRIETO P.
Location Manager .... PABLO BUELNA
Production Accountant .... ROSA MARIA GOMEZ
Assistant Production Accountant .... ELSA HERMOSO
Script Supervisor .... MARIO CISNEROS JR.
Director of Photography .... LEON SANCHEZ RUIZ
Assistant Director .... JOSE LUIS ORTEGA
2nd Assistant Director .... MIGUEL LIMA
Gaffer .... FERNANDO CALVILLO
Camera Assistant .... GUILLERMO MOYSEN
Camera Assistant .... LEON SANCHEZ/DEL ANGEL
Camera Assistant .... PEDRO VASQUEZ
Dolly Operator .... ANTONIO RAMIREZ
Camera Painter .... LUIS JIMENEZ MENDEZ
Camera Assistant .... MANUEL PAREDES
Chief Grip .... SALVADOR VASQUEZ
Chief Electrician .... SALVADOR GUTIERREZ
Generator Operations .... HUMBERTO GALINDO
Additional Casting .... CLAUDIA BECKER
Extra Casting .... CHUCHO GUERRERO
Actor's Delegate .... MANUEL TREJO MORALES
Wardrobe Master .... FRECERICO CASTILLO
Wardrobe .... MONICA ARAIZ
Seamstress .... MARIA JESUS LUNA
Assistant Wardrobe .... JAIME ORTIZ
Special Effects .... MARCELINO PACHECO GARCIA
Assistant 1 .... ALFONSO PACHECO GARCIA

Assistant 2 .... DANIEL CORDERO P.
Property Master .... RICARDO GIL
Assistant Property Master .... ADOLFO NAVARRO
Transportation Captain .... MIGUEL ANGEL GOMEZ
Videoman .... FLAVIO CASTILLERO
Make-Up .... ELIVIRA OROPEZA
Hair Dresser .... HUMBERTO ESCAMILLA
Hair Dresser .... BERTHA CHIU
Sound Operator .... MANUEL TOPETE
Sound Assistant .... JESUS SANCHEZ
Sound Assistant .... JORGE GOMEZ
Art Director .... MELO HINOJOSA
Chief Set Dresser .... ADALBERTO LOPEZ
Stand By Set Dresser .... FRANCISCO LOPEZ
Assistant Editor .... EDGAR PAVON

PROLOGUE

This film is based on events that occurred in El Salvador in 1980–82. For narrative purposes the time frame of these events has been condensed and some events have been combined without – the filmmakers believe – violating the spirit of that time. Living characters have been fictionalized.

> 'WITH LIES THEY TRIED
> TO MAKE US LIE
> AS IF THEY DID NOT KNOW
> THAT THE MOUTH WAS
> MADE TO SAY –
> THE EYE TO SEE.'
>
> Salvadoran Peasant

*INT: SAN FRANCISCO TENEMENT – TENDERLOIN – DAWN
Richard Boyle flicks open a battered eye, the landlord is knocking on the door. CREDITS roll.*

The baby starts crying. His tired, pretty Italian wife, CLAUDIA, bottle-feeding the baby to keep it quiet, makes her way to the door ...

Boyle sits up. It looks like another Major Bad Day is in the works. A battered body and face, a man who has seen far better days, and obviously has hit the bottle one too many times, his body is something that would make Jack LaLanne throw up, mid-forties, he looks like the ten wars he's been in – a survivor of countless accidents and broken dreams, the potato famines of a wiry Irish soul.

In background, the TENDERLOIN LANDLORD is arguing with Claudia, the argument moving across the flat to Boyle, putting on his clothes, one eye flicked to the morning news on the broken-down black and white portable.

NEWSMAN In the wake of the Nicaraguan revolution, chaos has descended on tiny El Salvador ... Today two more Catholic priests were found hacked to death in a ditch outside the Capital. So far in two months more than 1000 people have 'disappeared', many of them found murdered in ditches and dumping grounds along roads

136

outside the Capital and in the provinces. Government spokesmen attribute the murders to left-wing Marxist terrorists, while left-wing spokesmen point to the right-wing 'death-squads'. U.S. Government spokesmen will only identify these assailants as 'subversives' of both the right and left... In other news, the upcoming presidential election polls show Ronald Reagan leading...

Claudia handing him the crying baby as the argument continues. Boyle familiar with the child, rocks it, feeds it.

Claudia throws the Landlord's eviction papers on the floor, cursing in Italian. 'Fuck you, you bloodsucker, you black shit!' The LANDLORD, who is black and particularly vicious-looking, picks it back up, waves it at Boyle. (has a fistful of cash — just collected)

LANDLORD No bucks no Buck Rogers Boyle. You and this Italian bitch are out. Today!

BOYLE Hey man, come on, give me a break.

As he fumbles with the hot plate and the instant coffee. Outside on the fire escape are diapers and a flashing neon sign. His life is obviously a mess, papers and books everywhere, dirty clothes, Nikon camera, cyanide pills, cortison, war trophies, a VC flag, joints, cheap typewriter ...

The Landlord exits, muttering.

LANDLORD You'll see Boyle, you'll see. *(slams the door)*

Claudia suddenly can't take it any longer, snaps, crying.

CLAUDIA No! Basta! I've had it! I can't live like this! No more! I come from a family with class. I went to college. I have a Doctorate in Literature. What am I doing living like this! I didn't come to America for this! You lied to me! You lied to me all the way through!

BOYLE *(soothing her)* Look Claudia I'm going to get on the phone right now and get 200 bucks okay calm down ...

CLAUDIA Bullshit! You're drinking again. You make up any lie!

BOYLE No. No. No. I'm all there. No drinks, you'll see ...

CLAUDIA Bullshit! all you do is drink out the icebox. Anything. The other night it was his baby formula, you were so fucking drunk, you no good worthless bum of a bum ...

BOYLE You'll see, you'll see honey ...

As he clears his allergies, scratching himself all over. He gets a quarter from the retractable piggy bank.

INT: TENEMENT HALLWAY
He's on the pay phone with NANCY GOLDBERG at Pacific News Service.

BOYLE Hi, Nancy, it's Richard ... you know Boyle ... listen it's gonna blow in El Salvador. Real soon. Can you get me a new press card? And two grand and I'll get some great stuff for you. Promise ... ('No way.') Okay what about a press card? Come on Nancy.

NANCY VOICE Boyle we've had it with you. We gave you $2500 on that Lebanon gig and you ended up in Greece fucking it away.

BOYLE Nancy, I tried! I just can't stand Muslim night life. I got ...

NANCY VOICE Well we've had it with you. You go through money like Attila the Hun and no receipts! You lose tickets, passports, you drink too much and you're a general embarrassment in the business, Boyle.

BOYLE Yeah but I get you the story don't I! What about that IRA piece. Tortured by the Brits. And Cambodia – the last man out. I made Pacific News famous on that one. And don't forget freezing my nuts off for you in the Khyber Pass. And what about El Salvador hunh? Didn't I call that one right? ... Nancy? *(he clicks the phone)*

She's hung up, a woman in pin curlers waiting to use it. Boyle pauses, scratches his head – one of his mannerisms. He never quite allows himself to look defeated or depressed, his mind always racing ahead to the next possible strategy. He has another idea, picks up the phone.

BOYLE Larry ... Boyle, hey thanks for fixing my camera. Look, I need another favor.

LARRY *(rushed)* Look, Rich, I gotta be at the airport in an hour for Beirut.

BOYLE Look, Larry this is serious, I need 500 bucks to get back to El Salvador. 400 if you ...

LARRY El Salvador? They'll kill you if you go back there.

BOYLE Look what I need's the money, not a lecture.

LARRY Okay, 300 no more. Meet me at Pan Am in 40 minutes.

Boyle ('Okay!!') clicks off.

EXT: SAN FRANCISCO STREETS – DAY
In his racing green MG (circa 1968) Boyle is hunched over the wheel, eyes like marmosets as the COP SIREN interrupts his daydream.

CUT TO:

The Cop, holding Boyle's 1979 press card, has just run a computer check on him. Boyle is pleading ...

BOYLE ... honest officer I left my license at home.

COP Mr. Boyle, your license has been revoked ... you're driving without a license, registration, insurance, you have four outstanding speeding tickets all gone to warrant, you have 43 unpaid parking tickets, nothing's legal about your car, and even your Press Card's out of date ... I'm taking you in ... *(putting the handcuffs on)*

BOYLE I'm not that Richard Boyle! You got the wrong Richard Boyle. There's another Richard Boyle ... Officer where's your humanity. I just lost my job, I just got evicted, my wife's gonna leave me, I can't even feed my kid, gimme a break, come on.

COP *(putting him in the car)* ... you wanna break Mister, go to MacDonald's.

INT: JAIL – NEXT MORNING
Boyle's bleary-eyed, a growth of beard as he steps out of the jailblock to
meet DOCTOR ROCK, who's come to bail him out. Doc is an out-of-work
San Francisco rock and roll DJ, same age as Boyle, a whining, plaintive
tone.

BOYLE Hey Doc, thanks.

ROCK *(nervous, rushed)* Come on Boyle, get your car. We
    gotta get Bagel out. He's in Oakland. He got busted by
    the Nazis and he's in Dog Dachau ...

BOYLE They got my car Doc! I need $75 to get it out.

DOC *(examining pockets)* Oh shit! I just paid $125 to get you
    out! That's all I got *(gives him the $75)* Come on! They're
    gonna drop the pellet!

EXT: OAKLAND BRIDGE – DAY
Boyle and Doc speed across in the MG. A magnificent sunny day. But the
two gonzos got two different things on their mind. Doc passing a joint.

DOC ... faster Richie, willya, come on.

BOYLE ... hey I can't Doc, I don't even have a license man,
    they're gonna throw away the key, how long's he been
    in there ...

DOC I don't know, I left him with friends ... friends, hah.

BOYLE Don't worry Doc, they don't gas 'em right away ...

DOC Shit, everything's gone to shit. Miriam's thrown me
    out. She says I'm too old to be an unemployed rock and
    roll disc jockey anymore, she wants me to sell computers
    in Silicon Valley – computers!

BOYLE *(a pet peeve of his)* I can't deal with yuppie women.
    Fuckin' walkmans, running shoes, they'd rather go to
    aerobics jazz class than fuck. (Doc: 'They got these
    pussy exercises') Now Latin women are totally different,
    they're kind ... like Claudia, she doesn't give a shit what
    I do.

DOC ... best thing about Latin women is they don't speak English. Can I crash at your place Richie? I got no place to go ... I'll sleep in your shower stall, your toilet, I need a home, I ...

BOYLE Doc, have another joint, I got bad news for you, I got no place. We're being evicted. We were going to stay with you and Miriam.

DOC You mean I gave you my last 200 dollars and I don't have a place to stay now! Oy gevalt! I'm in deep shit. What am I gonna do now – I should've left you in jail.

EXT: OAKLAND DOG POUND
Doc races around the cages, 'Bagel! Bagel!' ... no answer. The ATTENDANT is a humane, earthy-looking woman in her 30's. Doc looking everywhere around the cages for his beloved Bagel. Boyle is scratching his allergies.

DOC Where's my dog?

DOG LADY What's he look like?

Doc pulling out an 11×14 glossy of Bagel.

DOG LADY Yes, I know him.

DOC Where is he!

DOG LADY I'm sorry. We put him to sleep. We kept him more than 14 days, we tried to ...

DOC Put him to sleep? Is he going to wake up? You mean killed him! You gassed him!

DOG LADY No, no, we don't gas them anymore. We give them an injection. It's much more humane.

DOC *(freaking)* What kind of humanity is that! You murderer! I just can't believe it. My best friend. My longest relationship! Seven years. My marriage only lasted four! It's not right, it's not just.

DOG LADY I'm very sorry, there are some puppies ...

DOC *(waving Bagel's empty leash)* My dog's leash ...

BOYLE She can't do anything. Come on ...

INT: BOYLE'S TENEMENT APARTMENT – DAY
Boyle runs up the stairs, Doc following.

BOYLE ... Claudia's got a few bucks in the bank, she'll help us but we gotta tell her real nice ... no more monster acts Doc.

The eviction notice is on the door. Boyle rips it off. On the back is scrawled in large letters 'FUCK YOU' in Italian. Doc looks at it over Boyle's shoulder.

DOC What's it say?

BOYLE 'Fuck you' in Italian ... Shit, she's gone back to Italy to her parents.

As he enters the apartment. It's stripped, except for his dirty clothes. And the black and white TV and the crib. His face registers a depth of sorrow and despair.

DOC Oh shit Richie, it's too bad ... at least she left the TV.

Boyle paces to the crib, rocks it, a dirty diaper left behind.

BOYLE *(desolate)* It was a marriage made in hell but I'm sure gonna miss my boy ... maybe she'll come back.

DOC *(laughs)* Sure Richie.

EXT: DESERT OUTSIDE LAS VEGAS – DAY
The skyline of Vegas as Boyle and Rock speed toward it in their MG. Rock smoking joints, listening to his rock and roll radio, Boyle intent over the wheel, looking now, suddenly, in his pockets. Crumpled bills, papers, money – a mess. He's pissed.

BOYLE Shit, she took my phone book! All my numbers. Fuck! Losing Claudia's one thing ... you really don't give a shit do you Doc ...

DOC ... all you got's my old girlfriend numbers anyway. I
got my own problems man. I'm really depressed about
Bagel. You don't understand what our relationship was.
He was my best friend. Now *you're* my best friend. That's
very depressing to me ... do you think it's easy not having
any responsibility. I'm 42 years old. I have no wife, no
children, no father, mother, no dog — I'm totally fucking
alone in the world, it's frightening. *(Boyle's half-listening to
Doc's litany of woe)* What other 42-year-old man do you
know who has absolutely no responsibilities? *(Boyle looks at
him)* except you —

INT: CAR DEALERSHIP – LAS VEGAS – DAY
*Boyle signing over his MG, handing over a crumpled postage stamp
size piece of paper (title to the car) to the fat car SALESMAN, who gives
him $1,000 in cash.*

Boyle bustles out, to Rock. 'Got it, let's go.'

INT: – CASINO
Boyle bets one roll of the roulette wheel. The whole $1,000. On red.

*The ball spinning. Doc tense, chewing gum. Boyle looking casual, not
at all worried, a look shared between them. Red!*

EXT: CAR LOT – DAY
Boyle buys his car back. With the thousand.

EXT: DESERT HIGHWAY – DAY
*Boyle races south across the endless desert. Doc's radio blasting road
songs, Doc doing an amphetamine and a joint, and drinking on a pre-
made margarita bottle, Boyle intent on the road, mind scheming, 100
miles an hour of concrete rolling under them.*

DOC Where we going now?

BOYLE Guatemala.

DOC Why?

BOYLE Why not. No cops, no laws. Sun. Cheap. Great marijuana. There's a great whorehouse in Guatemala. Takes credit cards. Fake ones, they don't care ... just like Saigon. Red Dragon ...

DOC You gotta go 2000 miles for a whorehouse Boyle. I know one in Oakland for 2 ½ bucks.

BOYLE *(a beat, interested)* Where?

DOC Your ex-wife.

DISSOLVING TO:

6 Days Later
More desert rolls by. Endless cactus and brush. James Taylor blasting 'Oh Mexico' now blending into a Salvadoran tune. The car's really beat to shit now, doors wired on, windshield busted, muffler's gone, speedometer reads zero, license plate fell off.

Boyle smoking a joint, an open tequila bottle between his legs, doing 100 mph. Past a road sign saying 'SANTA ANA 20 KM. SAN SAL-VADOR 100 KM.' A Vulture is sitting on it.

Doc, who is juggling the radio antenna to get signals, sees it, pissed. So pissed he has to take another valium.

DOC You said fucking Guatemala Boyle, you didn't say anything about El Salvador! Man I've never been out of the country. They kill people here.

BOYLE You believe everything you read in the papers man? You'll love it here! Look Doc this is serious, this is my last shot. If I get some good combat shots, I can sell em to AP, I'll get some money and we'll head for La Libertad, best surfing beach in the world, good time, kick back for a few months, you can live for a year on $300.

DOC Boyle, you've lied to me straight through.

BOYLE Doc, let's assess your situation, face the hard cold facts of life – you got no woman, no dog, no money, nobody loves you and you're ugly – here you'll have a life ...

DOC *(doesn't want to hear it)* Awright, awright, let's go.

BOYLE ... but you'll love it here Doc. You can drive drunk, you can get anybody killed for fifty bucks. Best pussy in the world. Where else can you get a virgin to sit on your face for 7 bucks.

DOC This pussy better be the best thing in the world or I'm going home. You're just lucky I'm fucked up Boyle.

BOYLE ... two virgins for twelve bucks. And drugs man, no prescriptions, they got stuff keep you hard all night long, all they want to do down here is fuck ...

DOC Twelve bucks? We can talk them down don't you think ...

BOYLE Doc, you're gonna be in pig heaven, believe me, you'll love it here. Oh shit!

Hitting the brakes, he dumps the joint, drains the tequila bottle, dumps it.

Doc puzzled. A DOZEN GUYS are out in the road, blocking it, dressed in civvies, with cowboy hats. They could be bandits, rebels, anything, but definitely not nice guys.

DOC Why are they blocking the roads man?

BOYLE Why, why, why, stop asking why, this ain't Gringoland man ...

Checking his pockets frantically now, finding his cyanide pills, gives one to Doc.

BOYLE ... hide this, be cool man, act dumb.

DOC *(looking at his pill)* What is this – some kind of tranquilizer?

BOYLE Yeah a permanent one – cyanide man ... put it away.

DOC *(throws it away)* I'm not taking this shit!

BOYLE Boy are you gonna be sorry when they cut off your balls!

Doc obviously thinks Boyle is overdoing it. His stoned POV — the approaching roadblock.

Boyle pulling the MG over. The Honcho comes over, peers down, a carbine slung inches from Boyle's face. The guy is now obviously dead drunk. And mean. Breathing Tic-tac fumes over Boyle.

BOYLE Hey Hola, como va amigo. Es turista. Americano.
Me gusto much El Salvador. Mi amigo ...

Gives him general bullshit Spanish, all smiles.

The guy obviously doesn't get it. A blank stupid look. The sun is pissing him off. He mutters something in slang Salvo about Santa Ana. Closed. No go. Boyle says something, the guy doesn't get it, waves, two more guys come over. Pidgen Spanish ...

Boyle now pulling out the cheap gold watch from his pocket, treasuring it with his eyes like the diamond sapphire of India. '... es puro oro ... dos mille dollars ... ' The guy eyes it like a python around a mouse, shakes it, sees it works, puts it in his pants as the other two guys get pissed at him. They talk among themselves.
Boyle, agitated under his smile, looks at Doc, gives him the intell.

BOYLE Tic-tac monsters, man. Fucking trouble man.

One of them points to the 'Periodista' Press Pass stuck to the front windshield. Mutters aloud 'Periodista!' The honcho suddenly throws the door open. 'Out! Now. Wallets! Money!'

JUMP CUT:

Boyle and Doc are spread against the car. They're being stripped. Of all valuables, wallets, money ...

BOYLE *(worried now)*
  Whatever they do, don't get down on the ground ... Kick
    em in the balls, fight, run, do anything, but don't get
    down on the ground!

DOC Why?

BOYLE Why! They get you on the ground, they can do what
    they want!

DOC *(anesthetized on joints)*
  This is fucking scary man.

BOYLE *(to himself)* Come this far ... Greased by a fucking
  Tic-tac monster in Salvoland, they won't believe this
  one ... aw who'll give a shit anyway!

The drunk Honcho pulls back the bolt on his carbine. Just as a jeep drives up. In it is SMILING DEATH, a Lieutenant in the National Guard. A young, thin, ascetic man with fixed eyes and the aforesaid smile.

SMILING DEATH Que pasa!

DRUNKEN HONCHO Subversivo!

Boyle seizes the opportunity, jumps out, waving his papers at Smiling Death.

BOYLE No! Periodistas! Es amigo Colonel Figueroa!
  Periodistas!

Death looking at him. He's obviously brainier than the Tic-tac Monster that almost offed Boyle and Company.

SMILING DEATH Figueroa?

Boyle nods vigorously.

EXT: STREETS OF SANTA ANA – DAY
SMILING DEATH and his driver roar up to a PLAZA in the heart of the city, next to an ARMORED CAR.

A DOZEN PEOPLE are laying in the dirt, hands over their heads. Troops stand over them – checking their 'cedulas' (papers, internal passports). Smiling Death goes over to another OFFICER, talks with him, points to Boyle and Rock.

DOC What's going on? What'd he do?

BOYLE Oh he's a student. That's the worst thing you can be
  here. They're checking his cedula.

DOC What's that?

BOYLE Birth certificates, voting papers. You don't have
one, you can get into deep shit.

*The Sergeant yanks a YOUNG MAN up by the hair and drags him,
yelling that he left his cedula at home, over to Smiling Death.*

*Rock and Boyle are forced out of the jeep by a pair of Soldiers and
marched over to the armored car, glancing at Smiling Death as he
questions the Kid. The Sergeant now hits the youth in the back of the head
with his rifle butt. The kid goes to his knees, praying for them to believe
him. 'Por favor, señor!' Little STREET URCHINS are all around,
fascinated to witness this stuff.*

INT: ARMORED CAR – DAY
*Boyle and Rock are shoved into the back of the car, the metal door
slamming on them. Looking out through the gunslips, they're in
complete darkness.*

BOYLE Yo estoy bueno amigo de Colonel Figueroa!!

*Their point of view – Smiling Death takes out his pistol, the Kid
begging. Smiling Death casually shoots him in the side of the head,
stepping away fast not to get blood on himself. He walks off.*

ROCK Holy shit! Holy Shit!! They're gonna kill us Boyle!

*The Armored Car suddenly takes off, Boyle and Rock bouncing back
and forth in the darkness.*

ROCK I thought you knew your way around here Boyle,
they're gonna kill us now aren't they?

BOYLE *(scratching his head, a grim laugh)* Well nobody ever got
into trouble for shooting somebody, only for letting
them go.

CUT TO:

Hours have passed.

*The Tank comes to a stop. Doc, tired, scared, crouched in a corner,
sweating. Boyle taking a pee in the other corner.*

DOC *(grimly)* This is it . . . you got any of that tranquilizer
left?

Boyle fingering his cyanide pill. The door cranking open.

SMILING DEATH is standing there with an AIDE. A tense beat.

SMILING DEATH   Colonel Figueroa is expecting you for
dinner.

EXT: MILITARY CUARTEL – DAY
*Boyle and Rock are marched out. A bugle call. Troops running in
formation. The Cuartel is built like an old US Cavalry compound.*

*As they step out of the carrier, a knot of kids and SOLDIERS are staring at
the corpse of the YOUNG MAN without the cedula. He's hanging upside
down from the top of the carrier, bloodied head staring at Rock, mouth
agape. Boyle hurries him along. Past a giant poster with dying soldiers –
'It's Our Duty to Die for the Fatherland!'*

INT: FIGUEROA QUARTERS – NIGHT

FIGUEROA   Boyle! How'd you get in here. No fuckin'
periodistas are allowed!

BOYLE   Snuck in through Guatemala Colonel ...

FIGUEROA   You damn bastards, you're lucky you still got
your huevos!

*They hug. FIGUEROA, a handsome, US-trained Colonel who looks like
Patton, two 45s, shiny knee boots, riding crop, stars all over the place.*

FIGUEROA   Come, caballeros, join us, more wine. Quero
pollo, pescado, muy fresco ...

*THREE SEMI-NAKED WHORES are running around his quarters,
which is decorated with purple couch, hula girl lamps, horrid paintings.
A parrot croaks. Figueroa is obviously a little drunk.*

FIGUEROA *(to the hookers)*   My amigo here ... write me up in
the American newspaper – the 'Patton of El Salvador'
he called me.

*Boyle and Rock sitting down to the feast, SERVANTS scurrying to
provide them with the food. Rock amazed and somewhat suspicious over
the sudden turn of events, is in pig heaven, pawing a fat hooker.*

BOYLE *(soaking him, to the others)* You were, Julio, it was the last great cavalry charge in history! In the Soccer war with Honduras in '69, he went all the way to Tegucigalpa! Not since Attila the Hun have there been such Cavalry tactics!

Figueroa loves it, squeezing the ass of the 2nd Whore.

FIGUEROA ... and this one takes it up the cula.

BOYLE ... looks like things are heating up again Julio. I guess that's one of Major Max's roadblocks outside of town.

FIGUEROA That puta! *(sotto voce to Boyle, eyes on servant)* There's a coup in the air. His men are everywhere. I don't even know who I can trust. Half my men are working with the 'escuadron de muerte', the other half are selling their weapons to the rebels and deserting ... fucking rebels got two more battalions in the north, the junta's got no power and the country's going to shit! Fuckin' Major Max talks about fighting Communism, all he fights is with his mouth. *(cuddling the third one)* ... pussy with hands inside ... squeeze you to death, no my little octopus! *(she mutters some obscenity back at him)*

Boyle looking at Rock, a lot of information being given here ...

BOYLE ... sounds like the rebels could take it all, Julio. If they take Santa Ana, they could split the country in two.

Figueroa chuckles, producing a cloth sack which he brings over to the table, pours out the contents.

FIGUEROA ... first they gotta get through me, and many putas have died trying ... Fuck em all ... Right-wing ears, left-wing ears – nobody's coming into Santa Ana. Santa Ana is *my* town.

Dozens of dried ears rustle across the tablecloth — right in front of Rock who reacts, disgusted, 'Ugh!' Boyle kicks him under the table. The Whores are very impressed, the Colonel muy macho now.

BOYLE That's real nice colonel.

FIGUEROA Yeah we're doing good . . . Enough of these fucking human rights.

Takes one ear, plops it in his champagne glass. It seems to come alive, listening to their conversation. A big hairy ear floating in the bubbles.

BOYLE . . . Say, colonel, maybe you can let me go out with one of your recon units or something. I could sure use some good combat shots y'know . . . I'll make em look good.

FIGUEROA You fuck this one Boyle, I fuck the skinny one. Your friend he can have the chubby one . . . Death to Communists! Death to all enemies. Let them hear me! Long live Salvador!

As he raises the champagne with the ear in it, toasts the table, drinks, gives it to the giggling whore, who drinks, passes it to Boyle . . .

Rock's eyes glued to the contents of the glass, about to throw up, the ears all over the table. The FAT HOOKER squeezing his balls.

FAT HOOKER Fuckee suckee you!!!

BOYLE *(in Spanish, drinks the toast)* . . . leave him alone! He got the clap in Guatemala and dysentery here. *(laughs)* He's dripping out both ends!

She draws back. Just in time. As Doc, eyes rolling, the champagne glass with the ear in it now pressed into his hand, throws up all over the white tablecloth.

EXT: ROAD TO CAPITAL – THAT NIGHT
There's a white flag on the broken antenna and 'TV' is taped on the crack in the windshield as Boyle and Rock speed towards the capital, headlight cutting the darkness. A song on the radio — 'every move you make, every breath you take, I'll be watching you. . .'

DOC Look Richie, it was fun travelling with you you know, but now I'd like to get a plane out of here, you know I got things to do in San Francisco, I got a *life* there, even with Miriam. I got you outta jail and you owe me a lot of money over the years, I think now is the time to part company ...

BOYLE *(peering ahead)* Later Doc! ... give me the mace outta the glove compartment. Roads can get tricky at night here.

DOC Mace?

BOYLE Don't worry Doc. Just a precaution. I'm covered ... I go for the jug. Two seconds.

Eyes glinting madly as he produces a big switchblade from his safari pocket. He grins.

DOC *(more seriously)* Look Boyle ...

As Boyle suddenly spins the wheel — a man drunk in their headlights, walking right at them down the center of the highway.

Boyle just misses him, not even breaking speed. Doc catching a glimpse of this creature who has been spun around by the velocity and now walks zombie-like after them.

DOC What was that?

BOYLE Fucking Tic-tac monster. Almost fucked up my car. Gimme the map.

EXT: STREETS – SAN SALVADOR – DAWN
Boyle roars into the parking lot of a MacDonald's in downtown San Salvador.

INT: MacDONALDS – DAWN
The place is filled with ghouls — Tic-tac Monsters, drunk Mariachi band playing out of sync, orphaned children begging, sleeping in a corner. A SECURITY GUARD with a sawed-off shotgun looks at them, goes back to sleep.

Rock gets his hamburger, menaced now by a Tic-tac Monster who starts drooling on him. Rock trying to be nice to him. Boyle, ignoring this, goes over to JOHN CASSADY in the back, loading his three cameras and four lenses at a table – real fast. The man is in perpetual movement, a nervous wreck, war correspondent for too long, 36 pushing 45, a handsome gaze.

BOYLE Hi John, figured I'd find you here ...

CASSADY *(a little surprised)* Boyle – I heard you were dead ...

Boyle, not liking this talk too much, tries a laugh.

BOYLE Do I look that bad? *(covered with dust and shit)*

CASSADY Yeah ... I heard they got you up in Guatemala. In some prison or something. Pulling out your fingernails. Tortured you to death.

BOYLE *(laughs, but not too much)* Fucking Guats. How was Beirut?

Rock coming over, sitting down, gobbling his Big Mac and fries like a ravaged man, Boyle barely introducing him, sort of ashamed about him in front of Cassady. The Tic-tac Monster trailing Doc, sensing a soft touch.

CASSADY Fucking awful.

BOYLE Great cover for Newsweek, John.
 (John nods, appreciates the compliment)

CASSADY How come you split so fast?

BOYLE Little beef with Major Max's boys, they didn't like the torture chamber story.

DOC What's this, you didn't say this Major Max character was after you on top of everything Boyle!

BOYLE That was a year ago Doc, they don't have yuppie computers down here.

DOC Look I'm getting out of here Boyle. First plane. I'm not kidding. This shit's gone far enough. You give me the rest of the money now. I'm serious. No bullshit.

Doc gives the zombie one of his french fries and the Tic tac Monster gobbles it down, eyes begging for another, drooling over Doc.

BOYLE *(annoyed now)* What money! Doc, you been on
    Valiums too long. The money's gone, that transmission
    in Guatemala, gas, border ripoffs, whores. We're down
    to 15 pesos and ... wait a minute, that Big Mac cost 12,
    asshole, we're down to 3 pesos – no 2! Shit, stop giving
    that Tic-tac monster french fries ...

Doc absent-mindedly gives the Monster another fry as he goes white now, really angry at Boyle, jumping up to shake him by the collar.

DOC Three pesos! You mean to tell me we have 3 pesos
    left! My dog is dead, Miriam is gone, I've almost been
    shot and I'm in El Salvador with 3 pesos! Hey I'm
    REALLY PISSED OFF.

The Tic-tac Monster now eating the distracted Doc's fries, drooling all over Cassady's cameras. Cassady is a professional all the way and is now getting really annoyed at this interruption by Boyle and his idiot friend who's brought the tac monster. Boyle, in a chain reaction, now getting pissed at Doc.

BOYLE Doc, don't let this Tic-tac monster drool all over our
    cameras, you can't get rid of 'em. You know why he's
    drooling – cause he drinks Tic-tac that's why. *(Boyle
    fishes out his own bottle from his safari jacket)* ... it costs 17
    cents and it blows their brain cells out and if you give
    'em anything you can't get rid of 'em.

DOC *(shaking him)* WHAT DOES THIS HAVE TO DO
    WITH ME!!!

BOYLE Everything! Your liberal shit is causing this guy to
    drool on us for hours, they'll follow us everywhere.

DOC *(half out of his mind now)* Look Richie, I can't speak the
    language! I got 2 pesos! I gotta get OUTTA HERE!

The Tic-tac Monster's eyes lighting up when he sees Boyle's Tic-tac bottle, goes for it, knocking over the coffee on the table.

BOYLE Shit! See you can't get rid of 'em ... so no more liberal yuppie shit with these zombies. OK!!! *(to Cassady)* Sorry John.

Doc staring at Richard, suddenly grabs the two pesos on the table and yells in his face.

DOC Fuck you BOYLE. I'M GETTING OUT OF HERE!

And runs out into the Parking Lot. The Tic-tac Monster shuffling after him. Cassady puts some money down on the table, gathering up his stuff.

CASSADY It's on Newsweek.

Boyle hurrying after him, not wanting to lose this chance.

BOYLE Hey John thanks for the burgers. Sorry bout ... Look, this is the truth, I got fired by PNS ... I really need a string down here real bad.

Cassady is finally impressed by Boyle's honesty, feels a little sorry for him.

CASSADY Look, Rich, there's no work here, nobody gives a shit about this stinking little war. Last week a sniper got a Mexican TV guy. They're aiming at us. Try Angola —

BOYLE *(knows the idea is absurd, tries one more tack)* Look I can get you out with Figueroa. I just saw him and I got carte blanche with his elite unit.

Cassady listens, but keeps walking. Out of MacDonald's.

EXT: MacDONALD'S PARKING LOT – DAWN
Cassady steps out. Boyle waiting for his answer ... Rock is pacing around the lot, trying to get rid of the Tic-tac Monster.

CASSADY *(noticing Boyle's MG)* Still got that green deathmobile, Boyle?

BOYLE *(opening the door for him)* Yeah. Wanna go on the Dawn Patrol, John?

An old look between them. Daunting devils both. Cassady finally smiles. 'Okay'. Boyle – 'Let's go!'

EXT: 'EL PLAYON' LANDSCAPE – OUTSIDE CITY – DAWN
A huge garbage dump. Rotting fruit. Flies. Stench. Wild dogs rooting around among the chickens and goats. Cassady shooting film. Three bodies, two young men, one woman, hands neatly knotted behind their backs. Lying in a ditch. Torture burns.

Rock sees it, reacts quietly this time, never having seen a dead person like this. Boyle talking to Cassady, not shooting, not wanting to cut into Cassady's gig.

CASSADY Go on. Take some ... *(moving on)*

Boyle taking his cue, moves to the edge of a gulch. We move with him to discover the horrible sight of dozens of fresh bodies strewn down the side of the slope. Vultures are everywhere, pecking out eyeballs and viscera.

Doc follows Boyle. Throws away the remnants of his hamburger. A vulture unseen to him, coming up to get it behind him.

Boyle crossing down to Cassady who is working his telephoto on the corpses, like a mechanic in some grisly mortuary.

BOYLE Look John, you know Alvarez, you can get me out
with the rebels. He thinks I'm a flake, some wino
journalist. I'm not. I've cleaned up my act ...

DOC *(interrupting)* GET OUT OF HERE!

Boyle and Cassady look up the gulch. Doc is freaking out. A vulture pecking at his foot. He tries to kick it away but the bird has no fear. Doc runs down the gulch toward them.

DOC Shit, it bit me! It bit me! It's got rabies. Man I'm
fucked. I need a rabies shot Boyle!

BOYLE Shut up willya. Ya big baby ... Nobody's ever got
rabies from a vulture.

Turning back to Cassady who doesn't even deign to bother with Rock. The two of them walk on.

BOYLE Come on John, I need one more shot at it. I'm down to three pesos.

CASSADY *(between shots)* You know who was a great photographer. Capa.

BOYLE Yeah, that was a great shot in Spain. Guy flying through the air.

CASSADY *(excited)* Capa got that point of death.

BOYLE *(stroking him)* ... you're right up there with him John – right there in that league, you're the best ...

CASSADY I want to get a shot like that Rich ... someday, fuck it, I want that shot ...

BOYLE Then you'll get it man ...

Doc popping a Valium, trying to calm down, moving away as another vulture seems to creep towards him, muttering 'Let's get the fuck outta here man.'

Boyle and Cassady heading back to the MG, Doc racing over, rubbing his leg.

DOC You sure you can't get rabies from a vulture?

CASSADY *(ignoring him)* Alvarez's people are staked out at the Cathedral these days. I'll talk to him ... You might check in with the new Ambassador – Tom Kelly, he's okay.

BOYLE Kelly? – from Cambodia. Sure. I know him real well. Good man.

ROCK What about the fucking beach man?

BOYLE Free party Doc, pretty Embassy girls, free munchies ... you'll love it ... *(to John, with effusive beggary)* Thanks John.

Tries to touch him in thanks but John pulls away. He's not the sort who likes to be touched.

CASSADY *(eyeing Doc)* ... I don't have to tell you to watch it.

DOC *(chasing the vultures off with a rock, to Boyle)* Asshole. If I got rabies man ...

INT: AP OFFICE – MORNING
Boyle races upstairs. The BUREAU CHIEF, a young man of 24, lanky, glasses, is asleep on the couch, wakes up as Boyle, impatient to get going, lays two 35mm rolls on the desk.

BUREAU CHIEF Boyle, I heard the Brits got you in Belfast.

BOYLE Fucking Brits. Come on Maurey, two rolls. ASA 800.

BUREAU CHIEF Bang bang?

BOYLE No. Death Squad stuff. Maybe one good shot.

BUREAU CHIEF We'll soup em. Same deal. Twenty-five bucks on acceptance. Full rights.

BOYLE How bout a little advance? Ten bucks?

BUREAU CHIEF *(shrugs no)* You know the rules.

Boyle, pissed, fingers the film a second, then changes his mind.

BOYLE Fuck it man, I'm not in that bad shape.

EXT/INT: CITY CATHEDRAL – DOWNTOWN SAN SALVADOR – DAY
Boyle with Rock jumps out of the MG. A car cruising past with loudspeakers hooked to the roof, making street announcements.

Boyle holds up his old crumpled press card, forces his way past a surly National Guard Sergeant, past all sorts of banners proclaiming Worker's Rights, Union Rights, Land Reform ...

The grounds outside the Church are jammed with campecinos, land reform types, farmers, students – getting up petitions, drawing posters.

Women – directed by a striking, dark-featured CARMEN SANCHEZ – are cutting up piles of vegetables into a stew for a line of workers. Boyle taking pictures with his Nikon.

DOC What's going on man?

BOYLE People come here to try to find out what happened
to their disappeared. *(points)* These people are in from a
land coop. They got run off by the police and they're
on a hunger strike.

DOC *(nervous)* I saw this in 'Zapata' man.

*Boyle leads Rock to the Human Rights Office, outdoors under a tent.
RAMON ALVAREZ, a young handsome leader of a left-wing party, is
passing photo albums among the women looking for their lost ones. As they
leaf through the albums, we see literally thousands of pictures of mutilated
death squad victims. Doc is further sickened, leaves.*

*A MOTHER suddenly recognizes the face of one of the victims – her son.
She breaks down. Ramon Alvarez trying to comfort her, 'lo siento, lo
siento'.*

*A Dutch TV CREW is there, led by JURGEN OLTIMANS, a big pushy
man, who instructs his camera crew to cover the tears.*

*Alvarez, annoyed at them, waves them off. Boyle slipping over to Ramon,
trying to get his attention before he moves away.*

BOYLE Ramon, hi ... did Cassady talk to you about my
going out ... with the muchachos?

*CARMEN SANCHEZ comes out, hands Ramon petitions. She acknowl-
edges Richard with a quick nod and smile, seems to remember him.*

BOYLE *(pressing Ramon sotto voce)* Ramon, I need a break real
bad. I did a good story on you last year ...

RAMON Look Boyle, I'm not a travel agency for you guys.

BOYLE If Major Max takes power, you people could sure
use some good press.

*Ramon snaps, throws the portfolio at Boyle. He points at the young
mother, crying, and the dozen other women searching through the
book.*

RAMON Good press. There are 10,000 desaparecidos and
every day the list grows and you pendejo talk about
good press.

Boyle is uneasy about the dressing down. One of Ramon's bodyguards comes up to him, a machine pistol wrapped in a newspaper ... Boyle eyes it.

RAMON Llevalo afuera *(get that out of here).*

The Bodyguard nods, tucks away the machine pistol and hurries out.

Carmen senses Boyle's uneasiness. Boyle looks at her sheepishly, pulls out his death squad negatives.

BOYLE ... listen I got some shots for you, I was out at El Playon this morning.

CARMEN *(takes them)* Thanks Richard.

Ramon sees this, nods at Carmen, 'montanas, si', and then goes back to comfort the young woman who has now totally broken down.

CARMEN Come back next week, I'll arrange it.

Boyle touches her, says 'gracias.'

BOYLE Ramon should be more careful, he's number one on Major Max's shitlist.

She nods knowingly, goes, as Doc comes up, totally grossed out by the scene, the grisly photos, the young woman sobbing uncontrollably.

BOYLE *(indicating Ramon and Carmen)* People like that make me feel like I blew my life ...

Behind the Church, in a courtyard, is a makeshift orphanage with TWO NUNS and about forty CHILDREN, ages newborn to eight, the Nuns dishing out lunch, the children huddling around Boyle and Doc, excited by the new visitors. They're orphans of war, children of the disappeared, burn marks and scars and mutilations on them.

BOYLE *(to Nun)* How are you Sister?

SISTER STAN *(recognizes Richard, but not his name)* Oh fine. It's good to see you back. Cathy's around here ... *(an Irish brogue)*

A little boy puts a clamp on Richard's leg.

BOYLE You look busy?

SISTER STAN *(with a tolerant smile for all misfortune)* Yes. All of
them within the last month. Parents missing, dead, lost
– it's getting very bad here. We even got a threat last
week against the orphanage ... *(points to a little girl
without a leg huddling around Richard)*
She's the last survivor from the massacre up at Rio
Lempa.

BOYLE I heard about that ... government helicopters
opened up as they were crossing the river?

SISTER STAN It's very bad now, very bad. Madness on both
sides.

*CATHY MOORE comes up with a box of medical supplies. A pretty young
Irish-American girl, in her twenties, a lay worker, tired now but still
energetic ...*

BOYLE Cathy Moore, the prettiest coleen in all of El
Salvador.

*Cathy smiles, distracted, setting to work to fit an artificial leg she pulls
from the box onto the little girl.*

CATHY *(in Spanish)* Anisetta, come ... Boyle, you
degenerate. Come back to visit all your old girlfriends
at the Noa Noa?

BOYLE Come on Cathy, you've ruined that by converting
them on me.

*With the help of Sister Stan, she starts fitting the leg. Boyle is obviously
affected, tries to chat with the girl in broken Spanish but she just stares
at him. He takes pictures as he talks.*

BOYLE Need a ride to Libertad Cathy, I'm going tomorrow?

CATHY Can't ... too much to do here ...

161

She curses. The artificial leg is too big. The little girl seems to realize it, looks back at them blankly.

CATHY *(pissed, to Sister Stan)* I told Cleveland the size! They promised me!

She throws it back in the box, frustrated.

SISTER STAN Now come on, Cathy, these things happen. There'll be another shipment next month. Anisetta can wait ...

A quietness in the eyes of the children that's heartbreaking. Rock looks away. Boyle, finished, puts his camera away, affected.

EXT: CAMINO REAL GROUNDS – DAY
The contrast is extreme. Crowded, everyone in good spirits, drinking heavily, eating from the massive buffet, chickens, hams, local foods, a mariachi band.

On the wall is a big blackboard, with 50 States marked in two columns – CARTER – REAGAN. Electoral and popular votes.

Boyle and Rock moving through the crowd in stinking clothing, Doc stoned out of his mind, limping on his bandaged vulture-bitten foot, getting evil looks from various white people. The hall is filled with military types, various uniforms, Chile, Argentina, Salvadoran army and air force, a dozen U.S. military types, an equal number of spook types, military wives.

AMBASSADOR THOMAS KELLY, tall, stately, handsome, is holding court with several reporters as CHEERS go up when early returns show Reagan sweeping New Hampshire.

KELLY   ... I really can't comment on that until all the returns are in but I will say this. It is my duty to support the policy of the President of ...

Boyle at the bar getting his whiskey glass filled, as Rock goes for the munchies like a starved convict.

DOC   ... can you believe some guy who was a straight man

to a chimpanzee is gonna be President of the United
States – doesn't it depress you?

*Boyle spotting somebody, going over, JACK MORGAN is a handsome,
Yale-educated civilian, every mother's dream.*

BOYLE Hi Jack. What are you doing here?

MORGAN Boyle? I heard you were dead.

BOYLE Takes more than wishing. What brings you down
here Jack? Reagan planning ahead?

*Morgan gives him a dirty look, introduces him to his party – which is
what Boyle wants.*

MORGAN Colonel Bentley Hyde, Milgroup, Bob Samuels,
USAID, Millicent Davies from USAFL-CIO ...

*Brief nods all around, they're in conversations, but Boyle pushes in, to
Colonel Hyde, a big, cigar-smoking assertive German of a man who
stands at the bar.*

BOYLE You don't remember me Colonel? Pacific News
Service. Vietnam? Richard Boyle?

HYDE Yeah, I remember. Last I heard about you was when
Thieu kicked you out.

*Hyde sizes up Boyle, towering over him. He takes out a cigar while
talking, offers one to Boyle. Boyle eagerly takes it.*

BOYLE *(laughs)* Yeah, but Mr. Thieu got kicked out after me.

*Boyle's joke doesn't sit well with Hyde, Boyle picks up on it and lights
his cigar, a gesture to show respect. Boyle even moves to light it, Hyde
smiles.*

HYDE You know, I never understand why you guys like the
commies so much. If you were a Vietnamese you'd be
working in a re-education camp pulling up turnips.

BOYLE Colonel, you don't find me applying for Vietnamese citizenship.

HYDE Yeah, they don't go for that funny stuff you smoke, old buddy. *(laughs)*

BOYLE Bentley, I need a big favor, can you get out on a Cazadore op?

Hyde puffs on the cigar, again sizing up Boyle. Boyle is an opposite of everything the Colonel is, Boyle is sloppy, the Colonel correct, but there is a sort of camaraderie, as Boyle has at least seen combat and knows his shit.

HYDE If I get you out, what's in it for me?

Boyle ponders the question, knows the implications. Hyde smiles, a sly, knowing smile and moves off.

Morgan slipping out of earshot with Boyle.

MORGAN You going out with the muchachos?

BOYLE *(cryptic)* Trying ...

MORGAN *(knows he will)* ... there's something in the wind. They're getting weapons, lots of em, through Nicaragua and they're gonna make a move pretty soon. So any information, pictures, anything you can throw my way, Rich ... we can make life easy for you down here ...

BOYLE *(vague)* I don't know Jack, that stuff's hard to prove. I hear they're getting most of their weapons on the black market in Miami or off Government troops.

MORGAN Last year. This year Castro's got them organized. It's Warsaw Bloc stuff and they're not fucking around.

BOYLE Same old Black Jack, communists fucking us in the ass everywhere right ...

MORGAN You're not going to think this is all one big joke when they take this place. Nicaragua was just the beginning. Guatemala and Honduras are targeted next, and in five years you'll be seeing Cuban tank divisions on the Rio Grande.

BOYLE *(laughs)* Jack, gimme a break, Cuban tanks on the Rio Grande. I'm more worried about Major Max on the Rio Grande. I'll call you. Buy me lunch. Say Jack can you lend me fifty bucks?

MORGAN *(laughs)* Yeah well from what I heard Major Max might be running this place real soon, so watch yourself old buddy ...

Boyle smiling, looking at him beat. Is he serious? AMBASSADOR KELLY COMES OVER. TALKS TO MORGAN. SHAKES BOYLE'S HAND. MOVES ON. Cheers go up. Reagan has just swept New York. An overwhelming lead. The military personnel in the room obviously pleased.

Rock, eating a giant sandwich with everything he can get from the buffet table on it, is trying to cozy up to a cleancut WAC in uniform, a chunky little tyke from Omaha.

DOC So what are you doing here?

WAC Oh, I'm a doorgunner.

DOC A what? Hey what's going on around here? I'm starting to feel like I'm on acid and it's 1967 and I'm listening to Jimi Hendryx.

WAC Uh, what do you mean?

DOC Mean? You know – Vietnam. We getting ready to invade or what?

WAC Uh I don't know what you mean, I was kinda young during that ... listen, I'm not supposed to talk to the Press okay. And you're weird. So fuck off.

DOC Hey I'm not the Press I'm a rock and roll DJ *(she's gone)* ... and what am I doing here?

BOYLE *(coming over)* Everything cool.

DOC Hey this is great Rich. I think I'm gonna get laid tonight.

Boyle leading him to a table where PETER CUNNINGHAM is just sitting down with PAULINE AXELROD and JOHN CASSADY. Cunningham is the Australian bureau chief for CNN News, Axelrod a CBS glamour puss down here to make her bones.

CUNNINGHAM Choy oy Richard – last I heard the Khmer Rouge put a pickax in your head ...

BOYLE *(a grim chuckle)* No, Peter, look I still got my head.

CUNNINGHAM You dinky dow Boyle. You know Pauline Axelrod ... Richard Boyle.

Boyle nods, 'sure'. Pauline lets her eye travel over his grungy clothes.

PAULINE Of course I know Boyle. Who you 'working' for now?

Boyle ignores the tone, pulling up a chair and squeezing himself in between her and Cunningham.

BOYLE Oh I got a great gig going. Got a book advance from City Lights on my Salvador stories ... you know Doctor Rock, the San Francisco rock and roll disc jockey?

Rock sits next to Pauline, eyeing her. She turns her attention to Cassady who doesn't socialize. Waiting for the election results, he makes logs and captions his grisly glossies of the Dawn Patrol corpses.

CUNNINGHAM I heard you got through the roadblock at Santa Ana.

BOYLE *(aside)* Yeah, you get me on as a field producer Peter and I'll get you out with Figueroa.

CUNNINGHAM Can't do that without an okay from Atlanta.

BOYLE Could you try Peter?

CUNNINGHAM ... at your age Boyle, with a broken back, you still humping with the kids?

BOYLE Gotta make a living somehow Peter.

PAULINE *(to Cassidy, looking at his pictures)* Jesus they took the fetus out.

The TV announces Texas has just gone for Reagan. A roar from the crowd. Boyle and Rock are now getting bombed, both totally depressed by the apparent victory. Cunningham, Pauline, Cassady show no emotion, if they have any.

PAULINE *(to Cunningham, fishing)* I got to do a standup from the roof at ten – boiling all this down.

CUNNINGHAM *(a little bombed)* Well you can't go wrong saying with Mr. Reagan in the saddle, the left is in 'deep shit'.

PAULINE *(producing a newspaper clipping)* I know that but the Journal is running with a rah-rah democracy piece, free elections all that, the nets are asking for the same thing, what do you think?

Cunningham glancing at the piece, Boyle reading it over his shoulder.

Rock, who doesn't like Pauline, slips a little tab of acid into her champagne. She doesn't notice.

BOYLE *(drunk now)* Pauline, this article is totally 100 percent and unequivocally full of shit!

PAULINE Look Boyle I resent ...

BOYLE *(pounding his fist on the table)* Yeah well I resent what I saw in Santa Ana. A kid shot in the head and dragged by a tank because he didn't have a fucking cedula. You know what a cedula is?

PAULINE Course I know what a cedula is ... You're a real pro Boyle.

BOYLE Yeah, well you want to analyze the situation, do it right! You don't have one of those cedulas stamped election day, you're dead, what kinda democracy is it when you *have* to vote and if you don't vote you're a commie subversivo ... these people will vote for Donald Duck or Genghis Khan, whatever the local cop tells them to do cause if they don't ... *this* is what happens!

Pushes the picture of the woman with the fetus ripped out in front of Pauline. She looks away, pissed at him.

CUNNINGHAM Come on Rich, calm down – and lay off the sauce.

BOYLE Fucking yuppies ... do a standup from the roof of the Camino Real for CBS. Think they got the whole story. 'My two weeks in El Salvador ...' Hiding under a bed in the Camino Real. Course they get their stories published. Cause they kiss the right asses in New York.

DOC *(whispering to Boyle)* Just gave that bitch 500 takes of pure blotter. Can't wait to see her 'boil down'.

Boyle gives him a glazed look like 'you did what asshole!' The table is already quite uneasy. Pauline is white, angry, drinks half her wine in one gulp.

DOC So what's your sign?

PAULINE Stop!

DOC Oh! 'Stop sign'. I was hoping it was 'Slippery when wet' *('Ugh!')* So, you like rock and roll?

PAULINE *(gets up abruptly)* No I hate it. Excuse me.

DOC So I don't want to fuck you either ... Have a nice trip.

Pauline stands, suddenly feels the acid, staggered. She walks unsteadily away.

BOYLE *(suddenly smiles)* Aw come on Pauline, I'm sorry OK, be a sport ... I'm an asshole.

PAULINE *(coldly)* Fuck you Boyle.

She leaves. Boyle shrugs, glazed.

CASSADY *(pause, shrugs)* Well I guess you just blew it stringing for CBS.

A climatic roar goes up from the crowd as Reagan takes Illinois. The crowd cheers. A band plays.

Another series of Firecrackers break and then there's a SMOKE BOMB on the lawn — and the crackle of GUNFIRE and it all blends in but it's suddenly real as an INCOMING ROUND cracks hard above Doc's ear. 'Hey what is this?'

People start to react, ducking, yelling. A long rattle of automatic fire overrides all noise. Guards whipping out guns.

A glimpse now of a CHEROKEE PICKUP TRUCK going by the gate. Real machine gun fire, tracers cracking the air above. Then a second and third smoke bomb. The Cherokee disappearing around the corner.

Guards running all over the lawn. Chaos.

Cassady in action, running around taking pictures.

DOC *(grabbing Boyle)* What was that! Guerrillas?

BOYLE I think Major Max's boys.

CUNNINGHAM *(getting back to his feet)* They're not too crazy about Kelly — and tonight's the end of Kelly. Gotta get my crew together ... *(goes)*

The Salvo band, all having hit the deck, now strike up and the party starts to resume, drinking, dancing, etc.

DOC *(grabbing Boyle, seriously freaked out on the acid)* Shit man this is the fucking American Embassy they just shot up! This is supposed to be safe.

BOYLE *(worried about Doc's hysteria)* Calm down, Doc, Major Max is just doing a little celebrating on election night.

ANNOUNCER Ladies and gentlemen, please do not worry. The disturbance is now under control. Eat, drink and be merry. Ronald Reagan has just swept California ... *(song of 'California Here I Come')*

EXT: STREETS OF ESCALON DISTRICT – NIGHT
Along the quiet tree-lined streets of upper class Escalon, the MILITIAS
are out in force, roaring along the avenues in jeeps, shooting off guns.
The sound of the Mano Blanco Marching Song blaring from radios.
Homeowners lean out their windows, firing rifles off.

A car with a loudspeaker on the roof drives by, announcing in Spanish
that Reagan has now won the entire nation – except Massachusetts – by a
landslide!

INT: MAJOR MAX VILLA – NIGHT
The camera moves to a GATE on the street, with civilian armed GUARDS
patrolling. The gate opens. A limousine slides out. A brief view – THREE
NORTH AMERICAN-looking MEN in the backseat – jowly, politician-
type men in suits.

The camera closing along the patio. Servants moving. Into a room. The
sound of a Marching Song. Men's voices. 'Tremble, Tremble, Commun-
ists' is the best English translation for it.

A white Arena Party Flag dominates the room. Twelve men are there –
some of them military officers, some wearing uniforms of the Mano
Blanco, some a youth guard. One of them is SMILING DEATH, the
Lieutenant at the roadblock.

The camera moving over their faces, raptly turned in the direction of
Major Max, who we hear now – short staccato, nervous Spanish ... a
monologue filled with obscenities ... the men laughing at the macho
language ... past the fat, wily GOMEZ, his second in command, to Max
himself – a handsome, short macho guy with wavy black hair in the Eddie
Fisher mold and elevator heels to compensate for his five feet six inches. He
is a strong man, muscular, intense, in the tradition of the Spanish
caudillo, packing a .38 on his back hip, chain-smoking, swearing freely, a
tough gangster guy.

MAJOR MAX ... this dumb shit Duarte now has to go back
and lick his puta's pussy, the shit-faced faggot everyday
looks more and more like a watermelon – Christian
Democrat green on the outside and when my machete
splits him open, Moscow red on the inside! ...

They roar with laughter at this. He raises the magic bullet in the air for all of them to see, and now walks among the twelve men, touching each on the back of the neck . . .

MAJOR MAX   . . . Yes, the time's come now for us brothers – former members of Orden, Patriots of the Maximilio Hernandez Brigade, brothers of the Mano Blanco – *(each sub unit reacting with pride)* and these fucking priests that are poisoning the minds of our Salvadoran youth are gonna be the first to bleed . . . they're pig shit and this Romero is the biggest pig shit of all – a shit . . . and with this bullet he will be the first to die . . . For every one of our people, we will kill 100 of them. We will avenge the killers of the South African Ambassador, of Colonel Rosario, of Molina, and Gutierrez and the Mayor of El Paraiso . . . all these shit-faced subversives that have sold our country out to the communists will die . . . Duarte, Kelly, Erlich, Zaun (runs off a whole list), the pseudo-journalists sent here by the Zionist Communist conspiracy, they will *all* die . . . Now who will be the one among you to rid me of this Romero?

The TWELVE MEN come forward as one.

MAJOR MAX *(proud of his boys)* Good . . . you . . . *(picks one)* You will be famous. Songs will be sung about you.

Gives him the bullet which the young SOLDIER accepts proudly. Max kisses him on the cheeks. Then they all snap out their Nazi salutes and start to sing the solemn, yet unintentionally – humorous Mano Blanco National Anthem – Patria si, Comunismo no . . . etc.

Smiling Death, his arm outraised, is prouder now than he has ever been in his life. He now belongs.

EXT: LIBERTAD VILLAGE – BY THE SEA – LATE DAY
Boyle comes speeding into the town. Past the Central Square. Vultures picking at garbage. A lively tropical beach town bordering the sea. Palms and garbage side by side.

INT: PHARMACY – LA LIBERTAD – DAY
A broken-down store with dusty pots, herbs, medicines. The toothless

old crazy-looking BRUJA, 60ish, is putting together a syringe from 6 or 7 various boxes of antibiotics. Boyle adding another one. She giggles, mutters with Boyle, Rock worried, his pants down, his ass exposed.

DOC What's she laughing about? What about a fucking subscription man?

BOYLE Don't need one here.

DOC What's she saying?

BOYLE *(a chuckle)* She's saying she's putting every kind of antibiotic she's got into this one and if it don't clean you out in one shot, it'll kill you.

DOC Not funny Boyle. I think I want the cyanide back.

The Bruja approaching him with the needle.

BOYLE Too late Doc. Listen, I gotta run. Meet you later at Roberto's. Don't pay her a thing. I got credit here. See you ... *(runs out)* A beer'll top it off good.

The Bruja trying to catch Boyle with her bill as she sticks Doc in the ass. He groans.

EXT: RIVER/BRIDGE – ADJACENT TOWN – TWILIGHT
Richard roars up in his MG, on the bridge, looks down eagerly. there must be FIFTY WOMEN doing their laundry on the stones in the river. He hurries down the bank, looking.

EXT: SNOW CONE STAND – LIBERTAD – DAY
Boyle driving past a snow-cone stand on the square. A Grandmother, white haired, 90's, erect, is scraping one ice for a truckdriver leaning out of his cab.

BOYLE *(concerned)* Hola! ¿Dónde María?

GRANDMOTHER *(recognizing him)* El Río. *(points)*

She's there. Maria, beating the clothes dry, a simple pretty campecina, early twenties.

BOYLE Maria!

When she sees him, she's flabbergasted. She thought he was dead. She goes white. Her son DUGLAS, 4, runs up to Boyle, barefooted, grabs him. REINA, the smaller baby, 2, is splashing in a mud puddle ...

All the tension seems to drain from Richard's face now. And we might understand why up to now he has been in such a hurry. This has been his destination.

He goes up to her. She raises to meet him. Maria is a little scared. She only speaks Spanish.

MARIA They said you were dead ...

BOYLE See for yourself ... Vamos a mi casa?

She's not sure. The neighbor women continue to wash but are vastly curious, smiling among themselves. The crazy gringo is back.

MARIA Are you still drunk (barracho)? You still crazy?

BOYLE No. No Maria. No mas cerveza. No mas tic-tac.

He goes up to her, runs his hands along her hair. She's not sure. Taking her by the hand, sweeping her along.

BOYLE Come, rapido, look, my new car. I sold my book ...
    I have money now.

CUT TO:
EXT: ROADSIDE NEAR BRIDGE – DAY
They go up the hill to the MG. Duglas loves it, dances around the car, Richard pulling out a Hulk tee-shirt for him and doing a Hulk imitation. Reina in Maria's arms is too young to appreciate it.

The topper is Boyle's pulling out the black and white portable TV and showing it to Duglas who goes crazy. It brings a smile to Maria's face ...

Boyle crosses to her. Hold her? Yes? She still hasn't committed to getting in the car.

MARIA I know you have another woman in the north.

BOYLE No. Terminado. Seguro. Solamente usted. Venga ...
    por favor. Maria.

He is incongruously docile with her, totally under her gentle control, trying to please her in every way. She is to him the apotheosis of latina beauty. She timidly gets in the car. He goes wild with happiness, puts the kids in.

INT: MARIA'S BEACH HOUSE – OCEAN – TWILIGHT
A palapa-type house fully open to the winds, hammocks, a stove. The sun sets.

Richard in the hammock with the naked Maria. A simple beauty, gracious and lithe, they've just made love ... Reina, the little girl, crawling up Richard's belly. Duglas watching cartoons on the black and white TV. A moment of pure peace for Richard – a sort of King with his adopted family. We dwell on his face as Maria strokes it.

A big ugly toad in the shadows croaks out a song. Duglas shrieks, points.

RICHARD Is that you Major Max? You still watching the house?

Maria giggles like a little girl, they tickle each other, the moment interrupted as Rock and CARLOS, Maria's 15 year-old brother, bang into the house, his radio blaster playing. He's a sharp little hippie in an L.A. Rams tee-shirt and a Grateful Dead hat, he talks an outdated slang. As he gives Boyle their old handshake.

CARLOS Hey Ricardo, you back from the dead man. I like your friend Doctor Rock, man he knows rock and roll *(grabbing Boyle's Nikon)* Ooooh – look at those tits.

Clicking off a picture of Maria and Richard in the hammock, he knows how to use the camera. She shrieks, innocent about her body, whipping on a towel on her pubic area but her breasts are still exposed. She runs off the hammock, into the toilet.

Carlos seeing a pile of Richard's weed on a table where Doc is rolling himself a joint.

CARLOS Wow! Hey Ricardo can I have some? Just a little? My main man ...

BOYLE Yeah go ahead.

He scoops up some into a newspaper, as Rock lights up.

CARLOS Hey man this guy's cool, where'd you find him,
Elvis is his main man ... Doctor R–O–C–K!

As Maria comes out, sees Carlos taking the grass and sharing Doc's joint. She gives Richard a dirty look, angry. He smiles back at her, shrugs.

BOYLE *(to Rock)* How ya feeling Doc?

DOC *(eyes rolling, joint smoke all over his face)* Oh man I don't know anymore Richie – place is getting weird. I can still see that vulture man, pecking out my eyeballs, y'know.

Loud Music as the Mano Blanco Party Theme comes on the Television. And Major Max appears – with a watermelon and a machete. As he gives his spiel about the Christian Democrats being green on the outside and – slash goes his machete – red on the inside ... Then back to loud music, which is so catchy that Duglas sings along merrily. Boyle joins in with Duglas, finding it pretty funny.

Carlos watches, sneers.

EXT: ROBERTO'S RESTAURANT – DAY
They're eating lobsters outdoors on the patio – BOYLE, MARIA, REINA and DUGLAS, their GRANDMOTHER (a feisty little monkey of a lady chewing on a cigar), CARLOS and two of his young friends, RAFAEL and JAIMIE. The rest of the place is jammed with diners. A mariachi band is playing and things are getting rowdy. Boyle is devouring lobster, Tic-tac, joints being passed around.

A DRUNKEN TIC-TAC MONSTER wanders just outside the restaurant along the beach, drops his pants and squats in the shadows.

Rock, eating, is turned off.

ROBERTO, the American exile owner of the restaurant, ex-surfer, straight, married to a Salvadoran woman, in his late thirties, comes over to Boyle with a check. Boyle giving him a thumbs up salute. Dinner was great. Looking over the bill.

BOYLE *(aside)* Say Roberto listen ... I uh ... I didn't get a chance to cash a travelers' check in the capital, how's my credit around here?

175

ROBERTO *(knew it was coming)* Your credit? Don't make me laugh, you asshole. Your tab's up to 400 colones. I run a restaurant, man not a fucking bank.

BOYLE *(sympathetic)* Hey I know, Roberto, have I ever stiffed you in 10 years? Look I got an NBC radio feed in the works and I got a CNN gig with Cunningham coming up, I'm hot again! I'll pay the whole tab next week, promise, scout's honor ...

ROBERTO Oh fuck, allright, just don't tell Elena about it okay, she'll kill me.

BOYLE Thanks man, you're a prince, listen throw in 100 colones cash and we'll make it an even 750. Walking around money y'know, don't want to look like a jerk in front of Maria *(sotto voce)* just a hundred ... come on man.

ROBERTO Fuck, what she sees in a jerk like you I don't know.

He laughs. Boyle laughs once he sees it's okay, and Roberto slips him a 100 from his pocket.

BOYLE Thanks. Place looks great man, really doing business ...

ROBERTO *(aside)* Only weekends, surfers don't come down from the states anymore. Too much death squad stuff...

His eyes going to a certain table. Boyle following it, subtle. A bunch of guys and chicks party in civilian clothing.

BOYLE ... don't worry, I'll put in a good word for you when the other side takes over.

ROBERTO *(not funny)* I hope not, fucking commies scare me even more. Close me down for sure, probably shoot me.

Two other DRUNKEN MONSTERS are drooling on the edge of the restaurant, begging for something – anything. One of them gets close to

Doc, an obvious soft touch, drools on him. Rock can't eat anyway, so he throws his lobster tail over the guy's head, 'go, get it'.

This confuses the two drunks. One of them lurches around looking for the lobster tail, finds it, dives down to get it. The other guy, knowing he can't get to it in time, picks up a giant rock off the beach, raising it high in the shadows. We see it coming down somewhere in the vicinity of the first beggar's head. All this seen faintly in the dark. The wash of the waves on the beach eclipsing it.

Rock is the only one at the table to have seen it. He looks around – the party goes on.

Carlos and Rafael and Jaimie are a little drunk and down doing a goose-step imitation of MAJOR MAX on TV, a toothbrush over his nose, singing the Mano Blanco Song ... 'Republicana ... patria, comunismo no ...' – catching the attention of the nearby tables.

Boyle picks up on it, immediately nervous, his eyes flicking to a table. They're looking over unfriendly. One of them, RHINOCEROS, is older (in his 40's), meaner and stupider than all of them. He is evidently the leader, a former National Guard Sergeant cashiered out for rape and murder.

Boyle whispering to Maria to cool it out. She says something to Carlos but he doesn't hear. Launches into another refrain from the song.

The four guys at the table huddle among themselves. The girls look real poisonously at Carlos.

Boyle makes his move, stands and jovially reseats Carlos and his buddy. Looking back quickly at the four guys. 'Cool it there ol' buddy.'

Grandma shakes her head. She's seen it before. A wistful tone, to Richard.

GRANDMA *(in Spanish)* It's a bad time, evil in the air ... it's like 1932 again. They came into the villages one night. They killed thousands ... some say thirty thousand in one night ... it was the 'matanza' – under that stinking tyrant Maximilian Emilio Hernandez ...

The camera has moved through her eyes to a MONTAGE – very brief, no more than ten seconds – of black and white newsreel images of the 1932 massacres ...

James Woods as Richard Boyle.

Tony Plana as Major Max (left) and John Savage as John Cassady.

James Belushi as Dr. Rock, James Woods as Richard Boyle, and John Savage as John Cassady.

James Woods as Richard Boyle.

*John Savage as John Cassady (left)
and James Woods as Richard Boyle.*

Elpedia Carrillo as Maria.

Violence in the piazza.

*Elpedia Carrillo as Maria and
James Woods as Richard Boyle.*

Opposite Page: *Elpedia Carrillo as Maria, James Woods as Richard Boyle,
and James Belushi as Dr. Rock.*

John Savage as John Cassady (left) and James Woods as Richard Boyle.

Michael Murphy as Ambassador Thomas Kelly.

James Woods as Richard Boyle and John Savage as John Cassady, killed in action.

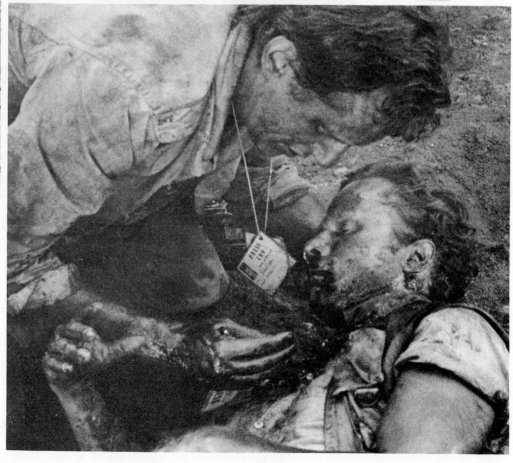

EXT: LIBERTAD TOWN SQUARE – LATE THAT NIGHT
Boyle, Maria, the children are playing Bingo, the main social activity.
A lot of people seem to know Boyle, who loses his stake.

He treats Maria and the kids to snowcones off a street-side stand.
Carlos, drunk on Tic-tac, with his two friends intersects with Rock who
is carrying his own Tic-tac bottle ('this stuff is wild man, white
lightning'), Boyle warns him 'you're gonna end up living in the street
here, begging for Tic-tac bottles' ...

The group crosses beneath the movie marquee – playing some Mexican
wrestling film with the masked avenger – to their MG parked on the
square – vultures pecking around.

Sitting on top of the little car are the FOUR GUYS from the restaurant –
the ex-Sergeant taking the lead.

RHINOCEROS Hey man you and your buddies are pretty
    funny. Maybe you can entertain us some more ...

MULE Yeah you're even more funny without your balls ...

Carlos is too drunk to be worried but not the intrepid Doc.

DOC Who the fuck are you ... Hey get off the car.

BOYLE Shut up man. *(trying to defuse it)* Hey amigos how 'bout
    some beers, it's all on me. *(doing his head count, center stage)*
    how many now ... uno, dos, tres ... quatro cervezas.
    Two seconds ... Doc ... you stay with Carlos. *(turning
    to go get the beers, to Maria aside)* ... Look Maria, take
    the kids now and put them in the car like nothing's
    happening ... okay ...

He hurries across the street to get the beers at a cantina. An awkward
moment, Maria casually putting the kids in the car. Carlos and his
buddies giggling among themselves, nervous. The four guys looking at
Boyle funny, back at Carlos, one of them singing the popular song to
the others (they're a little drunk too) 'vamos a la playa'.

RHINOCEROS Yeah, let's go for a ride to the beach. Come
    on man, we'll take you guys to the beach, we got a van.

A Cherokee Red Chief pulling up now. Trouble all right. Carlos steps back. Doc's puzzled. The guys start to move on the three kids, starting to surround them, yet not yet resorting to all-out coercion. The square is still full of people, it'd be preferable to con them into getting inside.

Boyle steps into it, real fast now, playing it diplomatic, giving out the beers to each of the four thugs, a little Spanish to each other ('there you go, drink up amigo').

In the same stride, grabbing Carlos.

BOYLE Let's go ... now!

Pushing him real fast into the car. Rafael and Jaimie jump in, overloading it. Rock wants to stay, drink with the thugs.

DOC I'll stay, they're not so bad. They got a sense of humor.

BOYLE *(grabs him)* Shut up asshole! Move!

He pushes him in the car. They speed out of there. The red Cherokee Chief trying to block their way. Boyle doing a shrieking U-turn across the square and cutting out of town.

EXT: BOYLE BEACH HOUSE – NIGHT
Maria helps the drunken Carlos out of the MG. Boyle sits in it, with Rafael, gunning the engine.

BOYLE *(to Maria)* Get him out of town a few weeks. Get him up to Santa Ana. *(to Carlos)* Mira Carlos, malo hombres! Gotta cool it now.

Maria and Rafael both muttering something at Carlos, angry at his attitude. Carlos, still zonked, dismisses it with a laugh.

CARLOS Don't worry, don't worry – they're assholes.

Boyle takes off with Rafael.

INT: BOYLE MG – ROAD – NIGHT
Boyle checking the rear view mirror, making sure they're not followed, to Rafael.

RAFAEL You can drop me here.

BOYLE *(pulling over)* Where you going?

RAFAEL Arriba, con muchachos in the mountains. *(points out there)*

BOYLE *(surprised)* What about your home? Where do your parents live?

RAFAEL It's not safe there any more *(gets out)* I go ... okay. *(they clasp hands)*

BOYLE *(surprised)* You're one of them? *(Rafael says nothing)* Vaya con dios amigo.

RAFAEL *(walking off, turns back)* In my country, amigo, there is no more God ...

As he goes off into the dark, silhouetted by the mountains.

INT: COLONEL FIGUEROA'S OFFICE – NEXT MORNING
Boyle is shown in with his safari jacket, three cameras, a tape recorder, ready to go ('Buenos dias Colonel').

COLONEL FIGUEROA is going over a battle map with a grizzled American mercenary, MIKE STANKOVICH – cold, steely eyes, crew cut, bandolier of ammo, and a strange mixture of a uniform – a cavalry cap from the Rhodesian Grey Scouts, a Montagnard charm bracelet, and a British Webley snub-nosed .38 in his belt.

FIGUEROA Boyle, this is Mike Stankovich. He says he doesn't want you on his recon patrol. Maybe another one ... I'm sorry ...

Boyle extends his hand to Stankovich who refuses to shake it.

BOYLE Por que, amigo?

STANKOVICH *(to Figueroa, ignoring Boyle)* I ain't taking this puta reporter nowhere.

BOYLE I ain't no puta, puta.

Stankovich reaches for his .38 revolver. Boyle whips out his switch-blade. Figueroa steps between them, smiling.

FIGUEROA Caballeros, come on, go down to the mess hall and have some coffee, you're both gringos, work this out between you ... go on.

INT: MESS HALL – DAY
Troops in battle gear are getting ready for patrol. Boyle and Stankovich both drink coffee, wordlessly staring at each other.

BOYLE Come on, lemme go out with you. No shots of you and if your boys want to do a little rape and plunder I'll look the other way. How 'bout it?

STANKOVICH Look, one of you cocksuckers got a shot of my stick in Mozambique. Sure we were messing with the Kaffirs but that shot cost us eight men drummed out. So fuck off.

BOYLE Come on man. I lost my hearing in this ear at Ben Het. I was with the lead counterattack of the Golanis in '73 and I was the last gringo to leave Cambodia, so give me a fucking break.

STANKOVICH *(rolling up his sleeve)* Yeah, fuckface, I got this at Ia Drang *(pulls up his pants)* and this at the Iron Triangle, so fuck off with your war stories. You sleazebags lost that fucking war with your fucking lies, no fucking way, fuck you asshole ...

BOYLE *(desperate)* What are you, afraid I'm gonna outhump you?

STANKOVICH *(tightens)* How 'bout some good clean arm wrestling, amigo, settle this thing?

As he pops a huge bicep.

BOYLE My pappy said never play another man's game, Stanky – but what about 'Knuckles'? Y'ever play? it goes like this. You punch my knuckles with your knuckles.

181

Then I punch you back. First guy to quit loses. You win I'll give you my gold wrist watch *(takes it off)* worth 2000 bucks. If I win, you take me out ...

Boyle clenches his fist, bony knuckles poised like a cobra ready to strike. Stankovich is challenged, but not dumb.

BOYLE *(taunting)* Come on, Stanky, arm wrestling is for wimps, putas and Alice Cooper. Knuckles is the real man's game. Or are you a pussy, Stanky?

Stankovich is like a dog unleashed. He leaps to his feet, as Boyle fingers the switchblade in his pocket. Stanky whips out his razor-sharp bayonet with a Special Forces skull and crossbones on the blade. But doesn't go for Boyle.

STANKOVICH Let's see who the pussy is here.

He cuts deep into his right forearm, blood seeping out, grins up at Richard.

STANKOVICH Who says I can't take pain, asshole!

Boyle at first amazed, starts to laugh.

BOYLE That's great Mike ... great game. Listen ... you win.

Stankovich now manages a triumphant laugh, as he whips out a scarf and with his teeth ties up his bloody arm.

STANKOVICH ... yeah well just so we know who's who in the zoo Boyle – yeah so now give me the watch.

EXT: BRUSH – PATROL – DAY
Stankovich, a lion stalking his prey, leads a nine-man 'cazadore' (hunter) patrol in full packs in the hot searing sun, Boyle trailing obviously, at 42, hurting, his back in sheer agony. Stankovich smiles at him.

They come to a cluster of houses, CAPTAIN SANCHEZ halting the column, having a quick conference with his second in command, CORPORAL SANTOS. Everyone except Stankovich is exhausted, sweat pouring off their bodies.

SANCHEZ *(to Stankovich, broken English)* My Corporal says
many subversivos in this house. We must go and see ...

STANKOVICH *(pissed off)* Come on Captain we both know
that's nothing but the local casa de puta. The G camp is
that way.

*He points north towards the high mountain range, pulling his plastic
grid map out of his back pocket. The men murmuring among themselves. No way they want to go up into those mountains chasing after
the dreaded Villalobos' crack commandos.*

STANKY Let's go!

EXT: MOUNTAIN RANGE – PATROL – LATE DAY
*Stankovich is walking point. He is reading his map. Ready to push on
when a burst of automatic fire rings out. Then a second burst, from the
other side.*

*One man is hit in the arm, yells out. Another is hit in the leg. The others
freak and break. All nine men fleeing down the mountain.*

*Stankovich yelling at them. 'Where ya going! Get your asses on Line!
Lateral Fire!!' Pissed off now, he stands there like John Wayne,
putting out raking fire.*

*Boyle clicking off shots at him. A great picture. One lone American
mercenary blasting away at the Commies.*

*A pause. No return fire. The snipers have pulled back. Boyle moving
in on Stankovich, taking pictures.*

*Stankovich sees Boyle, takes a fresh clip, slams it into his Uzi and aims
it right at Boyle.*

STANKOVICH You take that picture you sonufabich and I'll
kill you. Pop it out! Now! You heard me! ...

*Boyle realizes Stankovich is serious. If he can't kill a commie, Boyle's
probably the second best thing. He quickly pops open the Nikon and
throws the roll at Stankovich's feet. But Stankovich doesn't lower the
rifle. It stays pointed right at Richard's head.*

STANKOVICH I'm in a bad fucking mood Boyle ... and you
contributed to it ...

Boyle quickly rips his fake gold wrist watch out (his second of many) and throws it to Stankovich who picks it up and shakes it, holding the Uzi on Boyle.

STANKOVICH I swear asshole, if this thing is a phony, I'm gonna personally track you down, cut off your balls and stuff 'em down your throat ...

EXT: MARIA BEACH HOUSE – LIBERTAD – LATE DAY
Boyle drives up, bone weary. As he crawls out of the car, Maria, with the baby in her arms, rushes up to him, pure terror in her eyes.

BOYLE Que pasa mi amor?

MARIA Policia venga y captura Carlos y Doctor Rock. Los miran la marijuana! Es furioso, mucho problema!

BOYLE Donde!

MARIA El quartel o muerte!

Boyle races to his MG.

INT: LIBERTAD JAIL – NIGHT
Doctor Rock is in the back in one of the cells, sweating out the worst moment of his life. A .38 revolver is aimed right at his temple. A drunk POLICEMAN who looks like a bug-eyed Rodney Dangerfield laughs and pulls the trigger. Click. The THREE OTHER POLICEMEN, some of them without shirts, waving Tic-tac bottles, all laugh.

Carlos is there, beaten around the face and chest.

CATHY MOORE and BOYLE arriving not a second too soon. Cathy well known in the community, speaking rapid and excellent Spanish. Boyle plopping down the scotch and opening it. He's carrying his car radio and speakers which he's just ripped out.

BOYLE Aqui, amigo, muy suave.

Boyle chugs from the bottle and passes it around.

DOC *(freaked)* Boyle, get me outta here!!

BOYLE You wanna live Doc? Shut up. *(to Guard Sergeant)* Que pasa amigo?

The Bug Eye proudly holds up a bag of marijuana.

BUG EYE *(Spanish)* Marijuana. Subversivos smoke marijuana.

Boyle walks over to Carlos, grabs him by the collar, slaps him hard.

BOYLE Tonto puta! You dumb shit!

Then he goes over and does the same to Rock. Cathy meanwhile whips out 100 colones and promises that if they let this asshole go, he will get the daylights beat out of him at home.

BUG EYE No posible. Esta subversivo. Muy malo.

Boyle and Cathy huddle. Then Cathy explains how Doctor Rock is a famous American brain surgeon and was using the marijuana as an experiment to see how it would affect Carlos' brain.

Boyle going over to pick out one of Rock's joke cards strewn on the table with his other personal effects. He hands the card to the Sergeant who holds it up and tries to read it.

BUG EYE 'Doctor' ... Rock? What is this?

CATHY *(whipping out another 100 colones)* Oh that's short for Doctor Rockovsky, the world famous brain surgeon, I'm sure you know him, he won the Nobel prize ... the Nobel Peace Prize!

Bug Eye is skeptical, huddles with his second, this stupid-looking gringo doesn't look like a famous brain surgeon, but he trusts Cathy and he could get into trouble for killing a famous doctor. His eyes on Boyle's radio and speakers. Boyle slams them down on the desk, climactically.

BUG EYE *(to Rock)* OK, you can go ...

BOYLE Y otro? Libre?

Buy eye looks at Carlos, back at Boyle.

BUG EYE No es posible, no esta noche ... Now get out. Go!

Boyle shares a look with Carlos, who pleads with his eyes.

CARLOS Senor Boyle, por favor.

BOYLE Don't worry Carlos. I'll go to the Capital first thing in the morning. I'm going to see the Ambassador. I'm going to get you out. I promise!

Carlos looking at him. Boyle leaves, starts to take the radio but Bug Eye puts his hand on it.

No way. Boyle looks at him, disgusted, goes.

EXT: TOWN SQUARE – NIGHT
Rock, shaking, opens his rucksack and downs the whole bottle of valiums he has left, washing it down with straight Tic-tac.

DOC Those fucking guys man! They had my balls stretched out to here. They said they were gonna cut em off! Holy Shit man. I'm shaking ... I've really had enough of this shit!

BOYLE *(ignoring him, to Cathy)* Maria's in trouble man, she doesn't even have any papers, her brother's a suspected G, they could grab her any minute. I gotta get down to the capital, Kelly can do something.

CATHY *(tired now)* Look Richard, you're not helping Maria, you're nothing but trouble for her. And quit kidding yourself: she doesn't mean anything to you. She's just a nice little squeeze while you're here, instant family and all that. So why don't you leave now – before you fuck up the rest of her life!

BOYLE Hey I love her Cathy.

CATHY Sure. And what about your other wife and kid?

BOYLE She left me Cathy! She took my kid.

CATHY *(skeptical)* So you're going to take Maria back to the States? What's she gonna do? Sell snowcones on

Fisherman's Wharf? Here she's got a function. She belongs. In Gringoland she's a fish outta water. And besides – asshole – you got no money to support her or the kid you already got – so forget it! Leave her alone!

BOYLE *(suddenly dejected)* Yeah ... I know ...

Cathy, pissed off now at Boyle's stupidity, gets in her Van and drives off.

Boyle goes over to Doctor Rock, slumped in the front seat of the MG, passed out. He checks his pulse, it works. Bone-weary, he gets in the car.

INT: MARIA'S BEACH HOUSE – THAT NIGHT
Boyle in bed with Maria. The surf is pounding outside. She is sobbing heavily and he is gently stroking her hair. He tries to cuddle with her but she writhes free ...

EXT: U.S. EMBASSY – DOWNTOWN EL SALVADOR – NEXT DAY
A CROWD is picketing outside the gates. MANO BLANCO Party flags. Placards that read 'Kelly is a Communist!' 'Kelly Should Go to Cuba' 'Get Out of El Salvador, Communist!'

Boyle leaves his MG, negotiates the entry on foot. Accompanying him is CATHY MOORE.

INT: KELLY OFFICE – DAY
Pictures of wife and kids on his log oak desk, autographed pictures of Carter, memorabilia from nations he has served in, AMBASSADOR THOMAS KELLY cuts an imposing figure. Young-looking, handsome, a warm smile, he shakes hands with Boyle, but reserves his real warmth for Cathy Moore, of whom he obviously is fond.

KELLY *(hugs her)* Cathy, how are you? You look tired?

CATHY MOORE I'm all right, sir. Richard Boyle sir ... he did some stories on you in Cambodia?

KELLY Good to see you again, Richard ... please sit down.

BOYLE *(effusive beggary again)* You might remember sir ... the taking of Phnom Penh ... I was actually the last American journalist to leave Cambodia ...

KELLY Is that so?

BOYLE Yeah, I got out two weeks after Schanberg got out. He got the Pulitzer and I almost got cholera but we saved 1100 refugees from the Khmer Rouge.

KELLY That was awful what they did in Cambodia, weren't you one of the people who wrote them up as the good guys at one time?

BOYLE (*flustered*) Yes sir, I was really wrong on that one.

KELLY From our intelligence if those guys up in the hills ever took power here they'd make the Pol Pot episode look like a picnic.

BOYLE Are they as bad as Major Max and the Mano Blanco, sir?

KELLY (*flustered, looking at his watch*) I know, a pathological killer on the right and who knows what on the left and a gutless middle ... anyway Boyle, about your problem ...

Eyeing CAROL SNODGRASS, his aide, who sits in the room, taking notes.

KELLY (*sympathetic, a little frustrated but calm*) Miss Snodgrass has crosschecked with the National Guard, the Treasury Police, National Police and the regular army about the boy and they say they don't have him. We think this could've been overlooked and we're ...

BOYLE Ambassador, we all know they're lying ... he just didn't disappear – they've got him.

CATHY (*to Carol*) Carol, have you crosschecked with the human rights office?

CAROL No, nothing ...

BOYLE Fuck it sir. They fuckin' rearranged his fuckin' molecules and took their time about it. The kid's dying right now as we speak! Those fucks! He didn't hurt anybody. Those fucks!

The Ambassador uneasy with Boyle's violent reaction.

CATHY *(seeing it)* Richard, calm down please.

BOYLE That means his sister's gonna be on the shitlist now, sir. I gotta get a cedula for her, she's got none, they could come tonight and take her away ...

KELLY That's not up to me Richard, you know the laws here, she has to go to her hometown ... where's she from?

BOYLE Morazon sir – she can't get close to there, the Guard'll kill her as a suspected G.

KELLY *(looking to Carol for support)* I'll see what I can do but you know thousands of people have the same problem, it's not easy to ...

BOYLE What if I married her?

CATHY *(embarrassed)* Richard, you're already married ... I know you're very busy, sir, thank you for your time ...

KELLY *(rises, Carol ushering them out)* Sorry, really I'm sorry. *(to Cathy)* My wife and I are expecting you and Sister June for Thanksgiving, Cathy, all right ...

EXT: EMBASSY COURTYARD – DAY
MARIA, with Rock, waits in the courtyard, fingering her rosary beads, uneasy in her peasant dress, her eyes anxiously on Boyle as he runs up with the news. He takes her by the arms. Cathy Moore is not there.

BOYLE *(in Spanish)* They can't find Carlos yet but the American Ambassador is personally involved ...

She is silent, knowing. He walks her, with his arm around her.

BOYLE You're in danger Maria. Without a cedula they can grab you at any time ... I've been thinking about this very carefully. There's only one way out ... Marry me. *(she looks at him, shocked by the idea)* Look, we'll have a family, we'll take Reina and Duglas – and Carlos – back to America, you'll be happy there.

MARIA You already have a wife.

BOYLE No, no, that's over, that's been over six months *(scratching his head, lying)* ... we got a divorce, I just never told you.

She looks at him. Through him. CUNNINGHAM breaks it, driving up on his motor-bike fully equipped.

CUNNINGHAM Hey Boyle! Atlanta says they'll give you a shot. But you fuck this one up and I'll ...

BOYLE You're kidding!

CUNNINGHAM No! They want some stuff on the G's. You sure you're set with Alvarez?

BOYLE *(lying)* All set! No problem.

CUNNINGHAM OK, you got a camera, there's an Arena press conference tomorrow, Major Max is declaring for President, I gotta go to Venezuela so cover for me, willya. I gotta run.

BOYLE Sure. Hey Pete! How about advancing me fifty bucks ... I'm real low.

Cunningham reaches into his pocket, glances at Maria.

CUNNINGHAM ... my own pocket Boyle – but no whores; OK.

Boyle thanks him effusively, turns back to Maria.

BOYLE Maria ... por favor?

MARIA *(shakes her head)* No.

BOYLE Porque mi amor? Please ...

MARIA *(determined)* I'm a Catholic. I can't marry a divorced man and you Richard are a bad Catholic in *all* ways.

BOYLE What do you mean?

MARIA You know what I mean. You're living in sin. You drink *('not any more!')*, you sleep with many women *('no I don't!')*, you smoke marijuana *('it was Rock's')*, you lie, you scheme and scam, what's good or decent about you? What redemption can you expect?

Boyle scratching his head, his mind racing. None, I guess.

BOYLE Look, Maria – it's true I haven't been to church in 30 years – but give me a chance. We'll take communion together. We'll go to Archbishop Romero, he knows me, I'll get back in the Church ... si?

EXT: CATHEDRAL – SAN SALVADOR – DAY
Boyle driving Maria into downtown Cathedral where he visited Ramon Alvarez earlier. Demonstrators and police are everywhere. A tumultuous atmosphere, banners, protest signs. Maria is scared. Church bells tolling.

BOYLE ... it's even possible Romero might annul my marriage cause Claudia was a commie atheist anyway. I'm going to talk to him seriously ... *(making conversation)* You know the Archbishop? He's a great man, a man of the people. Man of God. They say he's going to win the Nobel Peace Prize.

MARIA *(quietly)* He's the only man that can save El Salvador...

RAMON ALVAREZ is on a megaphone arguing with some CAMPECINOS and POLICE. The air is filled with tension as a new Truckload of National Guardsmen arrives.

INT: CATHEDRAL – CHURCH DAY
A crowd has assembled for the sermon and communion. ARCHBISHOP ROMERO, a humble, handsome soul with a peasant's strong features, is in the pulpit.

ROMERO ... The governing junta has good intentions with their promises of land reform and their desire to control the so-called paramilitary forces in the army but sadly it is a failure because the power within the junta is

the Army and the Army itself is an obstacle to the reign
of God ... they know only how to repress the people
and defend the interests of the rich oligarchy ...

*Applause breaks from the peasant throngs. Boyle, repentent, serious-
looking, steps out of the Confessional to the side of the Cathedral and
joins Maria. They squeeze into a pew.*

ROMERO I have called upon the United States, repeat-
edly, to stop all military aid to this Army until it
satisfactorily resolves the problems of the disappeared
and submits itself to civilian control. Again and again,
American aid instead of promoting greater justice and
peace is used against the people's organizations fighting
to defend their most fundamental human rights – land,
education, health, food, shelter. We are poor. You in
Washington are so rich. Why are you so blind? My
children, you must look to yourselves in this sad time
for Salvador. Christians are not afraid of combat; they
know how to fight, but they prefer the language of
peace. However when a dictatorship seriously violates
human rights and attacks the common good of the
nation, when it becomes unbearable and closes all
channels of dialogue, when this happens, the Church
speaks of the legitimate right of insurrectional violence.
The spirit of God has led me to this ...

*The faces. Ramon Alvarez. Carmen Sanchez. A silence in the vast
church. Plainclothes POLICE shuffling.*

ROMERO I would like to close with an appeal to the men of
the Army and in particular the National Guard.
Brothers, you are part of our people. Yet you kill your
own peasant brothers and sisters. But before a man
may kill, the law of God must prevail and that law says
'Thou Shalt not Kill!' *(voice rising with emotion)* No soldier
is obliged to obey an order against the law of God.
Violence on all sides is wrong. Violence is wrong. In the
name of God, and in the name of this suffering people

whose laments rise to heaven each day more tumultuous,
I beg you, I ask you, I order you in the name of God:
Stop the Repression!

*More applause. Frail women in simple cotton dresses, hunched men
with wrinkled faces ... Maria praying silently.*

CUT TO:

The Archbishop is celebrating Communion.

*Maria, kneeling at the altar, sticks out her tongue as the
ARCHBISHOP, flanked by two ALTAR BOYS, presses the host onto her
tongue. Then Boyle takes the host.*

*They look at each other. A faint smile. She knows he is now blessed. The
body and blood of Jesus is with him. And maybe, yes maybe, she can love
him.*

*The Archbishop moves on, Maria and Richard rising to leave, Maria
crossing herself, Richard remembering to do so. The Archbishop moves on
down the altar, gives a wafer to a young man.*

*The kneeling young man, whom we may now recognize as the one who
took his own form of communion at Major Max's villa, spits in the
Archbishop's hand, curses him: 'hijo de puta!' and shoots him with the
silencer in his purse.*

*The silencer blasts blows the Archbishop back, his white raiments splashed
red with blood. Another blast follows.*

Maria turning around, screams. As do others.

The commotion spreads.

The YOUNG MAN walks away, unnoticed.

Richard grabs Maria, moves her out quickly as he can.

EXT: CHURCH – DAY
*A riot developing, people running in all directions. ARMY moving in,
making arrests.*

*Richard hustles Maria to the MG, waving his Press Card. The cops run
by him.*

*He gets a glimpse of Ramon Alvarez and Carmen Sanchez being dragged
protesting along with SEVERAL OTHERS. They are thrown into an army
truck.*

EXT: CAMINO REAL STREET – DAY
Boyle puts Maria into a taxi, gives the driver a big chunk of Cunningham's money.

BOYLE To Libertad! *(to Maria)* I'll be back tonight! ...

Tries to kiss her, but she can't, she's deeply upset. The cab zooms off.

INT: MAJOR MAX'S VILLA – ESCALON – DAY
GOMEZ, Max's Second, walks in with a suitcase which he throws open in front of MAJOR MAX. It's loaded with cash – $400,000. Gomez, a fat smart W.C. Fields type, with his .45 bulging out from under his shirt, is very happy. The deal is coming together.

GOMEZ *(looking at his watch)* ... our friends in Miami think you can be President. They send a little gift. $400,000 ... in unmarked bills ... *(Max laughs, in a good mood)* ... the two Madison Avenue clowns are waiting and the Reagan people are coming at 12, then the Press Conference ...

MAX ... Send them in.

EXT: MAJOR MAX'S COURTYARD – DAY
Two yuppie Madison Avenue ADVERTISING EXECUTIVES, McMahon and Johnson (a man and a woman), in neat suits and aviator glasses, the latest Gucci attaché cases, are waiting to sell Max. A little disturbed, however, by the yelling and now screeching and begging coming from one of the rooms in the Villa ... Followed by an ominous and absolute silence. The two Execs look at each other.

Gomez steps out, waves them in.

INT: MAX'S OFFICE – DAY
They have their demographic graphs set up, a tape deck, sales tools, poster designs, etc. – a professional presentation. Max playing with his .45, doing a roulette thing with the barrel.

McMAHON *(man)* ... you got to soften your image Major, you got to talk about positive things. The people want peace. In the TV campaign, you talk about *gradual* reform ...

MAX *(icy, reprimanded)* No. We don't want gradual reform. We want to *wipe them out.*

JOHNSON *(woman)* Well then I think you have to say that 'we need military vigilance to ensure human rights'.

Gomez does all the translating for Max, who has to stop and think about what that means.

McMahon rolls his eyes at Johnson. ('I think we're going to have a hard time selling this guy.')

MAX *(via Gomez)* People expect the truth from me. When I say we must destroy the communists and the appeasers, that is what they want from me ... This is why they loved Hitler, because he was a great speaker. He didn't talk a bunch of shit like that mushroom head Carter.

McMAHON Yeah, maybe you're right Max, but Hitler lost ...

JOHNSON ... and that Hitler stuff don't fly in the States ... Look, you're handsome Max, you look good in clothes, you don't look like a uh killer, you wanna be President you gotta play to that image, you want to close the gender gap, you want to pull the woman vote.

GOMEZ Listen to them, jefe.

McMahon puts a tape in the deck. A new Arana jingle comes on. (Or a videocassette). The jingle plays.

McMAHON Listen to this Max.

MAX & GOMEZ That's pretty good.

JOHNSON *(selling him now)* Yeah, and with it we're gonna win baby!

McMAHON *(preening now)* We know what we're doing Maxie. We're the best outfit in town. We sold Nixon, we had the Shah and Somoza up until last year, we still got Pinochet and he won his election. Something like 98%

of the vote. And we also did a great job on 'Save the Whales'.

Gomez translating all this, fucking it all up in Spanish. Max, an intelligent man nonetheless, is looking at Gomez. Are these guys for real?

MAX Whales, what are whales? These gringos think they're selling Coca-Cola here. They don't understand the issue here. They're *soft. (Gomez glossing over whales as some kind of political party, Max nods)* Somoza? You sure fucked that one up.

GOMEZ But they got Pinochet *(Max likes that, nods).*

MAX How much do they get if we lose?

GOMEZ *(conspiratorial)* If we lose we don't pay them shit.

McMAHON *(picking up the vibes)* I'm sure we can put this in some kind of contract form, can't we?

GOMEZ *(to Max, trying to convince him)* Look, you can become President with these jerks. They're smart Jews.

Max brings Gomez within whispering range, eyes on the execs, back to Gomez.

MAX You think – if I was President – I could kill all of them legally?

GOMEZ Yes of course ...

Max amused by that power, nods. Gomez turning to the two suits.

GOMEZ I think we can ... how do you say, make this 'package fly' ...

McMAHON *(relieved)* ... yeah I think so too, Gomez baby ... Thank you, Mister President!

On Max. Eyes on the future.

INT: ARANA PRESS CONFERENCE – THAT DAY
The Press is overflowing the room, cigarette smoke hanging heavy.
MAXIMILIANO CASANOVA, chainsmoking, is answering their ques-
tions, the party flag draped behind him. His wife, Yolanda, and 2
children are alongside him, a friendly family.

MAX   ... as you know I never agreed with the Archbishop,
     he sometimes got carried away in politics, he didn't
     understand ... but in my book, the Left killed him – no
     question – to provoke this kind of atmosphere ... no
     question ...

Pauline Axelrod writing down his response to her question ('thank
you'). Max looking around for the next question. A bunch of raised
hands. His supporters all wearing Major Max tee-shirts, 'Casanova
Youth', etc. Boyle pushes his way up to the front, a two-man
VIDEOTAPE CAMERA CREW, both Salvadorans, with him from CNN.
Cassady is there also, shooting stills.

BOYLE 'Mister' Casanova – it's widely rumored that you're
     the head of the Death Squads that are terrorizing the
     countryside and the city? Would you please comment?

Max looking at Boyle very cool. Murmurs all around the room. There
is pushing and shoving and it looks like Boyle is going to get beat to
shit.

CASSADY *(whispering)* You're pressing your luck, Rich.

Max grinds out his cigarette in the ashtray as he responds, very calm on
the outside. Gomez flicks his eyes at him.

MAX I really resent that question, because when you accuse
     you've got to present proof. Why do you never ask the
     Communists this? *(pause)* There are no Death Squads in
     San Salvador. The outrage of the people against the
     Communist threat cannot be stopped or organized by
     anybody ...

PAULINE Sir, polls still show you trailing the Christian
     Democrats, do you really think you can get the Catholic
     and Woman's vote?

MAX Yes.

EXT: MANO BLANCO PRESS CONFERENCE – DAY
The Conference is over. A table is stacked with weapons, which grim-faced PARTY REGULARS now return to their owners. Ashtrays, key chains, t-shirts, records, everything is for sale bearing Max's name. A sexy PLAYGIRL ringing up the sales.

Boyle and Cassady step out, get a filthy look from two heavy-set guys.

BOYLE Here he comes ...

As Gomez steps out of the Conference, Boyle moves, his camera crew following.

BOYLE Mister Gomez? A question please ...

Gomez muttering 'Who is this piece of shit!' to his bodyguards. A Bodyguard, suited, tied, carrying an Ingram now makes the move on the camera. Sticking his hand in the lens. The other two BODYGUARDS moving on Boyle, grab him, they shove and push. A brawl develops. The camera falls off the Cameraman's shoulder.

Cassady tries to interfere. They push him off.

Gomez moves in on Boyle, jowl to jowl, sheer hatred in his eyes.

GOMEZ *You* I'm going to get!

BOYLE *(taunting him)* Yeah, what are you going to do? Come on, come on fatso!

CASSADY Try to be objective, will you Richard?

Two Madison Avenue EXECS come tearing out of there, before the commotion gets out of hand, pull Gomez over to the side. Quietly.

McMAHON Hey Gomez baby, this isn't gonna fly, this isn't gonna look good. Think about our new image. You got 50 reporters here, okay ...

GOMEZ *(furious aside)* I don't give a shit about IMAGE. I want to cut his balls off!!!

Boyle, seeing the Madison Avenue execs, squirms free of the Bodyguard, ambles over, curious.

BOYLE Hi, how are you . . . you from New York?

McMahon and Johnson quietly freak out, and vamos. Gomez mutters to his Guards, stalks off.

INT: PUPUSERIA – STREET
In a grungy pupuseria right off the street where he likes to hang out, Peter Cunningham is furious at Boyle.

CUNNINGHAM Atlanta's really pissed off at you man. They got some call from some Madison Avenue outfit *and* State Department. Why are you such a fucking disaster Boyle? We sent you in there for a simple story man, not to get into a fight with Major Max! *And* you fucked up my camera. $3500!

BOYLE *(sheepish)* Peter, level with me – does this mean CNN doesn't want my services any more?

CUNNINGHAM *(throws up his hands)* I like you Richard but you're just too 'dinky dau'. What can I do? . . . They got the power.

INT: MG – ROADS – DAY
Racing back to Libertad with CASSADY, BOYLE has the radio turned on to some dinky music station playing sambas as he mutters darkly, passing the Tic-tac bottle back and forth with Cassady.

BOYLE . . . man I really screwed up with her, I can't even go to Communion without fucking it up. The *one* time in 30 years I go to Church, they kill the Archbishop on me, can you believe my luck?

CASSADY . . . aw stop crying in your beer, the shit's just starting. It was our war up until today. Now the whole fucking Press Corps is coming here. *(darkly)* I wish they'd close the fucking airport on 'em.

A news bulletin breaks in, Boyle raising the volume.

NEWSCASTER Six members of the Revolutionary Democratic Front were found dead today in a ditch outside the capital. There were signs of mutilation and torture. Among the dead were Kiki Alvarez and Juan Chacon ...

BOYLE Oh fuck! fuck! They got Juan and Kiki! There's nobody left! That was the last chance man! Now oh shit.

CASSADY *(drinking the Tic-tac)* ... night of the long knives, man, coming down. I were you Boyle, I'd lay low ... They're not fucking around any more.

EXT: TOWN SQUARE – LIBERTAD – DAY
Richard pulls the MG in as he sees ROCK drunk in the square with three Tic-tac monsters, begging for handouts.

BOYLE What the fuck are you doing!

DOC Boyle! They found Carlos man! He's all fucked up!

Boyle's running.

INT: CITY HALL – DAY
Boyle, followed by Cassady, pushes his way in past the assembled, silent crowd. On the Mayor's desk is the cleanly severed head of CARLOS. Several women in black saying litanies with rosary beads.

Boyle pushes his way over to MAYOR GONZALEZ, drinking out of a Tic-tac bottle, upset, arguing with FATHER CHANDLER and CATHY MOORE.

FATHER CHANDLER He was my altar boy goddamit! And I want him buried now!

MAYOR GONZALEZ *(Spanish)* Father I can't. They say to leave here for three days. Father what can I do?

Boyle walks out, past the National Guardsmen in uniform, indifferent.

INT: MARIA'S BEACH HOUSE – DAY

Boyle and Cassady come in, Maria cleaning out the last of Boyle's things, the children and grandmother gone.

Cassady discreetly goes to the refrigerator, mixing a Tic-tac screwdriver.

Boyle goes to Maria. She ignores him, emptying the dresser. A photograph of her and Boyle in the hammock taken by Carlos. She tears it up. Then a bag of marijuana. She throws it in Boyle's face, leaves.

He tries to block her, grabs her, tries to put his head on her shoulder. She recoils hard and fast, as if being touched by something evil.

BOYLE He was acting stupid. Why are you blaming me?

MARIA Because you were here he changed!

BOYLE Maria, please don't leave me.

MARIA (a cold, icy stare) Don't touch me ... I never want to see you again.

She goes. Boyle standing there – looking miserable.

Cassady stirring out of the shadows. He can't help but find Richard funny – even in his lowest moments.

CASSADY You're a pathetic worm Boyle. Have a drink.
    (gives him a drink)

BOYLE I love her man. She and the kids were the only decent things I had ... without her I don't really give a shit about living ...

He chugs the whole drink down.

EXT: PANAMA CLUB – NIGHT

Boyle, obviously drunk, scratches on his face, barefoot, takes a piss in the overweeded parking lot as Cassady crawls out of the MG, heading for the whorehouse, the HOOKERS out on the veranda in full strength, a juke box blaring, pigs rooting on the front door.

Boyle is really depressed as he pulls out his cyanide pill and fingers it, his bullshit bravado gone, a total desperation there until the pill drops through his fingers and lands in his puddle of urine. He picks it up, tries to wipe it off. Oh shit, he mutters.

201

Doctor Rock is slow dancing to Pat Boone's 'A White Sports Coat and a Pink Carnation' with WILMA, *his new girlfriend hooker, Cassady with another.*

In the back cubicle, CATHY MOORE *is conducting her clinic, giving penicillin shots to the hookers.*

MAMA MONCHA *is slapping pupasas together in her big fat hands giving Boyle a dirty look as he staggers in, asking for more credit.*

BOYLE Mama Moncha, mi amor, pocitito mas credito?

MAMA MONCHA No. You're already 200 pesos into me, you asshole ... You must be careful Boyle. Zihuanava has you in his evil grip.

BOYLE *(laughs)* What does he do?

MAMA MONCHA *(deadly serious)* ... he scratches your face and takes your shoes.

He begs with his best little-boy look. Rock coming over, throwing his arms on Mama Moncha, trying to get another freebee, mispronouncing everything in his neo-fractured Spanish.

DOC Mama Moncha, uno mas Tic-tac por favor, yo pago en dos menses. Promiso. Con interesso di 50%!

Even Boyle, drunk as he is, grimaces at his massacre of language, scolding Doc.

BOYLE You said you'd pay her in two menstrual cycles, you moron!

Mama Moncha barks out a laugh, gives up, motions Wilma to give them both two more beers.

Cathy, finished with the shots, is now distributing bundles of Christmas packages to the hookers and their children. Yo-yos, powdered milk, cookies, toys, food cans, 45 records, comic books — the center of attention.

Doc walking Rich back to a corner booth, trying to make him feel better about himself.

DOC Hey Rich I think this is God's way of telling us we gotta change our lives y'know – you and me, look at us – look at us, we're in deep shit – mentally, morally, emotionally ... every which way, we're a mess, we're *disgusting!*

BOYLE Are we really?

A toothless fat whore rubbing up against Richard. 'Fuckee suckee you,' Boyle extricating himself ('I'm afraid I don't know you miss').

Doc pulling out his last seven pills, codeine, darvon, perks, puts them on the table – the ultimate gift.

DOC Here Richie – the last of my pills. We get rid of these and tomorrow we start a new life together. For you ... and for me.

Dividing them, three for Boyle, four for Rock.

Doc gobbles down his four with the beer, Richie his three. Cathy Moore intersects on her way out.

CATHY *(disapproving)* Well I can't say I approve but ... here's a Merry Christmas to you ...

Pulls the last item from her bag, a small pint of Paddy's Irish Whiskey. Boyle's eyes light up as if it were the greatest gift he'd ever seen.

BOYLE Please Cathy, help me get Maria back. Talk to Father Paul. She'll listen to him.

CATHY Come on Richard, you're 42 years old, you're old enough to be her father. Forget her.

BOYLE Come on Cathy, I'm in love with her ...
  (Cathy laughs, drinks a beer)

DOC I love you too Richie.

As he keeps the Tic-tac Monsters and whores at bay, having now learned necessary vicious moves.

CATHY *(doesn't know what to say)* Father Paul has to stick to the papal orders. You were living in sin. *(Doc: 'Richard loves to live in sin')*

BOYLE I'll marry her!

CATHY Sure you will Richard, why don't you settle with
somebody who ... fits with you.

BOYLE I need to talk to you Cathy, about my whole life, it's
such a mess ...

CATHY *(touching him on the arm)* Rich, what are you doing
here, you're not making it as a journalist.

BOYLE *(brightly)* I'll make it again. *(she looks skeptical)* I love it
here, I can't go back. Look I can ask you the same
question my fair coleen, what the fuck are you doing
here? *(she looks upset at the word)* ... sorry. The white
hand's been painted on the parish house, your altar boy's
dead, even the goddamn peace corps has pulled out ...

CATHY I don't know, I guess I love it here too ... *(a smile
between them)* ... say that's a beautiful clonnard ring, Rich.
(touching it on his finger)

BOYLE You like that? It comes from Ireland – all the way
back to my great grandfather ... Have dinner with me?
(his head dropping on her shoulder, 'in love' again)

CATHY *(looks at her watch)* Can't ... *(Doc: 'I can')*

BOYLE Tomorrow night?

CATHY Going to the airport. Two of the sisters are coming
back from Nicaragua.

BOYLE Sometime?

CATHY Sometime Richard, yes ... but on one condition. No
more Tic-tac Richard ... you hear me?

BOYLE Cathy, you be careful on the road to the airport all
right? ...

CATHY Well I have to run ...

Her radiant smile, she pats his hand like she was handling a gentle Tic-tac monster. Behind her the entire focus of the room has shifted. Boyle notices.

SMILING DEATH, in a Lieutenant's hat, Mano Blanco Party shirt, black leather gloves, new pair of boots, sun glasses and his pistol in a purse, stands in the doorway. The campecinos drinking and talking more quietly, the little kids showing fear.

Two of his BOYS follow Smiling Death to the bar where they survey the scene, buy vodkas. The Hookers scurrying quietly.

BOYLE *(sufficiently cognizant)* I'll walk you to your car.

They cross the room, Smiling Death running his eyes up and down her body. RHINOCEROS is standing in the doorway, a t-shirt marked 'Grab 'em by the Balls and their Hearts and Minds'll follow,' leers at Cathy, as if he'd like to rape every orifice in her body.

EXT: PARKING LOT – PANAMA CLUB – NIGHT
Cathy gets in her car, Richard closing the door. 'God be with you Rich' ... 'See you in Ireland next year' ... 'You got it Cathy, Abbey Street, Easter Sunday' ...

She drives off. Boyle heads back to the Panama Club, but his way is blocked by Smiling Death and his Boys.

SMILING DEATH Anglo ... wanna go to the beach with us?

BOYLE *(takes a deep breath)* Look, yo no Anglo, yo Irlandes, comprende.

Smiling Death's boys surround Boyle, who whips out his mace and switchblade, still drunk and glazed. A red Cherokee drives up out of nowhere.

SMILING DEATH Come to the beach yes?

BOYLE If you think I'm going to the beach with you guys, you're crazy ... Okay asshole, tell your wimp buddies that besides an Irishman I'm also a Viking and I'd love to take as many of these creeps to Valhalla as I can.

One of the boys pulls back the clip on his uzi and aims it right at Boyle's head – about to fire.

SMILING DEATH   Alto! Yo quiero es puta viva. Entiendo!
   Viva ... *(to Boyle in English)* Come on Boyle it's no fun
   shooting you. Come with us ...

BOYLE   You ain't taking me alive motherfucker. Come on.
   Come on ...

*Doing his switchblade dance but the liquor has taken a toll and he
backs right into an UZI, which slams across his head. He goes down hard.*

*A Second Guy tries to grab him before he recovers, but Richard slashes his
cheek with his blade and the guy recoils. Rhinoceros takes aim but Smiling
Death waves him off, and kicks Boyle right in the gut — but not before
Boyle squeezes off his mace in Smiling Death's face.*

*Smiling Death reels in pain. Boyle crouches in agony. A Fourth Guy
cracks him in the mouth with his shotgun. Rhinoceros slams his Uzi into
Boyle's side and he goes down now, and almost out but blindly slashes out
with his blade, cutting into Rhinoceros' knee.*

*Boyle struggles to his feet fighting with all his spirit to at least take one of
them with him.*

*Smiling Death looks at his two bleeding men, totally enraged, grabbing up
his .45.*

SMILING DEATH   Okay Boyle, you wanna have fun! *(raises the
   pistol, takes aim)* First your arms, then your kneecaps, then
   your balls! Does that sound like a fun game!

MAMA MONCHA   ALTO!

*She comes running out, 220 pounds of her, with Doctor Rock and
Cassady trailing, drunk, Cassady yelling HEY! HEY KNOCK IT OFF!!
The HOOKERS follow.*

SMILING DEATH *(Spanish, to Mama Moncha)*   Stay out of this if
   you know what's good for you!

MAMA MONCHA *(holding her butcher knife)*   I don't care what
   you do, just don't do it here. I have friends in town can
   back me up!

This gives Smiling Death pause.

As Doctor Rock takes his beer bottle and tries to smash it against the side of a tree like he saw in a Western. It doesn't break.

DOC Okay cocksuckers, how you like these odds!

He tries again – without success. He looks frustrated.

Smiling Death's boys break into sneers and Boyle takes the moment to scoot over closer to Mama Moncha.

Everybody is now looking at everybody. A stalemate.

SMILING DEATH *(finally)* Vamos. Mas tarde. *(to Boyle)* We're not finished with you yet.

As they head for their Cherokee, Rock joins them, Tic-tacked out.

DOC Hey I'll go for a ride with you. You got some good dope?

SMILING DEATH *(to his men)* Ignore him. He's crazy . . . it's no fun killing crazy people.

CASSADY *(grabbing him)* Get the fuck over here! You dumb fuck!

The Cherokee takes off. Boyle suddenly slumps to the ground, injured and bleeding from his mouth, Wilma putting a compress on. From inside the club, the party goes on, Pat Boone crooning into the sultry night.

EXT: SAN SALVADOR AIRPORT – NIGHT
CATHY MOORE helps SISTERS MEGHAN BURKIT, CHARLOTTE WAGNER and DOROTHY KAZEL with their belongings into the curbside van.

Police patrol by them, watching. The van pulls out.

INT: NUNS' VAN – ROAD – NIGHT
The Nuns are chatting about Nicaragua as Cathy looks up in the rear view mirror. Sees the headlights of the trailing Cherokee. She accelerates.

The lights stay right behind her. In fact get closer. Cathy mutters something under her breath. But still thinks it's only a form of harrassment. 'Get your passports ready sisters . . .'

The Cherokee makes a sudden move, forcing their Van off the road into a ditch.

EXT: DITCH – ROAD – NIGHT
Five NATIONAL GUARDSMEN in civilian clothes step over to the van and the shaken nuns. They're drinking Tic-tac, muttering obscenities in Spanish among themselves, 'oh buenas chicas . . . juela cula' (good ass . . . me gusta la cula) – the leader looks like a frog.

FROG Good evening lady, how you doing?

Cathy standing right up there to him.

CATHY What do you want? We've done nothing. These are two sisters of the Maryknoll . . . I am a good friend of the American Ambassador Kelly . . . you are going to be in a lot of trouble. Now get out of here.

She walks steadfastly for the van. But the Frog, laughing at her speech, grabs her by the arm, whirls her around with incredible violence – and smiles into her face, rotten gold teeth, Tic-tac fumes.

FROG Get in the van, Sister. We go up the road. The fiesta is just beginning . . .

DISSOLVING TO:

EXT: ANOTHER ROAD – NIGHT
A deserted brush and arroyo. The headlights of the van snap on. Cathy and the two Nuns are revealed. The Mano Blanco Song is playing loud on the radio. The Frog and his second, the SCORPION, really getting up for the rape now, finishing the Tic-tac bottle.

FROG Let's see a little striptease. Take your clothes off.

Three drunk Guardsmen are stripping their possessions in the van – throwing passports into the ditch, taking the money. The Scorpion is lifting Cathy's skirts, giggling. She's trying to keep her skirt down. Gives her his Tic-tac bottle. She takes it now, drinks, tries to cooperate.

The Scorpion laughs. The Frog comes over now, really up for it on Tic-tac.

FROG The clothes! Off !! Rapido!

Two more of them come over. Then the Fifth.

CATHY *(to the nuns)* Go along with it. It's our only chance.

She makes the first few tentative moves of undressing. Two of the others follow, but the third, in her sixties, balks.

SISTER *(in Spanish)* What's the matter, don't you men have
   wives of your own?

This provokes a gale of coarse laughter. The men talking graphically as Cathy's body unfolds ... 'boco ... todo ... ' and more sarcastically about some of the older bodies, 'oh, que horror! ... que miedo, etc'

JUMP CUT TO:

The Scorpion ripping the clothes off the recalcitrant older Nun ... and throwing her in the ditch, staggering down to mount her.

Cathy is being fucked by two of the animals inside the van, which is rocking back and forth, the patriotic party SONGS still playing off the tape deck ... She has a look of resignation, yet tolerant, hopeful.

DISSOLVE TO:

Two hours later. The men are getting dressed, tired, hung over, sick and pissed off.

The Nuns are crying, gathering together their clothes.

Frog picks up his high-powered rifle, calls to his men.

FROG Vamos!

He casually turns the rifle on Cathy lying on her knees, trying to put her bra on. She looks up, understands. She looks right into the barrel, crosses herself ... and starts to pray as we cut to:

Long Shot of the Arroyo. And the shot is fired and she is dead. And the other shots follow in quick succession. As the nuns give up their souls.

209

EXT: NUNS' BURIAL SITE – BRUSH – ANOTHER DAY
AMBASSADOR KELLY, his SECURITY GUARDS, EMBASSY STAFF
look on, stony-faced as CAMPECINOS dig out the shallow grave where
the four women have been tossed. Kelly is very shaken. Cathy Moore was
like a daughter to him. The stench is terrible, rotting flesh, flies, her face is
blown away.

The Press is all over the place. Cassady moving like a cat with his camera.
Pauline Axelrod doing a stand-up for the mike. The Dutch crew, etc.

Boyle is the only Press Corps member not taking pictures. He is too shaken.
His face today looks like a bad dirt road . . . A young peasant girl brings
flowers and places them on the shallow grave . . . a sizeable campecino
population is there, reflecting Cathy's popularity.

FATHER CHANDLER and some Nuns are there, saying Mass with a
prayer shawl . . .

Kelly walks away – past Boyle who has tears running down his face. He
notices it, puts his arm around Richard, comforting him.

KELLY Stop it Richard . . . if you do that we'll all do that.

Boyle blinks at him. Rock is standing there with WILMA in mourning,
she's crying. He can't smoke a cigarette anymore, crushes it underfoot.
Kelly going over to the delegation from the town, led by MAYOR
GONZALEZ, the weak little mouse of a mayor, partially drunk on Tic-tac,
wide guilty eyes. Kelly's PUBLIC AFFAIRS OFFICER, CAROL
SNODGRASS, is talking quietly to Kelly.

CAROL . . . the rumor is five Guards did it for 15 colones
and a bottle of Tic-tac each and they got this clown to
sign the death certificate.

Kelly coldly eyeing the Mayor. His Security keeping the Press at bay.

KELLY Will he talk?

CAROL Not if we can't keep him alive?

KELLY What are the chances of that?

CAROL Slim and none . . . and he knows it.

KELLY ... well tell him he's got no business signing death certificates without an autopsy. I want one today ... I want to know if these bullets were government or rebel. *(Carol translating in expert Spanish)*

ROCK comes over. 'Want a cigarette? Want a valium? No. Want me to leave you alone?'

Pauline intersects Boyle who shakes himself out of his state.

PAULINE Boyle, you look like you drank too much and ran into a door.

BOYLE Yeah, I ran into four or five of them.

PAULINE What do you think ... Rumor is they might've run the roadblock and there was an exchange of gunfire ...

He looks at her venomously, but says nothing. She's too awful to waste words on. He walks away. She shakes her head. What a jerk.

Kelly is furious at the Mayor who squeaks out an answer to Carol.

CAROL ... he says the doctors refuse to do the autopsy.

KELLY *(addressing Gonzalez directly)* Why not?

GONZALEZ *(Spanish, terrified)* ... because the doctors say they don't have their surgical masks ...

KELLY *(incredulous)* ... they what? they don't have their surgical masks?

Furious, he walks away over to a tiny knot of U.S. embassy people, including Colonel Hyde, Priscilla Allworthy, an older State Department woman, and others.

KELLY Fuck it, I give up! I'm going to recommend to Washington we cut off all aid — military and economic as of now.

Hyde and Allworthy are stunned, look at each other.

ALLWORTHY Sir, the situation's just not that clear, I mean the nuns were not just nuns. They were political activists.

211

HYDE Sir, as I see it, they *were* coming in from Managua, they were Communist-oriented – maybe they got spooked at the roadblock, maybe they were pacing. It just got out of control: You got a bunch of low-level barbarians here. A little drunk, Cathy was pretty. They didn't need any orders from above.

KELLY *(livid now)* Pistol packing nuns my ass! I knew Cathy Moore and there's no way in hell you're going to sell me that shit Colonel.

HYDE Sir, General Garcia has personally assured me of a complete investigation of the matter.

KELLY Sure, have the fox investigate the chicken coop. You think I'm pretty stupid don't you Colonel. Let me tell you something. I know about you and Reagan's transition team coming down here last month without checking with me to meet with Major Max, and it's going into my report. 'Cause whatever they did they gave the Arana people the clear signal that resulted in this . . . and the price will be on your head *and* Mister Reagan's . . . *(pointing to another body being dragged up)*

Hyde flustered and surprised by Kelly's knowledge of this.

ALLWORTHY Sir, I think that's a little farfetched in view of the . . .

KELLY No it isn't! It's totally irresponsible that's what it is. You may think me a fool but America as I see it is dedicated to some kind of ideals, we do believe in something and these murdering bastards are not what we are about. And I'm not supporting them. Not one damn day longer!

He walks away.

Kelly's MILITARY ATTACHE comes running up from the Ambassador's car.

MILITARY ATTACHE Sir all hells' breaking loose at Alvarez's funeral. The G's've taken over the Church and about 8 blocks of downtown San Salvador!

Kelly and Carol split for their car . . .

The PRESS CORPS, overhearing, scramble for their gear. The news has shifted.

As they run like moths for their new source, we dwell a moment on the MONSTERS who don't run.

Boyle among them. One last look at Cathy's dirt-caked face. As he makes the Sign of the Cross, takes off his Irish clonnard ring, and puts it on her finger.

EXT: VOLCANO ROAD – DAY
BOYLE, studying a map, looks at his watch. He's sweating, as are CASSADY and the DUTCH CREW when a boy, about 12, suddenly appears on a white horse.

CUT TO:

EXT: GUERRILLA CAMP – BASE OF THE VOLCANO – DAY
The camp is in the form of a village, the old church converted to a military hospital, the schoolhouse now a Headquarters. The villagers are going about the daily business of fixing dinner, shucking corn, except they are all packing weaponry. Children are evident everywhere.

Boyle photographing a TROOP OF GUERRILLAS — men and women — going through a drill in the field.

The Dutch Crew filming, Oltmans obviously at home with the rebels, speaking with the SECURITY CHIEF.

OLTMANS *(Spanish)* . . . we want to spend a week with you, do a real in-depth and sympathetic portrait of you as heroes of the revolution . . .

The Security Chief is a tough 24 year old who's seen it before, nods with a hard smile.

SECURITY CHIEF Heroes shit, that's for the movies . . .

CASSADY is photographing individual GUERRILLAS posing with their weapons. They look like cowboys out of the Old West.

213

INT: GUERRILLA H.Q.
CAPTAIN MARTI, bearded, lean, tough, Cuba-trained – is giving the journalists a briefing with a map on a pedestal, explaining the military situation from their point of view. The battle flag is proudly posted – 1st Commando Company, 3rd Battalion, Acre Brigade. Several hardened PLATOON LEADERS look on.

MARTI *(pointing to the map)* ... for the first time our four armies are united. We now control the infrastructure of Morazon and Chatalengo provinces ... We're calling on all Government troops to join our Final Offensive and the people to rise up. We will take all the major cities, Santa Ana, San Miguel, San Vicente ... Then San Salvador will fall within 24 hours.

CASSADY ... when Captain?

MARTI *(cryptic smile)* ... before Reagan ...

BOYLE You really think you're ready Captain? With 4,000 troops take El Salvador? I mean the odds are the Pentagon's not gonna let that happen.

MARTI ... the will of the people or the march of history cannot be changed. Even by the Norteamericanos.

EXT: MAIN SQUARE – NIGHT
The guerrillas are holding a makeshift dance in honor of Christmas, symbolized by a tree and hangings. The radio plays some American rock tune and they jitterbug, pistols on their belts.

Van Slyk and the Dutch guys are filming. Cassady shoots stills all the way through, never seems to relax.

A GIRL studies a book by candlelight, making notes.

A COUPLE is kissing in front of an open fire.

Boyle interviews GABRIELLA, a young woman fighter, 15, with a shrapnel wound. Rafael, the friend of Carlos who escaped with Boyle's help, is cleaning her wound. Although she looks like a doe, she has a steely edge to her eyes and her words are hard. Her face warmed by the fire – the radio in the distance. Boyle is doing an audio interview.

GABRIELLA *(Spanish)* ... it was nothing. We killed six of them for one of us ...

BOYLE ... can you tell me why you're here?

GABRIELLA *(proud, defiant)* Why. My family was murdered. I was raped. That's why ... and you gringo? Do you understand – have you seen death?

BOYLE Much yes. But only once have I seen his face. Close.

GABRIELLA Where?

BOYLE In Vietnam. A long time ago.

GABRIELLA What did he look like?

BOYLE Dark, frightening ... real.

GABRIELLA *(nods)* I saw Death too, that night ... They took us out of the village, made us stand in the square. First they hacked to death my father and my brothers with a machete. Then they made the women take off their clothes. Then they raped and killed my mother ... she was pregnant. They cut her open. Then they raped my baby sister, made her do terrible things. Then they raped me. They threw the babies in the air and caught them with bayonets. Then they shot me ...

She pulls back her hair. There's a scar along her hairline. Richard reaches out to touch it gently.

BOYLE I'm sorry ... I'm sorry for your country.

GABRIELLA Yes I saw him too. I have seen the face of Death.

Rafael glances at Richard. The anger that fuels the revolution.

EXT: CAMP – NEXT MORNING
Boyle and Cassady are packed and getting on horseback to leave with a Campecino Girl. Oltmans and his Dutch crew shake their hands, Oltmans giving Boyle about a grand in cash.

OLTMANS I thought it was 2 days Boyle.

BOYLE Bullshit. 450 a day – guaranteed 3 days, come on man, I organized the parade now don't fuck me.

Oltmans gives him the money which he hungrily pockets.

OLTMANS Sure you don't want to stay?

BOYLE Nah I got all the photos I need. I gotta get back ... don't get yourself caught okay, it won't be fun.

OLTMANS *(laughs)* Don't worry I've been doing this long enough ... and thanks Boyle. Good luck.

EXT: CATHEDRAL – SAN SALVADOR – DAY
Close on a Photograph of the dead face of RAMON ALVAREZ, as we pull back to Boyle doing an audio interview with CARMEN SANCHEZ. The crowd around her is jostling, angry. A demonstration in progress.

CARMEN SANCHEZ *(into mike)* ... when we found his body, his fist was still clenched. They tortured him. Burned him. Poured acid on him! Cut off his balls and stuffed them in his mouth! Now I cannot control this anger ... the United States must understand before it is too late that the people and not the Government are the ones with the power ... you must negotiate with us, not kill us like animals! ...

Boyle trying to exit with Pauline Axelrod out of the crowd. She's hit in the face. Boyle shouting, 'Con permiso, Periodista Irlandes!! Irlandes!!'

EXT: CAMINO REAL BAR – DAY
Boyle is huddling with Morgan and Hyde, the bar quiet, a few military, no press. Morgan and Hyde are examining Boyle's photographs of the rebel weapons. Boyle's in a lousy mood, drinking too much, not liking what he's doing. Hyde buying another round.

HYDE This doesn't show much. You know I really stuck my neck out for you, Boyle, you're not too popular around here. *(looks again at the photos)* Where were these taken?

BOYLE I can't tell you that Colonel, but you can see it's mostly old stuff – shotguns, bolt action rifles, captured Belgian FLNs, some 50 cals and 120 mike-mikes they ripped off government troops.

HYDE Any anti-aircraft stuff? Any SAMs?

BOYLE Nothing . . . now what about a cedula for my woman and her kids?

HYDE *(shuffling the photos)* There's not much here Boyle or you're not telling us everything . . .

Boyle looks at him wearily.

MORGAN What about recoiless rifles, RPGs?

BOYLE Some. But not much ammo for the RPG's. Look they're in shit shape. They're getting nothing. The only modern stuff I saw was some of these . . . *(points to a glossy)*

MORGAN What's that? That new Czech 9 mm?

HYDE Nah it's an Ingram.

BOYLE Favorite assassination weapon of our NATO allies, the Brits – and you can buy it in Miami. I guess that blows your Warsaw Pact resupply theory Jack.

MORGAN Shit they could've got that stuff from Arafat.

BOYLE Yeah sure Jack – when are you gonna believe what you see with your eyes, man and not what military intelligence tells you to think.

HYDE *(eyes him, slams his finger on the table to make each point)* Listen Boyle, we got AWACs, infrared, statements from a defecting FARN Commandant and enough military intell to prove ten thousand percent that this ain't no civil war but outright commie aggression . . .

BOYLE Oh come on, you guys been lying about that from the fucking beginning, you never presented one shred of proof to the American public that this is anything other than a legitimate peasant revolution so don't start telling me about the sanctity of military intelligence. Not after Chile and Vietnam.

HYDE You don't know what you're talking about Boyle and I resent your ...

BOYLE Then resent it. You've been lying about the number of advisers here, you've been getting 'trainers' here on TDY *(Hyde: 'Bullshit!')* and you've lied about the switching of so-called humanitarian assistance money into the Salvadoran military coffers – and you've lied by saying this war can be won militarily. *('of course it can!')*

MORGAN Calm down, Boyle, I'm sorry Bentley.

HYDE I'm not gonna listen to this wino journalist's left-wing commie crap, Jack, we know where this guy's sympathies lie and I don't see why we're even talking to him ...

BOYLE *(his Irish up now)* Left-wing maybe Colonel Hyde, but I ain't a commie, you guys never seem to see the difference ... You trained Major Max at the Police Academy in Washington, you trained Rene Chacon and Jose Medrano in Vietnam, taught them how to torture and kill, then sent them here and what did Chacon give us – the Mano Blanco. What are Death Squads but the CIA's brainchild ... but you'll run with them because they're anti-Moscow *('Bullshit!')*, you'll let them close the universities, wipe out the Catholic Church, kill whoever they want, wipe the best minds in the country *('Bullshit!')* but as long as they're not commies that's okay. That, Colonel, is *bullshit!* You've created a major Frankenstein that's what.

MORGAN *(cool)* We can control him.

BOYLE Oh yeah, just like you control the Major Maxes in Guatemala and Chile and Argentina ...

MORGAN You think Pol Pot and Castro are any better?

BOYLE I don't know man but to some campecino out there who can't read or feed his family and has to watch his kid die from malnutrition ... well that guy doesn't really give a shit about Marxism or Capitalism.

HYDE Yeah well it was that kind of crap thinking that lost us Vietnam, this 'guilt' shit ... Look at that place now ...

BOYLE So that's why you guys are here, looking for some kind of post-Vietnam experience like you need a re-run or something. You got to turn this place into a military zone, pour in another 120 million dollars so they can get more chopper parades in the sky ... all you're doing is bringing misery to these people. *(turns to Morgan)* For chrissakes Jack, you gotta take care of the people first. In the name of human decency, something we Americans are supposed to believe in, you at least gotta *try* to have something of a just society here.

He stops, hearing himself, knows they are only words, his string run out. He chugs his drink.

MORGAN It's part of our national plan, Rich, we *do* do a lot of good here ... I'm often asked by people like you to examine my conscience and every so often I do examine it ...

BOYLE And what do you find Jack?

MORGAN Whatever mistakes we make here, the alternative would be ten times worse.

BOYLE *(shrugs, defeated)* Yeah ...

He leaves. Hyde also gets up as if to go to the men's room. When Boyle is out of earshot of Morgan, Hyde calls to him.

HYDE Boyle ... *(Boyle waits)* ... there's something you should know. My Salvo counterparts are mighty pissed about some 'muy malo periodistas' going out with the 'terrorists'. They figure they can catch one of these guys, they're gonna make a lesson out of him ...

BOYLE Look, I'll get out of your hair, just get me a cedula for my woman and her two kids all right and I'm gone.

HYDE Getting a cedula for your whore girlfriend's the least of your problems, Boyle. I personally don't give a shit if they kill you or not, I happen to hate the species you belong to, I'm just telling you: they're serious ... and if I were you I'd get my rubber shoes on. And get to the airport.

BOYLE You know you fit right in here Hyde. You sound just like another gangster.

He goes.

INT: CAMINO REAL HOTEL LOBBY – DAY
The lobby is now a scene of rioting chaos as the World Press has descended on El Salvador, vultures to the nuns. Also in the lobby is the unmistakable presence of American uniforms and guys with crew cuts, either spooks or military or USAID guys running around. The country is getting militarized.

Boyle, wearing a tee-shirt that reads 'Periodista. Don't Shoot Me,' coffee cup in hand, is on the telephone waiting for his call to go through long-distance. At the same time he's changing black-market money with ERNIE the Bellhop. The rate's jumping up.

CUNNINGHAM ... fucking zoo in here, every damn bleeding heart in the world's here doing nun stories, they got Dan Rather up on the roof doing an 'in-depth'.

BOYLE Hey change your money, never get a better rate, Ernie thinks the G's are gonna split the country any day.

As Ernie counts out the colones for Boyle, takes his dollars. They are interrupted by a yuppie college-type, FISHER, holding a telephone book, flashing his Press Card at Ernie.

FISHER Hi! Hustler Magazine. I can't seem to find the telephone number of the guerrilla headquarters here. I want to give them an exclusive interview, maybe you can ...

Cunningham turning away, disgusted, as Ernie looks at him, wondering how stupid a human being can be. Boyle's phone suddenly comes through, taking the mouthpiece off to the side, out of earshot.

OPERATOR Mister Boyle ... NBC Radio on the line, go ahead.

VOICE *(comes on, sharp)* What have you got?

BOYLE Four Dutch journalists were found dead this morning outside Chatelanango. The government says they were caught in an ambush but the powder burns were at close range. Also got a break in the nun's story. The Mayor of Libertad's been murdered.

VOICE *(cynical)* Not good enough. Today you'd need the second coming of Christ.

BOYLE What happened?

VOICE John Lennon just got popped.

Fisher is on the phone yelling.

FISHER That's right amigo, get me the number of the Frente Democratico Revolucionario ... I don't have all day.

> CUT TO:

Boyle's in the bar area of the lobby having a beer with Rock who's gone more and more 'native'.

DOC Boyle, let's assess the situation, the hard cold facts of life. You got no money, no job, no hope, no possibility of redemption – and you look like shit. But you got one thing going for you. Maria still cares about you, I don't know why but she does – you oughta go back to that woman on your knees ...

BOYLE *(doesn't want to talk about it)* Later Doc.

DOC *(proud)* Hey here's Wilma!

As she makes her way towards them with a shaggy mutt on a leash. A cute fat little chick, 16, no teeth, but a warm smile.

DOC Wilma, you know 'Boy-lah' *(they shake hands)* and look at this Rich – Bagel 2 ... isn't he cute?

Waxing sentimental as he hugs the dog.

BOYLE Great Doc ...

Rock is busy with Wilma and the dog as another voice cuts in on Boyle's other end.

VOICE Hey amigo ... can I buy you another one?

Boyle looks. A lean, tall SOUTHWESTERN GUY in short sleeves seems a little drunk. A face like leather, sparse hair. A chopper pilot maybe in civvies. Boyle nods.

SPOOK A Chivas for me ... Where you from amigo?

BOYLE Here and there.

SPOOK You one of them journalists running all over the godamn place ...

BOYLE Nah ... Parrots. I'm doing a wildlife documentary in Honduras. Jean Jacques Cousteau stuff.

SPOOK So what are you doing in El Salvador?

BOYLE Oh I got a bum steer. Not much wildlife left.

SPOOK ... must be interesting work. Me I'm just a boring old construction engineer.

BOYLE Oh really ...

A bespectacled Unitarian MISSIONARY interrupts.

UNITARIAN Mr. Boyle, I'm Reverend Abrams from the
First Church of Boston and we would like you as a
journalist to join our candlelight vigil for peace and
justice tonight outside Mister Casanova's headquarters.

Boyle looks at him like he has a few screws loose, 'No, thanks, I'm sorry . . .' the Spook overhearing he is a journalist.

UNITARIAN . . . you see we feel if we can show the media
that we will not tolerate the abuses by the Mano Blanco
Party that . . .

He's interrupted by a disturbance — Fisher from 'Hustler' protesting as he is hustled out of the lobby by THREE PLAIN-CLOTHESMEN with dark glasses.

Boyle turns his back on him. The tall Spook leaning close to Boyle, holding his elbow in a friendly yet menacing manner, a smile on his face, maybe a little less drunk now.

SPOOK . . . you know Boyle, mi amigo, you seem like a nice
fella even if you are a journalist. Let me give you a little
friendly advice out there in the bush . . . *(not too friendly
now)*

BOYLE Sure.

SPOOK Be careful . . . *(he goes)*

Cassady comes hurrying across the lobby in full gear, pulls Richard aside.

CASSADY Boyle, the offensive's just started. G's hit Santa
Ana and San Vincente an hour ago. Some Government
troops went over to them. Let's get going!

BOYLE *(hesitant)* John, I gotta make a quick stop in
Libertad.

CASSADY *(amazed)* Libertad? We'll lose 2 hours, I got film.

BOYLE Then go without me man.

Cassady reads his eyes, relents.

CASSADY All right, let's go.

BOYLE Doc catch you later . . .

Before Doc can ask, they're gone, racing through the lobby.

EXT/INT: MARIA'S SHACK – DAY
Boyle, wheels screeching on his MG, kicking up a cloud of dirt, brakes in front of Maria's. He's out of the car like a bat, running.

Duglas and Reina are playing in the dirt, see him. Jump up, run to him. Shouts of 'Papa!' . . . He picks the girl up and swings her in the air, giggling.

As we see the back of Maria's head watching through a window from inside the shack. He knocks on the door.

She opens it. He has a look on his face that she has never seen before, as if this is a matter of life and death and could be the last time . . . as if he needs her more than anything in his life . . .

He suddenly holds her, a frantic hold as if she would fly away if he let her go.

The wrinkled old GRANDMA looking on from the kitchen, slapping paupusas together.

BOYLE Maria . . . I'm . . .

She puts her hand on his lips.

CUT TO:

A back room in the shed, light filtering through the cracks, they make love.

There is a moment of stillness as they hold each other. Nothing to be said. Then he moves. She knows.

BOYLE Vamos.

MARIA *(sadly)* Si . . .

There are tears in her eyes . . .

EXT: ROAD TO SANTA ANA – DAY
Cars are lined up on the road. People running under them.

Pigs are squealing in the back of a truck.

BOYLE racing his MG towards the roadblock, CASSADY with telephoto lens hanging out the side, ready for anything.

ARMED MEN, rifles ready, flag down Boyle's car. Cassady holding up a white flag as they brake. It's apparent now the rebels are in control of the road. Distant artillery is crashing all over the place. Small arms fire.

CASSADY Periodistas. No armas.

REBEL Si. Alto aqui.

Boyle and Cassady jumping out of the car.

CASSADY *(Spanish)* Can we get pictures.

REBEL *(Spanish)* It's your funeral.

EXT: POLICE HQ – DAY
Boyle and Cassady move up through the streets to the Police HQ on the central square. Inside are several trapped NATIONAL GUARDSMEN, firing. A badly wounded man crawls into the Bunker. Another one is cut down as he tries to get in.

The rebels are in various pockets of landscape, not easily visible.

CASSADY We're not getting anything good here. Wanna try
   to get inside?

Boyle nods. Cassady sticks up his white flag. They go.

Racing across the street, we think they will be cut down any moment, but no one fires.

INT: POLICE HQ
Boyle and Cassady leap inside, out of breath. ELEVEN GUARDSMEN are left inside, two badly wounded, crying out without morphine, near death. They look fearfully at these two strange gringos.

CASSADY Periodistas!

LIEUTENANT *(young, terrified)* Que pais?

BOYLE Norte Americanos.

They look at him as if there were suddenly hope of salvation. Cassady whips out his Marlboros, passes them around.

LOUDSPEAKER *(Spanish)* Brothers of the National Guard.
You have five minutes, if you don't surrender, you'll die.

The Guardsmen choke up in terror, knowing death is near.

EXT: SANTA ANA STREETS – DAY
COLONEL FIGUEROA is in his lead tank, infantry behind and to the side of him, binoculars to his eyes. The rebels are pinning him down with heavy fire from various concealed positions.

RADIO MAN Colonel, the guerrilla force has penetrated the
cuartel!

FIGUEROA Shit! Get me the estadio major fast.

As CAPTAIN MARTI scans Figueroa's position from an adjacent BELLTOWER, says something in his radio.
RPG'S, mortar fire open up with renewed intensity on Figueroa. His tank is hit, and shrapnel blows Figueroa down into his tank, wounded.
His lead armored personnel carrier goes up in flames, blocking off his street.

INT: POLICE HQ
A new volley of heavy fire and a MORTAR SHELL rips a great hole in the roof above them, indicating the attack has begun. A GUARDSMAN is hit in the head. Cassady right there with the shot, Boyle not as dedicated a photographer, looking around as he hears horses, war cries.

INTERCUT:

EXT: POLICE HQ
The REBEL CAVALRY is charging down the central square, Boyle amazed.

BOYLE CASSADY – LOOK, CAVALRY!

Cassady exposing himself to get the shots of the oncoming rebels. The Guardsmen cowering behing the concrete, unable to fire such is the density of the incoming. Boyle finally has to grab Cassady and pull him out of the fire zone.

BOYLE You crazy fucking fool you're not that magic.

CASSADY *(crazed)* Today I am Boyle!

The CAVALRY charges right up on top of the stairs, unloading their fire. Others dismounting and racing into the HQ, yelling 'HANDS UP!' in Spanish.

INT: SANTA ANA CUARTEL
Mortar and machine gun fire. TROOPS retreating.

INT: FIGUEROA OFFICE
SMILING DEATH is on the radio with STAFF, barking out instructions, running to the map.

RADIO MAN The line is dead sir!

SMILING DEATH Dead! What the hell's happening! Where are the Americans?

Suddenly there's a burst of fire from just outside the door and it's kicked in and several of the TROOPS burst into the office, leveling their guns at him — followed by the REBELS.

The staff throw up their hands, as the REBELS move into the room with red armbands, several of them women, one of whom recognizes Smiling Death, yells something about 'let's kill the death squad pig' pointing at Smiling Death.

A hardened YOUNG KID, about 15, steps forwards, levels his Uzi at his belly, looking in Smiling Death's eyes. The smile is gone, an intense martyrdom in them now.

SMILING DEATH You can kill me but you can never destroy El Salvador — you commie puta, swine, traitor . . .

The kid emotionlessly cuts him in half at close quarters.

INT: U.S. EMBASSY – MILGROUP BRIEFING ROOM – SIMULTANEOUS
THE HALLS ARE CROWDED WITH US OFFICERS, CIVILIANS, briefcases, guns, action, cables, quick movement as KELLY walks into the briefing room over to BLACK JACK MORGAN, who rips off a report on the telex. The room is filled with computers, tracking satellite scans, the latest commo equipment.

MORGAN Sir ... there's a sighting that Sandinistas have landed a major equipment load in the Gulf of Fonteca ...

KELLY *(shocked)* Any backup on this Jack ...

MORGAN *(doesn't answer, under strain)* Sir, there's *no time*. Santa Ana has fallen, the country is cut in half, the first armored is getting wiped out, the situation is deteriorating faster than we expected. El Salvador *will fall* in the next 48 hours!

HYDE *(hostile)* ... 24! Their air force's got no gas, no ammo. We either restore military aid right now or we go to Phase Three. We got the 82nd Airborne on alert and the Marines are in position on the Ranger. *What do you want to do Sir!*

KELLY I will not be stampeded like this, Paul. *(to Morgan)* Substantiate that Nicaragua stuff right now.

HYDE Then sir if we don't give the order to evacuate soon I cannot be responsible for the safety of this Embassy or the American community here!

Kelly wavering, Morgan going for the jugular.

MORGAN ... listen Ambassador, we all know you're going to be out in a few days, that's not the issue here, the issue is – do you want to go down in the history books as the man who lost El Salvador?

Hold on Kelly. A man torn by his conscience, who as he says it, regrets it.

KELLY   All right, I'm going to recommend to the President that we resume military assistance. *(to his aide)* Get me Washington. Give the order to release the ordinance and gas stockpiled at Ilopango.

HYDE   Yes sir!

EXT: SANTA ANA STREET – DAY
Figueroa on the radio, his troops pinned down, taking heavy casualties.

MARTI VOICE   Figueroa . . . do you hear me? . . . Santa Ana has fallen . . . further resistance is stupid, futile . . . Join us . . . we need men like you in the new government. We can build a new Salvador.

Figueroa looks back to his depleted troops. Trucks are burning, dead bodies everywhere in the street.

FIGUEROA   Chinga tu madre! *(Go fuck your mother!)* *(into separate radio)* Fuckit, we're not gonna sit here and be picked off! We're pushing out of here! All units – follow me!

As he personally takes control of his tank pushing the wounded driver aside. Cursing, he rams his tank into the lead APC, pushing it out of the way. His radio man pleading with the Estadio Major for air support, he churns his vehicle at top speed through withering mortar and machine gun fire.

EXT: POLICE HQ
The surviving seven NATIONAL GUARDSMEN, including the LIEUTENANT, are hogtied.

RAFAEL, the young medic, is treating a badly wounded rebel.

GABRIELLA, the rebel girl from the camp, is now in charge of the company, on the radio. A runner tears up to her.

RUNNER *(points)* Figueroa's broken through. He's coming up the street.

Boyle and Cassady nearby, reloading cameras, dirt all over them, exhausted.

BOYLE Tanks man! Panhards! Can you lay on two more rolls of TRI-X.

Cassady gives them to him wordlessly, cleaning his lens.

CASSADY My 120's fucked up.

Boyle looks up. One of the NATIONAL GUARDSMEN is screaming, pleading for his life. Gabriella stands over him, her .45 at the back of his head. She fires.

Boyle gives up his camera, gets by the man, but is grabbed before he can stop Gabriella. She is standing over the young LIEUTENANT who is begging. The others remaining are all crying or praying silently.

LIEUTENANT I never hurt anybody. Please. In the name of the Father! I have a wife, a son!

A shot terminates his life. She moves down the line.

Boyle, disgusted, turns away, sees RAFAEL, who looks away. He goes up to him, grabs him.

BOYLE Is this your justice! You've become just like them.

RAFAEL It's war. You don't have the stomach for it, get out.

He packs his medical kit. The Guerrillas fanning out fast as we hear the sound of Figueroa's oncoming tanks. One last coup de grace shot rings out. Then a roar of machine gun fire and rockets as the rebels engage Figueroa's lead unit down the street.

EXT: STREET — FIGUEROA'S ARMORED COLUMN – DAY
Figueroa, driving the lead tank, is taking intense fire from Gabriella's unit. His units start appearing at various streets leading into the marketplace.

From his POV, he and the radioman ram a shell into the chamber and fire a HEAT ROUND which crashes near Gabriella's command post in the Police Headquarters.

Another APC comes up alongside Figueroa's tank and fires a white phosphorus shell at the rebels.

RADIO VOICE Congratulations Figueroa, now you must retake the cuartel immediately.

FIGUEROA Tell those shitheads running this show I can't take anything without air support and I need it now!

EXT: GABRIELLA'S POSITION – POLICE HQ
From her point of view she sees the tanks firing into her position. Her position is hopeless unless she can get more mortars and ammo. She gathers her last few fighters from the headquarters platoon to personally lead a desperate counterattack against Figueroa's tanks.

EXT: FIGUEROA'S LEAD TANK – DAY
Figueroa is personally directing his few remaining tanks to fire down into the rebel position. He grabs the radio from his radio man.

FIGUEROA Where is that air support, goddammit!

RADIO VOICE The Americans have released the ordinance and fuel, a squadron of fighters will be on your target in two minutes, out.

FIGUEROA Well, it's about fucking time.

FIGUEROA raises his hand, and motions for his armored column to charge forward.

EXT: SANTA ANA STREET – SIMULTANEOUS
CAPTAIN MARTI on the radio to GABRIELLA. His church tower is now besieged by Figueroa's INFANTRY. A REBEL is up in the bell tower ringing both bells furiously, trying to rally the troops.

MARTI You are a great fighter compadre! You must hold the Square! At all costs! Do not retreat. The people will rise up any moment. Venceremos!

But as he looks up, THREE CHOPPERS come zooming over the church, machine guns crapping, chewing up his troops.

EXT: SANTA ANA SQUARE – SIMULTANEOUS

Civilians are dying everywhere. A FATHER runs for a doorway with his DEAD CHILD draped naked in his arms.

Another CHILD dies quietly in his MOTHER'S sobbing arms as BOYLE and CASSADY move, getting great shots but obviously they're taking heavier and heavier fire from Figueroa's tanks and infantry.

Gabriella at the Police Headquarters is now barricaded on the steps outside, under tank fire, on the last of her ammo.

Boyle looking up into the sky with a sense of dread as he hears it. He sees four black dots off in the distance. They're coming. Reapers of his destruction.

Cassady resets his telephoto lens. Boyle tries to advance his camera but the advance lever now breaks off – rendering his camera useless. He throws the lever away and kicks himself, frustrated, a symbol of his wasted life, missing the greatest shots of his lifetime.

The four black dots are getting closer, fighters – pilotas – in a tight formation, on a low strafing run.

As the rebels scatter, Cassady edges up for the shot of the plane coming right up main street, laying out death on the dime. Boyle yelling for him to get down but lost in the encroaching roar.

Cassady, in his apotheosis, shooting the plane coming right at him, bomb racks unloading. Catching that moment of death as Gabriella is hit square in the head, mortally wounded ...

Boyle throwing himself into a doorway.

Cassady shooting.

The moment of death.

His death. The plane at 100 mph, engine roaring, right on top of him!

He finally makes his dive for safety. Too late.

As the magic bullet finally rips out his throat.

Boyle screaming – No! No!

Then a CHOPPER appears out of nowhere. Vietnam, '67. A U.S. DOORGUNNER glimpsed in the sun, shades, helmet, with his

SALVADORAN pupil. But it is the U.S. trainer who is firing – as he rakes Boyle with machine gun fire.

Boyle, hit in the heel, crashes to the pavement, yanking his leg, making his painful way towards Cassady. The chopper mopping its way down the street.

The rebels are dead or dying, the INFANTRYMEN swarming up over the streets and marketplace to finish them off.

Rafael and the remainder of the Rebel Force, about 30–40 men, are withdrawing, putting out fire, keeping this from becoming a total rout. Rafael's face the last thing we see as he vanishes across a wall.

Boyle yelling 'Periodista!' at the Infantrymen, who stop, scope him out, continue on – gets to Cassady, his chest now a mass of blood. Boyle pulls open his mouth, but sees he can't breathe, too much blood. He takes out his pen and jabs it into Cassady's throat hole, performing a crude, emergency tracheotomy.

BOYLE John, can you breathe now?

Cassady, gurgling, tries to talk. He reaches for his camera, for Boyle to take the film, as Boyle performs mouth to mouth, Boyle's ear right next to the poor man's mouth, now hears the painful whisper.

CASSADY ... I got it, Boyle, I got the shot. Get it to New
York man, put it in their hands!

As he struggles to press the filthy blood-soaked camera into Boyle's hand. Boyle quickly grabs it, presses Cassady's hand hard, close to his ear.

BOYLE I promise John. You got the shot John. You got the
magic shot ... You're the best!

John's blood-encrusted hand releases all its tension and slides off his camera and flops on the ground.

As the pilotas make another ear-splitting, death-whining turn over the town.

Boyle burying his face in his hands.

233

EXT: TOWN SQUARE – LATER DAY
The VULTURES have arrived en masse.

As have the Press. Several CREWS working the battle, competing with the vultures, who are fighting for their food, not afraid of the intruders. Four Press Guys haul John Cassady back down the street, chased by Photographers.

PAULINE AXELROD doing her stand-up. CHOPPERS are landing and setting off in background. A knot of Salvadoran military brass is with Pauline – a GENERAL being interviewed. He's incensed, hands pointed at the dead Guardsmen.

SALVADORAN GENERAL Show that, periodista, show that to the American people, show what the Communists do!

Pauline on cue panning to the corpses.

Boyle going by in his litter, he tunes it all out – on his way to the waiting Medivac chopper. A silver chopper just landing now in a cloud of dust – MILGRP 7648 and an American flag marked on it. But the dust blurs out his vision. BLACK JACK MORGAN and a Military Man coming alongside Boyle.

MORGAN Hey Boyle, you all right? Sorry 'bout Cassady. You okay?

BOYLE Foot's fucked. Hey, who's winning the war man?

MORGAN *(laughs)* Who do you think? We got Santa Ana back and the Indians are running for the hills ... Oh by the way, you hear about Kelly?

BOYLE What?

MORGAN *(rubbing it in)* He's been bounced. Looks like the new boys are in.

BOYLE Makes you wonder who the real vultures are here. See you 'round amigo.

Morgan moving away, Boyle's eyes moving back to the silver chopper, now lifting off in a cloud of dust. Through the whirring blades and rotor wash, squinting, Boyle now sees COLONEL HYDE in animated conversation with a figure wearing shades and light jacket. It looks like MAJOR MAX – then the chopper is gone.

INT: SALVADORAN MILITARY HOSPITAL – DAY
The ward is crowded with wounded personnel and their families, in
some cases up to half a dozen surrounding each bed.

The DOCTOR is operating on Boyle's foot right at the bed – a tendon is
cut, some nerves severed, a messy wound, Boyle gripping a whiskey bottle
which he drinks, screams at the doctor in Spanish.

BOYLE FUCK, GIMME A PAINKILLER FOR
CHRISSAKE!!! YOU DUMB SHIT.

The Doctor, inured to pain and screams and practically everything,
simply wipes the blood off his scalpel on his filthy smock and with the
NURSE's assistance, starts sewing Boyle up like a turkey.

FIGUEROA a few beds down, is drunk on his own whiskey, laughing at
Boyle's expressions of pain.

FIGUEROA Ah Boyle – you're always good for laugh! Listen,
you're lucky. He told me he wanted to amputate your
foot. But I told him you're a friend.

BOYLE *(cursing them all out)* Chinga tu madre, you puta, you
dumb shits clean the fucking scalpel at least willya!!

DOCTOR ROCK comes bursting in with little REINA in his arms and
DUGLAS trailing . . . then MARIA follows, a little frightened.

DOC Rich, you okay!

BOYLE NO!! GIMME A VALIUM, A JOINT,
ANYTHING!!

Rock pulling out a packet of pills and a bottle of Tic-tac. Maria
trying to comfort him. But the DOCTOR is suddenly
called away as CAPTAIN MARTI, badly wounded, is
brought in, a LIEUTENANT yelling that this case takes
priority.

The Doctor and Nurse hurry over, leaving Boyle. Doc sotto
voce, looking around.

DOC I got some cedulas Rich. From the bruja. For the kids
and Maria. They're pretty good.

Waving the fake cedulas but Boyle can't see, blurred with pain.

DOC She tried to fake your exit visa but she fucked up a bit but I think it'll work.

Showing him a blurred exit visa in his crumpled passport book.

DOC You gotta get outta here man, the Hacienda police came by Roberto's last night. Said you were illegally in the country. Roberto told 'em he thinks you're dead.

On Boyle. He feels like he is at this point, grips Maria's hand. Maria changes expression. Rock follows. Boyle looking at what they're looking at — now sees TWO MANO BLANCO MONSTERS burst into the ward, obviously looking for somebody and obviously packing something in their waistbands. They come right up to Boyle.

MANO BLANCO MONSTER *(looks at Boyle)* Gringo?

DOC Uh ... muy importante. Dan Rather. CBS. Si. Ese. Amigo de Ronaldo Reagan.

They don't care about Boyle, cast their eyes around the ward.

Figueroa quietly going for his .45. One of the Arena guys yells something to the other one.

They go over to Captain Marti, rip off the top sheet, the Doctor trying to protest.

MANO BLANCO MONSTER *(pushes him away)* I'll finish the operation for you Doc ...

As he blows Marti's brains out.

They run away. Everybody is shocked but no one says anything. As the Nurse turns off the life support system and the Doctor throws up his hands, wipes them, and crosses back to work on Boyle, pulling his scalpel out.

Boyle seeing him come, takes a big swig of Tic-tac, eyes getting woozy, grips Maria's hand.

EXT: ROAD – NEAR SALVADORAN BORDER – DAY
Boyle driving Maria and the kids, Doc in back. The car is smoking badly, actually falling apart now. As is Boyle, who is evidently very

sick, stuffed with painkillers, codeine in his weaving eyes, he can barely keep his infected foot on the gas pedal. Maria is very worried.

Tensing now as they pass a sign, 'Frontera – Guatemala – 500 metros.'

BOYLE Doc, when we get there you hang back. Any trouble you get on the phone to Kelly. If he's gone, Morgan'll help ...

DOC I heard you the first time Rich.

BOYLE Least you don't ask 'why?' anymore.

DOC Yeah, now it's 'why not?'

BOYLE You take care of yourself, Doc, don't become a Tic-tac monster *(tries a smile)* and don't stay too long. They kill people here.

DOC *(echoing Boyle)* You believe everything you read in the papers Boyle? I love it here in El Salvador. No cops, no laws, no yuppies. I got Wilma, I got Bagel 2, I'm going into partnership with Roberto on a nightclub, I'm gonna be a DJ again, my life is going great – and I owe it all to you Richard. Thanks for taking me.

He means it in his own sarcastic way. Boyle gives him a heartfelt look.

BOYLE I'll miss you Doc.

DOC Yeah for 'dos menses'. Say hello to Gringoland for me.

EXT: BORDER STATION – DAY
TEN NATIONAL GUARDSMEN are milling around a semi-busy check-point. A bus trying to get through to Guatemala. The Guards are finishing breakfast, in no great hurry, coffee, beans, rice, meat. They're bored with the flies and heat, mariachi radio music blasting out, crap strewn all over, empty Tic-tac bottles; they're obviously hung over and not looking forward to another boring day of shit duty.

Boyle sits there in his MG on a line, nervous. His foot killing him.

Doc watches him from a CANTINA across the street. Smiles. Good luck. Nerves.

INT: CUSTOMS SHED
Boyle, Maria and the kids give their cedulas to a BORDER GUARD, a thin, intense man in a grubby tee-shirt, military cap, .45 pistol, he looks like a grasshopper. He studies the papers, them. The cedulas seem to be all right but it's Boyle's exit visa that catches his interest.

Boyle is sweating, nervous, looking weird with his drugged eyeballs circling his head.

GRASSHOPPER *(holds up exit visa)* This is phony.

BOYLE *(shocked, a look of dismay and hurt)* No phony. Seguro.

He calls to his bull-like BOSS who comes over, burping, chewing on a toothpick. They hold up the exit visa to the light. Smudged ink, sloppy. Boyle and Maria sharing a look of fear.

Grasshopper and the Bull share a brief monologue.

THE BULL It's fake ...

BOYLE Look allright, it was a rush job. I have to get back to America. I'm a journalist. Newsweek. Time. CBS. Big shot ...

As he produces his outdated Press Card in Spanish. With it twenty-five U.S. dollars.

The Bull sees it, takes it. Pockets the money, takes the card, goes back into the rear office, saying nothing.

BOYLE Where's he going?

GRASSHOPPER Telefono. Capital ...

Boyle shares a glance with Maria who is gripping Duglas — making sure he doesn't blow it. Reina starts to cry — the situation getting out of hand. Boyle looks at his last fake gold wrist watch, pulls it off his wrist.

BOYLE Look, I just remembered I have a meeting in the capital with Ambassador Kelly and Mr. Jose D-U-A-R-T-E, my friend Napoleon ...

As he glances at the Bull on the phone, his phone connection has come through.

THE BULL Si ... 'Boy-lay, Rich-ard Boylay ... si ... '
(*rattles on in Spanish*)

BOYLE *(to Grasshopper)* So look I gotta get going back to the
capital. I'll be back ...

*Leaving his gold watch behind and ushering Maria and the kids out
quickly.*

EXT: SHED
*Boyle tries to get into the MG, eyes crossing immediately with DOC across
the street. A thumbs down gesture.*

*As he pulls open his door, something cold is at his temple. A rifle barrel. He
raises his hands.*

*Maria and the kids are pulled out of the car, the kids starting to cry, Maria
trying to keep them quiet.*

*Boyle is pushed along by the Guards, led by the Grasshopper, who rattles
on in Spanish – the gist of which is Maria and the kids are hauled off for
separate questioning to another shed. Boyle throwing her a look as he is
pushed back into the main shed.*

INT: SHED – BACK ROOM
*Boyle is smacked in the side of the head with a pistol butt. He goes
down. His clothes, papers, camera, and bags are dumped on the floor,
tossed and searched by SEVERAL GUARDS, all talking to each other.
('Get his film!') One of them occupied with his Playboy magazine.*

*Boyle looking up. PEDRO, the biggest of them, a pot belly, no shirt, an
Oakland Raider hat, looms over him. Boyle crawling to his painkillers
that have spilled out on the floor, gobbling them up. Then sees his cyanide
pill – gets it. Thinks about it. He pockets it.*

*They're now stripping his film reels – exposing them to the light. Ribbons
of film everywhere.*

LAUREL Any photographs? Subversives? Communists?

HARDY Nada. It's all blank ... maybe it's blank to fool us. A
commie trick.

Boyle crawling to get his Mano Blanco hat and Major Max tee-shirt.

BOYLE *(a man for all seasons)* Mira! Mi amigo de Maximiliano Casanova. El mucho macho hombre. Me gusta Mano Blanco! *(breaks into the theme song)* ' ... tremble, tremble Communists'.

Pedro, furious now, grabs him by the neck to shut him up, smacks him against the wall.

PEDRO ... but Mano Blanco doesn't like you, fuckface, you make trouble for Mister Gomez!

BOYLE Gomez? He's my friend!

PEDRO ... that's why he wants you dead. Shut up!

Grasshopper points to Boyle's boots.

GRASSHOPPER What's in your shoe!

Boyle tries to bullshit again about being Major Max's friend but Pedro kicks him hard right in his wounded foot. Boyle screams and hits the deck. Pedro pulls off his two boots. Out plops Cassady's rolls of film of the final battle – marked 'John Cassady, Newsweek, 400 ASA.'

The Bull looks at it, starts exposing it.

Boyle, hollering in pain, holding his freshly bleeding foot, sees it.

BOYLE No! The best film of the war! Cassady died getting it! You FUCKS!!

As the Bull quickly ruins each roll – they're blank (to him) and he's pissed about it. He goes and kicks Boyle again in his bleeding foot. Boyle howls.

Cassady's classic shots rolling to the floor, never to be seen.

CANTINA PHONE BOOTH – DAY SIMULTANEOUS
ROCK is trying to get Kelly in the capital, struggling with his novice Spanish to make the operator understand.

DOC ... muy importante ... emergencia ... Embassadio Estados Unidos.

She rattles back something in Spanish which he can't understand. The line goes dead. Frustration. He bangs at the phone, then calms down. Nervous. Puts more money in.

EXT: SHED
They drag Boyle, barefoot now, hobbling painfully, out the back of the shed to their waiting Cherokee Chief. Past the pigs and chickens.

BOYLE *(begging)* Look no problem. Yo muerto okay. Yo comprende. Pero en America una ultima comida para el hombre. Okay. Me gusta pollo.

Looking at the chicken running around. They laugh. Pedro kicks him in the foot, laughs again.

PEDRO This gringo is gonna look like a chicken with his balls stuffed down his throat.

Laurel and Hardy are starting up the Cherokee but it rolls over dead.

BOYLE Ah! Me numero uno mecanico. Mira! Ayudo!

Hobbling over to look under the hood with Laurel there and Grasshopper coming over, impatient.

GRASSHOPPER *(yelling at Laurel)* How many times do I have to tell you to pull maintenance on this piece of shit! You dumb shitbag! *(hits him)*

Boyle, during this, quickly takes the distributor cap and yanks out the spark plug wire.

BOYLE Ah si, es problema aqui.

He thinks he's gotten away with it, but Pedro's been watching, comes up furiously, grabs the wires with one hand and Boyle's head with the other. Smashes it on the hood and kicks him in the foot. He's groveling on the ground.

GRASSHOPPER *(pissed off)* Fuck it. Take him in the back room. We'll do it here.

They pick him up bodily, march him back in.

CANTINA PHONE BOOTH – SIMULTANEOUS
Rock is on the phone, out of his mind, bullying, cajoling, pleading in his best DJ's voice.

DOC   ... matter of life or death man! Boyle is *about to die*! And if he does, man, your fucking next job is gonna be in *Ruanda* counting spears! so ...

EXT: AIRPORT TARMAC – DAY
Kelly is walking towards a Lear Jet with State Department markings. His aide is carrying his bags; as another aide runs up and talks urgently with the ambassador in long shot. Kelly, looking at his watch annoyed, turns back with the aide.

INT: DEATH ROOM – SHED
They drag Boyle in, throw him down – pull off his pants.

Pedro, in his Oakland Raiders hat, pulls out his bayonet, sharply honed, an evil smile directed at Boyle's balls.

PEDRO   Me gustan los huevos rancheros.

BOYLE   Momento ... look I'm not kidding now – I have $50,000 in traveler's checks hidden. A few kilometers from here Pedro ... listen let's make a deal ... you can walk out of this thing a rich man.

PEDRO   You lie, you stupid gringo.

Grasshopper comes in, pissed at Pedro.

GRASSHOPPER *(Spanish)*   No. Not here. Too messy, too much blood. Shoot him. We say he's escaping like that ...

Pedro argues with him, explaining how they can get away with cutting off his balls instead. Boyle meanwhile pulls out the cyanide pill, eyes it ... now puts it under his tongue.

INT: AIRPORT – SIMULTANEOUS
KELLY is yelling into the phone, furious. AIDES hovering nearby, his plane to Washington ready to depart.

KELLY   You tell General Martinez I am still the Ambassador in this country for one more day. And I want Boyle and his friends out of there NOW or I am going to make that day hell for you bastards – you got that Mister!

INT: CUSTOMS SHED
The Phone rings loud. Twice. THE BULL, chewing on his toothpick, reading a foto-novella, picks it up. Stiffens. His boss.

THE BULL Colonel? Si! ... Boy – lay ... si ... aye, *(worried)* mas tarde ... pero un momento ...

The voice yelling at him. The Bull padding slowly to the Death Shed.

INTERCUT TO:

INT: DEATH SHED
PEDRO slamming the bolt on his carbine. He's pissed at losing the argument with Grasshopper, who checks his watch.
Boyle knows that is it. And there's no way some miracle is going to happen.

BOYLE All right, fuck – get it over with ...

Crosses himself one last time. For real. Spits out the cyanide pill.
Pedro raises the rifle.
Boyle waits.
Pedro pulls the trigger.
Nothing happens. They all look at each other.

BOYLE *(pissed now)* You dumb schmuck, can't you even get the goddamn ammunition right!

Grasshopper yelling at Pedro as they slam the bolt open, check out the bullet, Laurel and Hardy joining the argument. They all seem to agree. A new bullet is put in.
Boyle is pissed, cursing them out. Pedro slams the bolt shut. Raises the rifle.

BOYLE Chinga de madre!

The door opens, the Bull jovially calling to Pedro.

THE BULL Hey Pedro! He's a good guy ... Hey Boy-lay, amigo, come, big mistake ...

On Boyle.

INT: CUSTOMS SHED
Boyle is drinking beer, his Major Max hat on his head as the
GUARDSMEN bring him fried chicken, returning all his possessions,
treating him like a major dignitary now, all smiles. Pedro drinking a beer
with him, showing his dirty pictures and guffawing. Grasshopper offer-
ing him an autographed picture of Major Max.

The Bull giving him back the exposed rolls of film as if they were still good.

THE BULL Con permiso?

Claps him on the back as MARIA and the KIDS run in. They haven't
been touched, Maria so relieved to see Boyle alive — her face says it all as
she runs to embrace him.

DISSOLVE TO:

EXT: NOGALES, MEXICO – STREET – DAY
A few days later. Boyle with a hula shirt buying Duglas an L.A.
Dodgers baseball cap that goes with his Hulk t-shirt. Maria has a
UCLA t-shirt on, a skirt, chewing gum, she looks like a perfect American
housewife hauling Reina in a Mickey Mouse outfit.

EXT: U.S. BORDER STATION – NOGALES – DAY
Boyle, looking bored and hauling gifts, bottles of Kahlua, goes
through the turnstiles on a crowded Sunday afternoon, Maria and the
kids right behind him.

He hands his press card to the CUSTOMS OFFICER, who glances at it.
It's not a particularly tight checkpoint.

OFFICER Where you been?

BOYLE *(shifting bags, busy)* Oh, just took the wife and kids to
    Nogales for the afternoon. *(to Maria)* Sweetie, did you
    remember to take the roast out for tonight?

MARIA *(in perfect rehearsed English)* Sure honey, I take care of
    it . . . hold this.

DUGLAS *(in good English)* Daddy, when can we go to
    Disneyland?

OFFICER *(bored, looking to next person)* Okay next.

They cross. Maria unbelieving at the ease of it.

INT: GREYHOUND BUS – DAY
As it zooms up an Arizona highway – desert on both sides. 'Phoenix' ahead.

Inside the bus, Maria, very content, snuggles up to Richard.

BOYLE Es todo muy bien, mi amor?

MARIA Si ...

BOYLE *(Spanish)* Gringoland. It's a wacko joint but nothing like El Salvador. You can do what you want here, be what you want – long as you got money. I'm gonna sell some Salvador stories, maybe a story on John ... things are gonna work out okay now – things are gonna be okay, mi amor – okay? *(hugs her cozy)*

Duglas and Reina are staring wide-eyed out the window at Gringoland.

... the shiny car wash palaces, the diners with their crazy signs, the fast cars, it's all new to him.

The bus coming to a stop, air brakes.

Boyle looking around. What the hell is it.

The door opens. An IMMIGRATION OFFICER comes on. Looking like Erik Estrada, six feet, dark sunglasses, shiny gun, radio on his hip, he struts down the aisle, checking the papers on certain Latino types – ignoring the Anglos.

Boyle, freaking out, grips Maria's hand. She obviously knows, terrified by the uniform on the large gringo.

The OFFICER comes up to Richard, looks at Maria, the kids.

BOYLE *(handing him his Press Card)* Hi ... took my wife and kids to Nogales for the day.

SUNGLASSES *(to Maria)* Are you his wife?

Maria is unable to answer, frozen in terror. The Officer senses it.

BOYLE Sure she is. What is this anyway.

SUNGLASSES *(to Maria)* Papeles, passaporte ... carta verde.

MARIA *(defeated)* No, nada.

BOYLE *(standing up, ready to fight)* Hey man, why don't you leave her alone, she's with me, she's been through hell in Salvador and I'm a journalist and she's my researcher and assistant.

The Officer has whipped out his radio.

OFFICER Three suspects. One Latin female adult, two kids. Call the wagon ... ten four.

BOYLE COME ON MAN – YOU CAN'T DO THIS TO HER!!

OFFICER Stay outta this buddy.

Boyle is on him like a bat. Gives him a chop to the face and the ribs. Tries to get Maria out of there.

BOYLE MARIA – GO! – NOW!

But it's too late. TWO MORE SUNGLASSES hit the bus, wielding handcuffs and guns.

SUNGLASSES 2 Awright buddy – freeze!

MARIA Richard! – STOP! I GO.

Her voice imperial, cutting through all the chaos. Richard stops, throws up his hands. Sunglasses 1, pissed, grabs Boyle by the neck and jerks him into an empty seat – handcuffs him to the seat.

Meanwhile the other two have handcuffed Maria – and start pushing her towards the front of the bus – with Duglas and Reina.

DUGLAS *(calling back)* Papa! Where are they taking us?

REINA *(terrified)* Papa – come with us ...

Maria gets a hold of them, talks to them. Looks back at Richard. One last heartbreaking look. Richard can't take it, starts screaming at the cops.

BOYLE If you send her back – they'll KILL her. They'll
RAPE HER AND MUTILATE HER – do you
HEAR ME YOU BASTARDS?

*SUNGLASSES 1 loses his temper now and rushes back and punches Boyle
hard in the face.*

SUNGLASSES Allright, you're under arrest asshole!

BOYLE Please – they'll kill the kids too. You don't know
what it's like in El Salvador.

*Sunglasses handcuffs Boyle's hands behind his back and moves him
down the aisle. His moving POV through the bus windows of Maria
being put in the first squad car.*

An OLDER GUY, leathery face, squinty eyes, mutters to his OLD LADY.

OLDER GUY He's on drugs.

Boyle being led off the bus – across to a 2nd Squad Car just arriving.

*A YUPPIE COUPLE, 30's, watches all this, the wife visibly upset, her
husband reassuring her.*

YUPPIE HUSBAND ... but honey somebody's got to keep
these people out or we'll be overrun. *(to Driver)* Driver,
we're running late as it is. Can we get going now?

The bus doors swish closed with a hiss of air.

EXT: HIGHWAY – DAY
*Boyle pushed into a Squad Car. Sunglasses on the radio. General cop
bullshit – 'One WMA, Boyle, Richard David, 2/26/42 ...'*

As Richard twists around, looking at the other squad car.

*One last glimpse of Maria, handcuffed, and the Kids looking at him
through the backseat window. They're all crying, Duglas pounding on the
glass. Siren whining, Erik Estrada flashing by, their squad car now goes.
Back to the South. Gone forever.*

*As Richard heads north. A stunned look, never so lost or alone – tears in
his eyes.*

THE END

AFTERWORD

FROM OLIVER STONE'S SPEECH TO THE NATIONAL
PRESS CLUB, WASHINGTON, D.C., APRIL 7, 1987

I was born in 1946, in New York City, at the dawn of the
Cold War. My father raised me Republican and instilled in
me a fear of the Russians and Communism. By the standards
of the fifties, he was right, but he never expected me to go
to war – and was horrified when I did – to fight for those
beliefs he had been raised with. I arrived in Saigon in June
1965 at the age of 19 – the day the My Canh floating
restaurant blew up. The Marines and First Infantry troop
were drinking in Tudo Street, carrying weapons at that time
and firing them off in the air in the first blush of our victory.
We were the good guys, we *were* going to win. It was the
war of my generation. It was *glorious*.

When I returned in 1967, as a combat soldier, the first
thing that struck me was that it had all started to change for
the worse. The Vietnamese that had welcomed us in 1965
had now started the slow process of taking our dollars and
hating us for it. Corruption and prostitution were rampant.
PX supplies were being ripped off by South Vietnamese and
American lifer sergeants, who were later implicated in scan-
dals over this war. Many people came home in body bags
while others made millions of dollars. There were six or
seven noncombatants for every combatant, many of them
eating steak and lobster dinners each night at Da Nang or
Cam Ranh or Saigon or Quin Hon or Quang Tri or Bien
Hoa and the many other pig heavens. The situations in the
rear in fact began to resemble, to the boonie rats and grunts,

249

a Las Vegas or a Miami Beach. We brought a corporate Miami Beach/Las Vegas mentality to Vietnam.

When Johnson pulled out in March 1968, it was metaphorically over. The grunts sensed it right away, we were never going to win, but we had to withdraw with a semblance of dignity. That semblance of dignity took four more years of deceit and death, and in the moral vacuum, there was never any clear reason to us why we should die. Dissension and mutiny grew in the ranks between draftees and officers and lifer sergeants. Fraggings on a scale never seen in modern war occurred, black/white relations grew worse with King's assassination. Marijuana and eventually heroin usage engulfed a portion of the troops. The ultimate corruption was, of course, President Johnson sending only the poor and uneducated to the war – in fact, practicing class warfare wherein the middle and upper classes could avoid the war by going to college or paying a psychiatrist. I am sure to this day that if the middle and upper classes had gone to Vietnam, their mothers and fathers – the politicians and businessmen – would have ended that war a hell of a lot sooner; in fact, politicians' sons, if not politicians themselves, should be sent to every war first. So I think that ultimately we were destined to lose this war even before we started; or, to paraphrase Sun Tzu, 'every war is won before it is ever fought.' We were destined to lose because this war had no moral purpose and it was fought without any moral integrity. And we did lose because basically, as a character in *Platoon* says, 'We were not the good guys anymore.'

I walked away from that war, 21 and benumbed, and something of an anarchist in my thinking. It took me several years to recover some form of social identification, and when I did, in the mid-1970s, I thought that as an American the nightmare was behind us. The Pentagon Papers had come out, then Watergate . . . we were on a roll. Never did I expect to see these events occur again. But they did. The combined weight of the three great shocks of the 1970s had shaken America to its core. Watergate, the defeat in Vietnam, OPEC, and the Japanese emergence were blows to our political, moral, and economic confidence and sent us reeling back into a desire for escape and reassuring Reaganism. By 1979, liberalism was dead or dying, murdered by the hostages in Iran. Whatever resolve Jimmy Carter had had been killed off. And with Reagan's election, the nightmare in Salvador climaxed. An archbishop, 18 other priests, and 4 nuns were murdered by death squads – founded, as I pointed out in my movie *Salvador*, by people like José Medrano and René Chacon, who studied with our Green Berets in Vietnam and the International Police Academy in Washington and at the Jungle School in Panama. But this was the time of the Jeane Kirkpatrick school of thought that manages to distinguish between authoritarian and totalitarian government, and in the crusading name of anti-communism, from 1980 to 1985, we poured 1.7 billion dollars' worth of military and economic aid into a military mafia that was, in fact, a death squad responsible for some 30 to 50 thousand civilian deaths. All in the name of anti-communism.

When I arrived in Honduras, Guatemala, Salvador, and Costa Rica in January of 1985, I had a flashback on the order of a *Back to the Future* Spielberg movie. I thought I had returned to Vietnam, 1965, Saigon. It was hot, wet, and the American kids were 19 again in green uniforms. Except this was Tequcigalpa, Honduras, and I was 38 years old. I talked to the young G.I.s in uniform – technicians, many of them–and they were gung ho, no doubts about it, they were fighting communism once again in Nicaragua. We were 'saving' Honduras. Some of these people were women now, and I suddenly felt like a forgotten older man who was wandering around wondering how this could happen again so quickly in his lifetime. Yet when I went out on the streets with my rascally journalist companion, Richard Boyle, who was played by James Woods in *Salvador*, I was hearing and seeing a different story than the official line: how the dollar, like in Vietnam, had inflated the Honduran economy; how female law students and female members of the middle class were turning to prostitution in bars just to make ends meet; how the *contras* had become the corrupt South Vietnamese of 1968; how the Hondurans, who used to like America, now hated us or at least wanted to steal from us; how we are militarizing Salvador, Guatemala, Honduras, and Costa Rica. And when I asked these kids in uniform, 'Do you remember Vietnam?' they looked at me with a kind of vague, disturbed 'Why are you talking about this?' look; they were uncomfortable. The fact was, gentlemen, they did *not* remember Vietnam, it's that simple, amnesia has set in, and what's worse is moral amnesia has set in, because the guys who run the country don't remember Vietnam! They don't remember what war means in terms of suffering to the body and the soul. The power of forgetting, I have found out as I have grown up, is *not* to be underestimated – ever.

Well, I've gone around in my head and tried to sum all this up, and at least in this stage of my thinking, the only systematic explanation I can derive from all this is the concept of ideology versus, for want of a better phrase, the 'Six Inches in Front of my Face' theory. It's a term I came up with from Vietnam, where I had to stop being this cerebral, educated creature from New York and start dealing with the six inches in front of my face in the jungle, to start really using, for the first time, my sight and smell and sound, to deal with the world the way it *is*, not the way it ought to be. The ideologues like Khomeini and Hitler, and, on a smaller scale, Reagan can justify repression and killings because they're not there, they don't feel and taste and smell it.

When the legitimate left wing of Salvador was dragged out of a meeting in a schoolroom in November 1980, tortured by a death squad, and left with their balls stuffed in their mouths by the side of the road, Jeane Kirkpatrick's reaction was 'those who live by the sword shall also die by the sword,' ignoring the fact that these men – Juan Chacon and Kiki Alvarez among them – were unarmed. This act of horror is, I would say, the equivalent of dragging out the Jesse Jackson wing of the Democratic Party in this country and killing them. The idealogues will tell you it's okay if we do it south of the border. When the nuns were killed, Alexander Haig made some comment about their packing pistols and running a blockade. What Jeane and Ron and Al really need, I think, is to rub their noses in Nicaragua. To talk to people. To deal with the 'Six Inches in Front of *Their* Faces.' But the idealogues never do. They point their finger at communism as a monolithic evil, but they never settle on the specific. So I guess what I'm saying is let's praise the practical man – the man who negotiates his way through life, who values peace as the supreme domestic virtue, and is willing to make a few compromises and sacrifices to achieve it. The man who can sit down and negotiate with the Russians and the Nicaraguans. Being in the movie business, I've learned only too well that *everything* is negotiable in life – and certainly human lives.

The Cold War, which has governed my generation's life span, has given us Korea and Vietnam, a defense industry that like a black hole takes thirty percent of our budget and creates nothing with it and justifies our financial neglect of education, health and welfare; has given us cities with the highest crime rate in the world; has let us decline to eleventh place in the world in per capita income, to forty-sixth in literacy and put us two trillion dollars in debt. And now has brought us an active participation in a sinister repression of revolution in Salvador, and the desire to destroy another one in Nicaragua against all legal sanctions, including the illegal mining of the harbors in violation of the World Court and to me, more heartbreaking, in defiance of our Declaration of Independence, which calls for the right of revolution and the right of self-determination. We are now – no question about it – fighting an illegal war financed by our shady arms deals with Israel and Iran and the even shadier drug deals of the C.I.A. with the Cuban right-wing mafias and *contras*. With such minds as Ed Wilson and Ted Shackly, with the government now run by people with gangster morals, who've totally forgotten truth, who've totally forgotten the meaning of our own revolution as defined by Jefferson and Washington: What are we becoming? What has happened to us? Where is our sense of outrage? It's not there because we've become or are becoming, in fact, as rotten and corrupt as the Russians once were and seem to be trying to do something about.

It is time for a change, it's time for a corporate raid, it's time for a buccaneering spirit to take over the corporation called the U.S.A. and unload the fat-cat management. The Cold War has eroded America and will *most certainly* ruin it unless my generation brings forth a new voice of reason and intelligence – possibly a political cadre of Vietnam vets hardened by the sad truths of Vietnam that can take us out of this Cold War mind set. To take us beyond existing definitions of left and right in a true anarchic fashion, anarchy being defined here as redefinition. To redefine communism in its many forms. As Confucius said, 'To rectify the language that declares a city saved by bombing it to pieces,' to attack the shibboleths like the defense industry, to say no to tyrants, left or right, to pull our troops from Europe and Korea. To redefine our goals; to remember our Constitution was conceived in a spirit of revolution and self-determination. To bring forth the twenty-first century with a spark of hope and a true and generous revival of the American spirit of liberty for all.

ABOUT OLIVER STONE

Oliver Stone was born in New York City in 1946. He attended Yale University, leaving in 1965 to teach at the Free Pacific Institute in Cholon, Vietnam. He joined the U.S. Merchant Marine the following year and sailed the China seas and the Pacific as a wiper. From September 1967 to November 1968, Stone served in the U.S. Army in Vietnam with the 25th Infantry Division and the 1st Air Cavalry. He was awarded the Bronze Star for Valor as well as a Purple Heart with a 1st Oak Leaf Cluster. When he returned, Stone studied film at New York University, graduating in 1971. Among others, his screenplays include *Scarface* and *Midnight Express*, which won an Academy Award for best screenplay adaptation. He is currently at work on a film about Wall Street.

ABOUT RICHARD BOYLE

Richard Boyle has been covering wars as a photojournalist for twenty years. Besides covering El Salvador, he has reported on Vietnam, Ireland, the Yom Kippur War in Israel, Cambodia, Laos, and Nicaragua. He has been wounded twice in combat. The last American journalist to leave Cambodia after the Khmer Rouge occupied Phnom Penh in 1975, Boyle left journalism in the late 1970s and worked in a variety of jobs. He managed a nightclub in Italy, counseled low-income ghetto youths in San Francisco, and acted as national security adviser on the staff of Congressman Paul N. McCloskey. Boyle returned to journalism in 1979 to cover the civil wars in Nicaragua and then in El Salvador, where he reported for NBC radio and Cable News Network. He is the author of a book about Vietnam, *Flower of the Dragon*, and has produced several documentaries, including *Below the Volcano* on El Salvador.